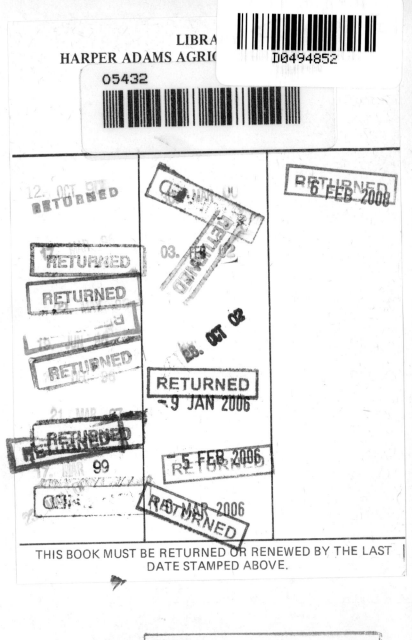

Nontariff Agricultural Trade Barriers

NONTARIFF
AGRICULTURAL
TRADE BARRIERS

Jimmye S. Hillman

FOREWORD BY D. Gale Johnson

UNIVERSITY OF NEBRASKA PRESS
LINCOLN AND LONDON

c

Library of Congress Cataloging in Publication Data
Hillman, Jimmye S. 1923–
 Nontariff agricultural trade barriers.

 Bibliography: p. 221
 Includes index.
 1. Nontariff trade barriers. 2. Produce trade.
I. Title.
HF1430.H54   382'.42   78-16054
ISBN 0-8032-2301-3

5432

CONTENTS

TABLES AND FIGURES

viii

FOREWORD

The growth of nontariff barriers affecting international trade in agricultural products that has occurred since the mid-1950's represents a major threat to both international cooperation and the future of efficient agriculture in the world. Nontariff barriers are becoming the most important form of agricultural protection, either replacing or supplementing tariffs. If the recent trends are not reversed by the General Agreement on Tariffs and Trade (GATT) negotiations or negotiations in other forums, the fragmentation of world markets for agricultural products will increase, and efficient and low-cost agriculture will face increasing economic difficulties. More and more of the world's agricultural products will be produced in the wrong places and at high cost.

As Professor Hillman shows conclusively, the variety of nontariff barriers nearly defies the imagination. Some, such as quantity restrictions or import quotas, are very obvious, with known effects on trade. Others, such as the variable levies imposed by the European Community, are nearly as definite in limiting quantities imported. But others are much more subtle and subject to administrative discretion and discrimination and much more difficult to evaluate in terms of their effects. These include marking regulations, package and container specifications, state trading, licensing arrangements, and an enormous number of sanitary and health regulations. At times sanitary and health regulations are just that— measures that are designed to protect plants, animals, and humans from harm. But many such measures are based on minute differences in standards of sanitation or in sanitary procedures and are clearly designed to protect local producers.

Why have nontariff barriers increased so in importance? Professor Hillman demonstrates that such barriers have not increased in importance because of deliberate and overt trade intervention,

ix

but have resulted from domestic decisions with respect to agricultural policies and programs. Domestic agricultural policies that seek to stabilize prices received by farmers require that the flow of trade be regulated. An ad valorem tariff will seldom do; if international market prices fall low enough, imports will be increased and the domestic market price will decline. And if domestic farm prices are both high and stable, more output may be forthcoming than can be disposed of at these prices. An attractive alternative, at least in the view of many policy makers, is to resort to export subsidies so that the excess supply can be moved into international markets.

Few countries—perhaps none—are willing to engage in negotiations about their domestic agricultural programs. And most countries consider their nontariff barriers quite direct extensions of their domestic programs. The unwillingness to negotiate about matters that are considered to be domestic in nature goes a long way in explaining why there has been little success in negotiating reductions in nontariff barriers and why it will be difficult to achieve such reductions in the future.

In addition, most governments excuse their use of nontariff barriers as a response to similar barriers imposed by others. For example, a major reason given for the imposition of import quotas on beef and veal by the United States was that the European Community was restricting its imports of beef, and the United States market would be inundated with the beef that formerly went to other markets. Unfortunately, there is some validity to this position, both in the specific case cited and in general.

One cannot be optimistic that past trends with respect to the increasing importance of nontariff barriers are likely to be reversed in the near future. The developing countries are quite rightly calling upon the industrial countries to permit more favorable access to the markets of the latter countries. While many of the nontariff barriers are used to restrict imports of Temperate Zone products, such as grains, the restrictions on sugar imports, numerous fruits and vegetables, and livestock products directly and seriously restrict markets for the developing countries.

The approaches being taken by the developing countries, especially those being orchestrated through the United Nations Conference on Trade and Development (UNCTAD), are likely to result in more nontariff restrictions rather than fewer. The emphasis is upon arrangements that would control the flow of trade in order to stabilize prices, presumably at profitable levels, and to assure access to import markets. To the low-cost producer it really doesn't make any difference whether his export expansion is prevented by the actions of importers or as a result of agreement among importers and exporters. I have yet to see a commodity agreement—and this is what is being proposed for a considerable number of agricultural and other raw materials—whose objective was to free and expand trade. The objectives are always different— to control and restrict trade.

While I doubt that the initiatives now being taken by UNCTAD will result in many new or at least many new lasting commodity agreements, one serious consequence of the efforts to negotiate such agreements is that attention is diverted from the reduction of barriers to trade in agricultural products. A cynic could argue that one of the reasons several industrial countries continue to discuss the possibilities of new commodity arrangements is to delay serious negotiations on reducing trade barriers and the required modifications of their domestic farm programs.

In this book Professor Hillman has called to our attention an exceedingly important problem confronting world agriculture. It can be hoped that his efforts to show the enormous variety and extent of nontariff barriers to trade will result in some pressure upon those countries using such barriers to consider appropriate modifications. This may be little more than a faint hope; the final chapter of the book makes it all too clear how difficult it will be to negotiate the reduction or elimination of such barriers.

D. GALE JOHNSON
Eliakim Hastings Moore
    Distinguished Service Professor
Department of Economics
The University of Chicago

PREFACE

The idea for this study came to me in mid-1967 in Washington, D.C., where I was concluding work on the President's National Advisory Commission on Food and Fiber. Kennedy Round tariff negotiations were phasing out; nontariff trade barrier problems and agricultural trade policy issues had been pushed into the background and had not been dealt with. A common agricultural policy for the European Community had been developed and the future of that policy was contingent upon high prices and a variable levy system. The United States had implemented import quotas on beef and the costs of its restrictive domestic farm policies were exceedingly high. The outlook for trade liberalization was not bright in 1967. In fact, today, more than ten years later, despite the turnaround in the world supply situation during the 1972–75 period, domestic agricultural policies and attendant nontariff trade barriers still pose a threat to international specialization. Therefore, the GATT negotiations are still very much appropriate for their traditional purpose.

My interest in the subject of nontariff barriers was kept alive by professional involvement and intermittent contacts with public and private trade agencies, particularly those in Washington. A sabbatical leave at Oxford University in 1972–73 made possible the project and manuscript outline. Research projects on policy at the University of Arizona Agricultural Experiment Station have sustained the manuscript to completion.

Like many projects of this nature, the original outline and my intentions were much larger than the final product would indicate. Limited time and a lack of budget for additional personnel were major constraints. Particularly, a second case study—one on the citrus industry—was eliminated from consideration for these reasons.

Much of the data and information appearing in the substantive chapters were gathered through personal contacts in England, Europe and Washington. Personnel in the GATT, UNCTAD, FAO, OECD, and the Foreign Agricultural Service, USDA, were quite generous with their time and suggestions. For materials contained in Chapter 7, specific mention should be made of help from the Australian Trade Commission, the New Zealand Meat Board, and the Animal Health Division of the British Ministry of Agriculture, Food and Fisheries.

To enumerate all the persons to whom thanks are due would necessitate another small manuscript. Obligation and courtesy demand, however, that some be mentioned. The Charles E. Merrill Trust was generous in providing financial support; Robert A. Magowan merits my special gratitude. The Social Science Research Council, London, also provided financial support. Mrs. Wendy Thompson, Secretary to the Economics Committee of the Council, was very helpful.

The late Kenneth Hunt, Director of the Institute of Agricultural Economics in Oxford, provided space, supplies, library and typing assistance, as well as the intellectual atmosphere conducive to a successful sabbatical project and study. George Jones of the institute made suggestions in early stages of the manuscript. Max Corden of Nuffield College in Oxford and Timothy Josling of the London School of Economics gave me intellectual stimulation throughout the stay at Oxford. Hugh Corbet of the Trade Policy Research Center, London assisted in many practical ways. Jan Tumlir and J. M. Lucq of GATT, James O'Hagan and Eric Ojala of FAO, and Paul Lamartine Yates in Geneva, all reacted to ideas and were sympathetic to my problems. Thanks are due to Ernest Koenig, George White, and William Rodman of FAS, USDA, who throughout the study provided data and information basic to the study. Barbara Huddleston and other FAS personnel were also helpful.

D. Gale Johnson of the University of Chicago read the manuscript and made helpful comments. Jack Belck, University of Arizona Agricultural Editor, made a major contribution in the editing process.

Finally, special thanks are due my wife, Helen, and daughter, Brenda Hillman Michaels, for their typing and proofing of the original manuscript, and to my secretaries, Mrs. Harriet Gregg and Mrs. Kathy Stark, for their general assistance in putting the chapters in final shape.

Nontariff Agricultural Trade Barriers

Chapter 1.

AGRICULTURAL TRADE AND PROTECTION

Despite the overhang of farm surpluses, especially in the United States, trade developments were reasonably favorable in the 1960s and early 1970s. But the underlying trend and basic outlook for agricultural trade suggest a dangerous decade ahead for agricultural trade,[1] even though as of this writing (spring 1978) it is difficult to come to grips with the future direction of world agricultural production and trade.

Unusual events from 1972 to 1975, like those of 1965 and 1966—severe droughts in the USSR, India, and the Sahel; the reduced Peruvian anchovy catch; two U.S. dollar devaluations; the quadrupling of oil prices; and other aberrations—tend to obscure international policy and trade problems of the post-World War II period. These problems include long-term excess capacity in commercial agriculture, the lack of adjustment between the agricultural and other sectors in major industrial countries, the propensity of nations to use import restrictions and commodity policies—e.g., for sugar, coffee, cocoa, and other products—to insulate themselves against price fluctuations in the world market, and the inclination of nations to use agricultural export subsidies to help solve domestic farm price and income problems.

Events during the past several years have given rise to governmental actions (for example, the imposition of export controls on farm commodities formerly in surplus and of import quotas) which can camouflage the basic problems of agricultural trade and adjustment. There are also some signs that severe problems in energy and other areas will precipitate nationalistic approaches which will degenerate again into shortsighted protectionism.

It would be hazardous to presume that the difficulties which have obstructed the path of agricultural trade liberalization for fifty years or more will be swept aside by the current circumstances.

1

Put in another way, it would be presumptuous to believe that major changes in farm programs of the industrialized countries can be accomplished without strong demands from producers that they be protected against the risks involved in trade liberalization. The general thesis of this study, therefore, is that agricultural trade restrictions will remain and that nontariff barriers will increasingly present the stickiest of these difficulties.

WORLD TRADE IN AGRICULTURAL PRODUCTS

The current level and content of world trade are quite different from those of the past, and in the decade or so ahead a more radical change will likely be experienced in most aspects of commerce: trade in finished products, movement of raw materials, travel, and that all-important category, accounting for the invisibles. The value of world exports increased more than five times, or from about $60 billion to more than $310 billion, between 1950 and 1970.[2] It almost tripled again by 1975, reaching approximately $876 billion. Despite the inflation during this quarter-century, the volume of trade in agricultural and finished goods also rose significantly, as will be seen shortly.

The value of world exports of agricultural products (which here include agricultural primary materials and forest and fishery products) increased from about $20 billion in 1953 to $40 billion in 1960 and $150 billion in 1975; this growth was, however, much less rapid than that of minerals and manufactures, so that the proportion of agricultural products in world exports fell from more than a third in 1953 to only 17 percent in 1975. Agricultural production was sluggish in many developing countries; hence, much of the increase in agricultural exports came from traditional, Temperate Zone food and fiber producers.

During the 1960s there was only a slight acceleration in agricultural trade in value terms over that of a decade earlier, an acceleration due mostly to recovery in prices. In volume terms, the growth of world exports of agricultural products slowed, whereas the expansion of world exports of manufactures accelerated. In other words, during the 1960s there was a pronounced widening of the gap between the volume growth of world exports of agricultural products and that of manufactures.

Looking at annual data only for the decade of the 1960s, the story is similar: a slower rate of growth in the value of trade in agricultural products than in industrial goods, which is attributable to slower rates of increase in both domestic agricultural prices and volume of agricultural products traded. This is illustrated in table 1.1. The volume of agricultural exports grew at an annual rate of 4.3 percent, compared to a 2.5 percent increase in production, indicating that a rising proportion of agricultural output entered channels of international commerce. The impact of the "price explosion" in agricultural products and raw materials, beginning in 1972, can be observed by comparing the compound annual growth rates in the last two columns of table 1.1 (1960–70 compared with 1960–74). Again, the price effect in the agricultural export sector far outweighs quantum data.

Even so, taken at face value, these data on agricultural trade could be misleading. It is important to point out that for many years much of the increased volume of agricultural trade resulted from farm policies in the industrial countries which subsidized a major portion of exports. It is probable that in the immediate future subsidized and/or regulated trade in agricultural products will continue undiminished among industrial countries and between them and the rest of the world, because it is unlikely that protective agricultural and trade policies which have existed for over forty years, and which have accelerated in many countries since World War II, will be altered greatly.[3] In addition to the trade-distorting features of export subsidies, there is increasing emphasis on policies of self sufficiency and import substitutions in many large food-importing countries, which follow from attempts to reduce food import bills and pressure on foreign currency reserves. Export subsidies gave way to quantitative export controls in the "great turnaround" in 1973. For whatever reason, real agricultural protection appears to have risen considerably since World War II and shows no current sign of abating. This may be a pessimistic appraisal, but it is probably a realistic one.

For most industrial countries, with the possible exceptions of Great Britain and Japan, imports of agricultural products tend to be marginal; that is, there is not a heavy dependence on imported food and agricultural raw materials for national survival. Relatively small changes in world production or demand can, therefore, cause large changes in the volume of world trade and market prices, which in turn explains the pronounced instability of world

TABLE 1.1 World Exports and Production in Agricultural Products, 1960-74

	1960	1965	1970	1974	Compound Annual Growth Rate, 1960-70
(World exports)					
Value					
Agricultural products (billion $)	40.0	49.6	64.6	148.0	4.9%
Percentage of world total exports	31	27	20	17	
Value index (1960 = 100)					
Agricultural products	100	124	162	370	5.0
World total exports	100	146	246	657	9.4
Unit value index (1960 = 100)					
Agricultural products	100	101	106	238	0.6
World total exports	100	103	114	225	1.3
Quantum index (1960 = 100)					
Agricultural products	100	123	152	155	4.3
World total exports	100	140	217	293	8.1
(World production)					
Quantum index (1960 = 100)					
Agricultural products	100	113	128	140	2.5
All commodities	100	130	169	208	5.4

Source: OECD, *Policy Perspectives for International Trade and Economic Relations,* table 14; U.N. *Monthly Bulletin of Statistics;* GATT, *International Trade, 1970.*

Note: Agricultural products, including agricultural primary materials and forest and fishery products: S.I.T.C. (Standard International Trade Classification) Secions 0, 1, 4, and 2 (excluding 27 and 28).

When the intratrade of the EEC is excluded, world exports of agricultural products are $38.1 billion for 1960 and $57.6 billion for 1970, and their compound annual growth rate is 4.2 percent between 1960 and 1970, and 9.6 percent between 1960 and 1974.

markets for agricultural products. The period 1972–74 is a good example: a 3.5 percent deviation from trend in world grain production caused considerable trouble in world markets. Likewise, relatively small disturbances which occur in the processes or channels of trade can cause disproportionate gyrations in commodity movements.

Statutory and regulatory actions with respect to international marketing of agricultural products, and the administrative procedures which accompany these actions, can and do raise many avoidable obstacles to growth and stability in world agricultural trade.

PROTECTION IN AGRICULTURE

There is a proposition which implies that agricultural protection, and the failure of agriculture to adjust to changed circumstances, inevitably lead to general protectionist policies and to all the bad effects which go with such policies. This is a corollary to the old proposition that "depressions are farm-led and farm-fed." Though there might have been some economic evidence in the nineteenth century to substantiate this—for example, the economic malaise of the 1880s and early 1890s in the United States—no hypothesis has been accepted which will support this as inevitable today. Moreover, while advocates of protection once proposed high tariffs as a general policy to avoid depression in the rural sector, there is little evidence that they were ever very successful in that regard. Neither is there evidence that protectionist policies were ever responsible for lifting a country or its rural sector out of a depression.

Despite the lack of evidence (which may be due to the lack of research) to support hypotheses about protectionist policies and economic depression or recovery, one should not conclude that agricultural policies are of no importance in the search for more liberal trade policies.[4] Indeed, a major problem for the 1970s is that nations do not appreciate the latent danger built into protectionist farm policies since World War II. D. Gale Johnson pointed that out vividly in his book:

The disarray in World agriculture is clearly significant because of (1) the distortion of prices and trade, (2) the large costs imposed on taxpayers and consumers, and (3) the uneconomic expansions of farm output in the

industrial countries and the associated effects upon the developing countries.
*But these serious consequences may be of secondary importance, being far
outweighed by the possibility of protections and intransigence that persist
in agriculture to erode, and perhaps destroy, the basis for liberal trade policies
generally.*

It is difficult to over-estimate the dangers of current trends in agricultural
protectionism to the future of trade liberalization generally. . . .

The 1970s may see a reversal of the trend towards trade liberalization that
has persisted for almost four decades. If it does, it will be to some considerable degree because no progress is made to reduce barriers to trade in agricultural products.[5]

In short, though there appears to be no immutable economic
and statistical proof of linkage between protection of agriculture
in a domestic economy and any recession or recovery therein, it
may be dangerous to rule out the influence which general agricultural policies have on the propensities toward trade liberalization
throughout the world and on the mood for trade negotiations in
international bodies such as the General Agreement on Tariffs and
Trade (GATT).

If substantial agricultural adjustment is not achieved soon and
if agricultural protectionism is not reduced or checked, there is a
danger that, as on two occasions in the past, the agricultural sector
will be associated with a mass movement toward general economic
protection, trade wars, and political breakdown. This happened in
the mid-nineteenth century, when agricultural producers in continental Europe led the way to commercial disintegration after a
free trade interlude had followed the Anglo-Franco treaty of
1860. It happened again in the 1920s when American and European agricultural producers were in the forefront of protectionist
movements that ushered in unprecedented trade restrictions and
restrictive devices. Such restrictions were among the forces which
led to world trade chaos and economic breakdown.

Prior to World War I, international agricultural trade restrictions consisted principally of a customs duty or protective tariff
imposed on products at national frontiers. After the commercial
trade breakdown of the 1930s, a wide variety of nontariff protective devices were invented and instituted by countries all over
the world to bolster sagging agricultural prices and incomes. These
devices were used chiefly in countries with large Temperate Zone

agricultural product trade, but they were used also in developing and tropical countries.

Various schemes and agricultural programs were created to stabilize and increase domestic farm prices and incomes; and, in order to prevent world exports from disrupting these actions, government after government erected formidable barriers to trade, many very complex. In summary, the world, particularly the industrial countries, turned increasingly to nontariff barriers rather than to tariffs as protective measures for its internal agricultural programs.

NONTARIFF PROTECTION

Nontariff barrier problems, as well as agricultural policy issues, were pushed into the background during the Kennedy Round negotiations. This was not only because they were tedious areas for negotiation. There was also an initial underestimation of the nature and level of their ultimate significance to the countries involved. This negligence was also due in part to problems involved in developing common agricultural policy for the European Community. Not until the smoke had cleared did participants in the bargaining realize the real importance of and difficulties involved with both issues.

In any event, the agricultural sector with its many difficulties and issues affecting nontariff barriers has burst upon the world trade scene as a real problem child, while GATT participants are involved in yet another round of negotiations. Agricultural protection and nontariff barriers are now being recognized as key subjects in broad areas of negotiations which are necessary to policy formulation, decision making, and adjustment. Neither issue can be pushed aside any longer and ignored. To do so would endanger gains already made in trade improvement through tariff reduction, particularly during the Kennedy Round.

Currently, one of the most universally applied nontariff barriers is the quantitative restriction introduced in Europe in 1926. It spread rapidly there and in the United States and became part of the agricultural trade and policy tenets, especially in post-World War II legislation. Quantitative barriers were joined by export subsidies, licensing, and exchange control, as well as other, more elusive, nonquantitative nontariff restrictions and measures such as state trading and bilateral agreements, "voluntary" agreements or executive negotiations, and rules and regulations on health, safety, and sanitation. Uncertainty in production and in the flow of products internationally has resulted.

The present study analyzes nontariff barriers to trade in and the production of agricultural commodities. It also treats selected problems of adjustment in agriculture which arise because of these barriers. Special attention is given to those obstacles which have hindered a smoother adjustment process of the agricultural sector within countries and those which have prevented agricultural and rural area adjustments between them. Recognition is given, of course, to the fact that, as countries develop, as trade increases, as agricultural production inputs become more mobile, and, particularly, as price inflation in agricultural products increases, the subject dealt with here could be deemed of lesser importance. This is especially the case under conditions of fixed tariff rates of the traditional kind. Under present circumstances in which the spotlight of world trade matters is focused on the subject and the traditional tariff is declining in importance in comparison to other protective measures, it is difficult to believe this will happen. Nevertheless, the agricultural sector and the nontariff barrier question are subject to the oscillations which take place in broad worldwide economic indicators. They are also subject to the fiscal and monetary policy decisions within the confines of many countries. Hence, when corrective action is occasionally needed on a nontariff agricultural trade barrier, for example, little attention is given the problem and there is little recourse to action by those such as private firms seeking relief from the "fallout" of protective action. In such a situation, the firms, rather than trying to remove the barriers, tend to add the cost of overcoming them to normal costs of doing business.

Added to the *apparent* decrease in the relative importance which was attached to nontariff agricultural trade barriers during the post-World War II period is the fact that they present a knotty conglomerate of legal, regulatory, and administrative phenomena with which to deal. The word *apparent* is emphasized because, as this study unfolds, the actual importance of the nontariff question will be revealed.

As pressures were relieved on exporters through the removal

of traditional protection devices, through GATT procedures, Kennedy Round negotiations, and the like, country after country began searching for more oblique methods to protect domestic producers and traders. So the form and substance of protection changed and became more complex; in the case of many agricultural products, effective protection increased. A case in point is the complicated legislation surrounding the U.S. Meat Import Act of 1964. Even though this legislation has never been applied, voluntary restraints by exporters to the U.S. market have been negotiated in order to keep imports below 110 percent of a quota. But in 1970 and 1971, when meat prices in the United States were increasing sharply, import quotas were invoked, the president immediately suspended the quotas, and meat was "free" to flow into the U.S. market. In October 1976 the president imposed quotas on imports of fresh, chilled, and frozen beef, veal, mutton, and goat meat to limit 1976 imports to about 560,000 tons (36,470 tons of beef from Canada). This action resulted from continued large shipments of beef from Canada caused by the substitution of cheaper Australian and New Zealand manufacturing beef in the Canadian market.

The uncertainty surrounding the annual negotiation procedure on quotas further complicates the trading process and prevents long-range export programing by foreign suppliers for a product—meat in this case—which is already complex in its economic relationships.

Despite attempts to push aside the subjects of agricultural adjustment and nontariff trade barriers, they continue to recur, each time stronger than before. In the case of agricultural adjustment, it is now evident that it constitutes one of the most fundamental questions in the United States and the European Economic Community (EEC). In developing countries, also, agricultural trade is finally being recognized as strategic in the solution of many of their growth and income problems. As to nontariff barriers, unprecedented research and action programs are now underway. Following the end of the Kennedy Round, GATT drew up a lengthy inventory of all nontariff measures suspected of interfering with trade. Successive stages of examination, discussion, analysis, and exploration of avenues for the removal of barriers have continued, and no doubt nontariff barriers will be one of the most important subjects in future trade discussions.

The general subject of nontariff trade barriers is treated in detail elsewhere.[6] Moreover, the topic of agricultural trade policy has been in the mainstream of professional economic discussion for some time. For this reason, this study will be more narrowly focused. It is limited to the treatment of nontariff barriers and their relation to agricultural trade and adjustment. It will consist principally of introductory observations about the problem and its evolution, a pragmatic survey of nontariff subject matter in agriculture, observations based on case studies, conclusions, and, in certain instances, suggestions relative to the nontariff barrier problem for trade negotiation.

Chapter 2.

THE NONTARIFF BARRIER PROBLEM

Nontariff barriers to international trade, which had been on the world scene for some years, proliferated after the 1962–67 Kennedy Round of tariff negotiations. They now have gained the attention of governments, commercial traders, and economic and political analysts as far stickier obstacles than tariffs to the flow of goods and services. The issues involved are complex and reflect the nature of the revolution which has been taking place in production technology and the distribution of goods and services since World War II. They also reflect the seeming inability of man and his traditional institutions to adjust to new developments and new conditions in political economy. It's hard to describe the situation in ordinary language. Only the most current bibliographies and abstracting services contain the term *nontariff barriers*. Economic analysis is hard-pressed to accommodate phenomena which encompass not only traditional tariff theory and political economy, but also law and property rights, and a vast area in public administration.

The area of nontariff barriers, because of its complexity and lack of specification, is in danger of becoming one of those vast repositories of residual subject matter into which nasty problems are swept and which, when confronted directly, result in frustration for the investigator. The subject has been difficult for those dealing in the affairs of world trade to identify, rationalize, and negotiate. Moreover, there is a tendency for negotiators on trade problems to deal principally with policies related to tariffs, prices, and other quantitative indicators and to leave in abeyance the more abstract and complex points and questions, even though the latter might be identified with some of the fundamental issues in trade liberalization. Be that as it may, international trade in agricultural products is of great importance to the world, and though

11

it is beset by many problems of a nontariff nature, an attempt must be made to push understanding a bit further.

Why has the subject of nontariff barriers suddenly become so important to the world? There have been many recent expositions on the subject,[1] but a few simple suggestions, most of which will be treated in greater detail farther on in this study, may suffice to introduce it. First, technology has introduced a flood of phenomena into the late-twentieth-century trading world which either did not exist or which were introduced in a more orderly fashion in the classical trading world. Traditional institutions in many countries have had trouble accommodating to the changes brought about. For example, the introduction of motor transportation has revolutionized the movement of agricultural products. Countries have had difficulties in investing in new facilities and in creating new national safety and environmental agencies necessary to accommodate the burgeoning trucking industry. As another example, the creation of entirely new lines of consumer products, such as frozen foods, and the introduction of these products into countries where they did not exist before have created all types of problems in distribution.

Prior to World War I, world trade was dominated by the movement of a rather homogeneous group of a few agricultural and related raw materials on the one hand, and relatively few standardized items of capital equipment on the other. This is no longer true. Science and technology have fostered the creation of hundreds of new products and have changed the form of old products so as to create a need for new standards, new health and safety regulations, and other forms of control mechanisms. Yet another example may be drawn from circumstances which arise out of the international transmission of technology. When a rapid transfer of technology from one country to another results in immediately improved efficiency and lower costs of production in the second country, one might expect a relative reduction in levels of protection in that country on that product. But this does not always happen because inefficient producers in the second country generally insist on protection against "somebody" so they won't have to make adjustments, and the "somebody" is almost always an outsider. This particular case is illustrated by what happened in the famous "Chicken War" in Europe vis-à-vis the United States in the 1960s.

A second explanation of nontariff barriers phenomena is that their visibility is much greater and their effects are felt much more, now that tariff and related direct protective measures have been reduced or removed. Where a tariff had previously been the first line of protection, its removal may have resulted in replacement by a different type of protective measure previously unused. Denton and O'Cleiracain point out that the removal or reduction of tariffs has an "incitement" effect in that it gives incentive to the introduction of new, or the extension of old, nontariff measures in order to maintain previous levels of domestic protection.[2] Certainly the removal of tariffs and the reduction in their relative importance in international agricultural trade has focused a spotlight on the nontariff question, an area which had been smoldering since the dramatic increase in nontariff barriers in the 1930s. This visibility was accentuated when, after the Kennedy Round of tariff negotiations, bodies such as the Organization for Economic Cooperation and Development (OECD) and the General Agreement on Tariffs and Trade turned their attention to national policies which distorted trade by nontariff methods. Before this, there had been little organized work on many of the indirect obstacles to trade. GATT has drawn up an inventory of nontariff barriers consisting of over eight hundred separate items based on notifications submitted by governments and consultation with traders about measures that were met in their export markets.[3] Visibility as well as the protective effects of nontariff barriers is likely to become more apparent if further effective moves are made among trading nations to eliminate tariff and other direct forms of protection.

A third reason for the recent rise in importance of the nontariff barriers problem is the vast public bureaucracies which have grown so fast during the past half-century. It is a moot point whether existing agencies are causes or effects of the large array of regulatory activities in international commerce today. Some of these agencies have no doubt derived in part from the need to regulate and administer the results of technological discoveries described above, but in many cases they have grown out of a shift of power from legislative to administrative authority. Such power has enabled governments to mobilize themselves in indirect fashion for purposes which are not always obvious in a sense of economic measurement. There is good evidence, however, that this administrative power has been used to discriminate strongly against foreign competition in many areas. For example, it has been used in negotiating in the areas of public purchase of goods and services, in implementing import quotas, in formalizing executive agreements, and in administering the vast complexes of state trading. In any event, apart from the multiplication of formalities, with their direct and indirect costs, there has been an increasing tendency by governments to equip themselves with extraordinary powers to cope with various types of imports whose competition is deemed dangerous or unfair. A mass of rules and regulations in international commerce, many of which are obstructive to legitimate trade, has resulted.

DEFINITIONS AND LANGUAGE:
WHAT IS A NONTARIFF BARRIER?

Protection is a subject that is laden with emotive and obscure language; but as has been said by many language analysts, the purpose of language is as much to conceal thought as to reveal it. Other researchers have dealt with the language problem, and even the semantic problem, which is involved in describing nontariff barriers. While recognizing that there is a communication problem even in the use of terminology, this study will not differentiate between the terms *nontariff barriers, nontariff distortions, nontariff obstacles,* and other, similar nomenclature. The reader is referred to the study by Denton and O'Cleiracain for an excellent treatment of the clarification of terminology.[4] Viewed rather simply, the term *nontariff barriers* has come to mean all those restrictions, other than traditional customs duties, which distort international trade. These include impediments at national borders, domestic laws and regulations of all types which discriminate against imports, and assistance programs aimed at stimulating domestic production. There are also many programs of governments which provide unusual subsidies to exports, including direct price guarantees or export restitutions, tax incentives, favorable financial rates for exports, and domestic programs of assistance to production which not only help substitute for imports but also promote exports. The definition used for nontariff barriers in this study is *any governmental device or practice other than a tariff which directly impedes the entry of imports into a country and which discriminates against imports—that is, does not apply with equal force on domestic production or distribution.*

Generally speaking, nontariff barriers include several types of policies or practices which interfere with or distort trade: (1) measures which restrict imports; (2) measures which provide assistance to domestic production in order to substitute for imports and which, in effect, promote exports; and (3) measures which provide direct assistance to exporters. Malmgren has described the scope of nontariff barriers as follows:

In essence, NTB's are usually linked to domestic economic and social objectives: Promotion of employment in low-wage unemployment areas; protection of key political constituencies; protection of priority sectors in national growth plans; preservation of government control of production and distribution of certain types of products; protection of a minimum production capability for national security reasons; import substitution for balance of payments reasons; protection of consumers, and similar objectives. Sometimes the NTB's are intended by governments to discriminate against foreign trade. At other times the NTB's have come about unintentionally, often as an outgrowth of some domestic policy decision which never took the trade impact into account at all.[5]

Nontariff barriers, then, are trade restrictions usually backed by national legislation or administrative law which are based on the power of a nation to regulate its domestic commerce as well as any other activity in the name of the public health, safety, and well-being of the nation's citizenry. In addition to including restrictions on international commodity and factor movement which arise because of clearly enunciated, well-defined, and properly administered laws and regulations, they also include certain potential barriers to trade. These barriers arise because of unwritten, ill-defined, or irregularly administered laws and regulations, and result in economic uncertainty. It is a well-recognized fact in international commerce that producers in many countries refuse to initiate the processes of production and distribution necessary to penetrate markets which may be currently unrestricted because of uncertainty over commercial policies in countries where the markets are located.

The protectionist principle is essentially the same, whether it is invoked through direct or indirect methods of legislation or regulation; whether it is effectuated by a well-recognized market impediment or as a psychological obstacle to trade on the part of all those against whom it is possible to discriminate. Whatever the technique used and whatever the reason for market exclusion, the result is a destruction of the benefits of geographical division of labor and industrial specialization. The inevitable consequence is a limitation of national and international incomes.

In the sphere of nontariff barriers, trade restrictions exist not only on account of "what the law says," but also because of what the legislative and regulatory potentialities are, or "what the law doesn't say." The element of uncertainty is far greater in the latter situation. Uncertainty of this type—political and administrative in nature—is far more elusive and potentially destructive than the kind of economic uncertainty involved in price changes, because in the former there is little quantitative information available for hypotheses. Statistical probability observations about legal and administrative procedures amount almost to pure guesswork. Hence, it is necessary to point out that, while a nation may be restricting "trade"[6] very little by law or administrative edict, behind the scenes there may exist a deep sentiment against foreign competition, and for protection, which may erupt in the form of a variety of market impediments once trade begins or increases to a sizable amount. What constitutes the restriction in this sense is the uncertainty surrounding trading potential because of what shippers and dealers *think* might be forthcoming *after* such moves as they might make have, in fact, been made.

Nontariff barriers to trade are also composed of dormant and temporarily unenforced legislation and regulations. In fact, these may constitute an even more dangerous obstacle to trade than unwritten law and arbitrary administration. Shippers move their products into a "legitimate" market, when suddenly the dormant law or regulation is enforced. This happens frequently in the case of perishables where supply conditions can build up or deteriorate rapidly. For example, when there are shortages of meat and poultry and when prices are abnormally high, local inspection and conditions of sale in certain European markets are known to have been relaxed, only to be rigorously enforced later when supplies became more plentiful and prices lower.

FACTORS AFFECTING LEGISLATION AND REGULATION

How and why do trade restrictions arise and thrive? While the same reasoning might be applied to all types of barriers, this section will present briefly some rationale for nontariff barrier legislation and regulation, and will be followed by a discussion of administrative issues in the next section.

Obviously, there are times and conditions more conducive than others to the imposition of trade barriers. There are certain factors the frequency of whose emergence influences the frequency of such periods and the intensity of cries for protection. Perhaps the foremost among these, and a factor to which allusion has already been made, is the influence of economic crises and depressions. *Crises* used in this context means not just localized or industry-wide setbacks, but general, national, worldwide, and structural depression. During such a state of affairs, the volume of business contracts generally shrinks, incomes fall drastically, and alternative employment possibilities for all production inputs are limited. Concomitantly, many sources of revenue for local and national governments dry up, their normal functions are reduced, and a variety of problems arise.

Historically, it is in such times of economic crisis that levels of protection rise and discriminatory practices of all types abound. Competent observers attribute the dramatic rise in protectionism in the 1920s and 1930s to depression and to the economic disintegration of Europe after World War I when Austria was partitioned into independent economic entities, followed by attempts on the part of European nations to fence one another off from various markets as competition increased and as business slackened. Certainly, the drive toward nationalism and self-sufficiency all over the world during the 1930s was accelerated by the aggravated state of national and world economies. Even within the United States, where constitutional powers prohibit trade restrictions among the states, economic conditions of that period were such that many interstate trade barriers were introduced.[7]

A second general factor tending to promote trade barrier legislation is competition due to innovations in production, transportation, and marketing techniques. This is exemplified by the methodical growth of mass distribution arrangements which circumvent older marketing channels. These methods are likely to be feared by producers and distributors in certain nations and localities lest their positions in the marketing system be undermined or bypassed. Direct selling, avoidance of central markets, and chain-store merchandising all bring new forms of competition and produce fear among existing interests. Also falling into this category is the growth of motor transportation through improvements in truck design, favorable common carrier rates, fuel-use efficiency, and highway expansion.

Specific improvements in commodity marketing techniques such as mechanical refrigeration, technological changes in food preservation, standardization in packaging, revolutions in communications procedures, and the streamlining of services have extended the area of competition and have allowed heretofore unknown intermarket penetration. Because they lead to the deterioration of local market structures in many areas, efforts are made to protect and preserve these markets for national or locally established producers and distributors. Of course, not all changes in production and distribution generate such negative reactions and effects. As will be pointed out shortly, many such changes facilitate the expansion of the trade process.

When rapid advances are made in production and marketing, national and local legislative and regulatory bodies may react in a variety of ways. If they fail to keep abreast of the times by their slowness in enacting progressive legislation and by repealing or revising outmoded statutes and regulations, efficient marketing will suffer. This occurs quite frequently because of the lack of uniformity in sanitary laws, grades, standards, and labeling regulations, and sizes, weights, and measures requirements. The intent, frequency of occurrence, and discriminatory intensity of nontariff barriers which arise in this form need not be connected necessarily with economic conditions or with deliberate attempts to protect local business from foreign competition. The force underlying such trade barriers is hesitancy or failure to accommodate a nation's legislation and regulatory activities to changes in social and economic circumstances. A simple change in demand may call for a different container, package, or quality which is not permitted or provided for by law in a particular country or locale. Such differences in requirements which arise and which are not attainable because of the slowness of legislative and administrative bodies to act may exercise a cumulative burden and act as a barrier in international commerce.

Outright retaliatory legislation against foreign imports may be directed against real or imaginary legislation in other countries. In effect, there is an inclination among legislative bodies to try to offset or to counteract the ill effects of restrictive legislation by other countries. Retaliatory legislation is probably correlated with some other motivation. For instance, in times of economic crisis not only will original barrier activity increase, but one would also expect an increase in retaliation.

Another factor responsible for trade barriers involves the raising of public revenue. As national and local government procedures and roles grow, multiply, and become more complex, new sources of revenue are needed to meet increased demands for funds or to replace old sources which have become inadequate. The recently enacted value added tax in certain European countries may be cited as an example. Taxes and licenses also seem to be correlated with economic crises and recessions, and may reinforce or be superimposed upon other barriers which arise in periods of commercial stress. The net result is a burden on international commerce and noticeable business instability. The same reasoning might be applied to the motor trucking industry, where tax evasion and instability of revenue are the twin results of high registration and license fees, high fuel taxes, third structure taxes, and lack of reciprocity between nation states.

ADMINISTRATIVE PROTECTIONISM

Nontariff subject matter involves the fields of law and commerce as well as economics; hence, an attempt to describe and invoke a world in which welfare would be scientifically optimized through the manipulation of nontariff barriers becomes a highly involved and tenuous undertaking. The discovery of motives for economic policy, therefore, cannot be simple or clear-cut in a world composed of nations, some of which are willing to suboptimize a welfare function, and which transfer power increasingly to the hands of administrators who are only indirectly responsible to public opinion. (In the case of the private corporation this problem is expressed in terms of management and stockholders.)

National economic policies vary widely. At one extreme, the analysis of motives involves an attempt to appraise the dispersed and conflicting individual decisions that in the aggregate produce an equilibrium of social forces. At the other, the principal thing that matters is the aims and the ambitions of a small administrative group and the means by which it is able to secure for its policies the continued acquiescence, or support, of the public.

Accompanying the relative decline of tariffs and other direct forms of protectionism during the past forty years has been the dramatic rise of an indirect, or administrative, protectionism, most of which has had a symbiotic relationship with nontariff laws and regulations. The passing of power from legislative to administrative forms of government has resulted in increasing opportunism in policy making and interpretation and has rendered it necessary for decisions to be made more quickly and in more complicated detail. One has but to observe the decision-making possibilities in the Common Agricultural Policy (CAP) at Brussels to appreciate the strategic position of certain administrators. In such a situation, what pressures are actually effective in the making and interpreting of policy? Who has the ear of those who must take action? Whose judgment and advice are used? How far are decisions based upon practical considerations concerning which responsible officials alone have, if not full, at least the best, information available? Do the administrators tend to consult experts who must almost necessarily be individuals with a direct personal interest in the decision to be made? Are the administrators more or less open to the pressure of vested interests when their actions are further removed from public criticism?[8]

Even though these questions defy clear and decisive answers, certain generalizations can be made. In the first place, however high-minded and able the administrators who conduct day-to-day policy, there is a real danger in their progressive withdrawal from direct and detailed public criticism and responsibility. Those who would question this should go into the burrows of officialdom and try to pinpoint who *really* is responsible for decisions and their implementation with respect to the United States under Section 22 of the Agricultural Adjustment Act, in the compensatory payments on grain in the EEC, and so on. The real danger is not so much possible graft and corruption, but the more subtle danger of the concentration of power in those who are not subject to direct public action and whose cumulative errors in judgment are not brought to immediate account.

Another fact appears clear from recent experience. The concentration of policy-making power in administrators puts a premium upon organized pressures from directly interested groups and lessens the consideration likely to be given to the general public interest, particularly unorganized consumer interest. In the case of agriculture, the result is that government policy and regulation in the area of nontariff barriers has historically been dominated by organized producers. Agricultural marketing schemes, export programs, and regulatory activities are in many cases directly accountable to farming interests. The various international commodity control programs set up to regulate production, trade, and prices are designed primarily to protect the financial structure of existing investments, even at the expense of new investment opportunities in areas of developing production.

Administrative devices used to restrict trade range from the imposition of fees and the issuing of licenses at the discretion of government officials to the use of regulatory measures such as veterinary, health, quarantine, and similar restrictions imposed for specific purposes, or merely the literal application of wide powers taken by governments to ensure adequate inspection, classification, statistical recording, allocation of quotas, or valuation of imports. Since there is a well-recognized procedure of judicial interpretation and appeal in most countries, estimates of the effectiveness of these laws and regulations ought to be made by investigation of the actual administrative practices followed in each country rather than by analyses of the powers granted by legislation. This study proposes to attempt that in a limited number of instances.

Suffice it to say that in recent years in the case of quantitative restrictions—quotas, license fees, exchange controls, and the like—it has been possible to pinpoint rapidly discriminatory practices, whereas the interpretative norms for certain regulatory activities are difficult to discover. One official told the writer, "Honestly, it depends on the price of _____ as to how rigorously I apply this particular regulation."

What is being emphasized here is the administrative aspect of protection rather than the essence of law and regulations.[9] In many instances, however, appointive or elective administrative officers are invested with the power to formulate rules and regulations which may facilitate the interpretation of legislation, and which carry the same authority as statutes. There is no uniformity among countries in the manner and sequence of issuing administrative directives, e.g., as among, say, France, Germany, and the

United States. In many cases, new administrative officers may issue their own revisions or supplements to the regulations. This in itself creates problems of administrative procedure, as it is often difficult to ascertain details of the latest set of regulations. The implications are often political, since each newly elected administration of a country brings with it selected appointive officers.

Finally, as has been intimated, it is difficult to ascertain the exact extent of protection resulting from the prerogatives given administrative officials. During the struggle over internal, or interstate, trade barriers in the United States in the 1930s, it was stated that

in the national and municipal areas administrative action resulting from the grant of wide discretion to the enforcement officers and action extending beyond statutory authorization has perhaps been more often used for protecting local products and entrepreneurs from out-of-state competition than has purposeful legislation.[10]

There is little doubt that administrators use their flexibility to discriminate against foreign competition. It is evident that administrative protectionism occurs on a wide scale and that special interests avail themselves of opportunistic application of administrative authority to the benefit of particular groups. Further, in many cases where injured parties ask for judicial review of administrative practice, decisions and relief are slow in coming.

POLITICAL BOUNDARIES AS NONTARIFF BARRIERS

Even in the absence of restrictions which arise either because of discriminatory design or for passive reasons that are due to differences in laws and regulations, political boundaries of themselves produce nontariff barriers and affect trade in a number of ways. There exist a variety of forms to be completed, investigations to be made, and legal procedures to be followed before business can be carried on in another country. All these involve extra time and expense. Aside from the legal and regulatory nontariff barriers, how do political boundaries produce barriers? Stated in a different way, why do political boundaries by their very nature result in market imperfections?

A trade restriction which results in extra marketing costs produces an upward jog in the transfer-cost gradient at that point, distorting the pattern of market areas and supply area. Hence, market areas that extend across political boundaries are reduced in size and often eliminated. It follows that the higher the barrier in terms of costs, the more nearly will the boundaries of economic and political areas coincide with each other. And, if barriers prohibit trade in commodities and factors, the political boundary becomes an economic boundary.

It is not difficult to conclude that a most important effect of national laws and regulations is their influence on location or production and processing of commodities. Figure 2.1 illustrates the effects of an international boundary barrier plus the special "circuity effect." This effect is best exemplified by the traffic through border stations. Since large overhead costs are involved in their upkeep, these stations, like bridges across a river, are provided only at intervals. In the case of many border stations, natural features such as rivers and topography help determine where roads and bridges—and consequently the stations—will be. Moreover, since all legal traffic must pass through these avenues, it is clear that international commodity shipments are made more circuitous and, hence, slower and more expensive, entirely apart from any extra time and expense involved in the actual crossing of the boundary.

In Figure 2.1 producers of a particular commodity are located around *A*, and a boundary runs along the straight line *HK*. With market costs directly proportional to transport costs, producers can deliver their product domestically at the same total unit cost— say "X" u.a. per unit—anywhere on the circular arcs *BC* and *FG*. If no extra costs or circuity were involved in the international transfer, the product could be laid down at the same total unit cost anywhere on the arc *CSF*. Assuming that crossing the border does entail some extra costs—for example, an inspection fee or an indirect tax— but that crossing can take place at any desired point, producers at *A* can sell only as far as the arc *DRE* in the other country. The dark area represents the loss of distribution range because of the requirement that has to be met out of the country. If regulations necessitate that interstate traffic pass through a specific port of entry, say *P*, the limit of the "X" u.a. delivery is reduced to *GFMRLCB*. Thus, it is evident that there is a further loss of distribution range because of circuity, i.e., because of the necessity of funneling traffic through *P*. This area is shown by the striped area.

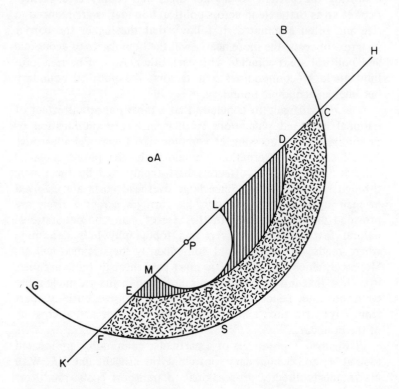

FIGURE 2.1. Effects of a Trade Barrier and Port-of-Entry Restrictions upon
the Distribution Area of a Production Center. From Edgar M. Hoover, *The
Location of Economic Activity* (New York: McGraw-Hill Book Co., 1948),
p. 220. Copyright © 1948 by McGraw-Hill Book Company and used by permission.

The effect of the boundary barrier is not uniform for all types
of commodities. Nor is the effect the same for productive factors
and finished goods. In the case of agricultural shipments, the
nature of the product (whether processed or unprocessed), the
location of the production area with respect to the boundary, the
susceptibility to insect infestation or animal disease, the existence
of grade and standard uniformity, the relationships between bulk
and value, and method of transportation, e.g., truck or rail, all

affect international marketing and location of agricultural production in their unique ways.

If international trade barriers were to return on the scale that existed in the early 1930s, the general effect on a production and processing localization would not be difficult to imagine. Points devoted to production near border areas would suffer under the economic consequences of smaller-scale production or higher average distribution of costs, or both. Processing plants located at strategic optimum procurement centers—which may be near national borders—may likewise suffer. In order to secure a steady flow of materials, the industry might have to move away from the border. However, on the other side of the border, protected trade areas and production centers are created and there arise certain advantages—artificially created—to border locations for industries in the "protected" country.[11]

ISSUES IN THEORY AND MEASUREMENT

While it is recognized that there are many valid arguments for protection made on narrower economic grounds of group, regional, or national welfare, the emphasis here will be on world welfare throughout. Attention is focused on those actions of governments or their representatives which disrupt the international movement of agricultural products and which, while disrupting trade, cause products or productive factors to be allocated in such a way as to reduce potential world income.

This study will not be normative, but, instead, a positive analysis. In other words, it will not be concerned with assessing the desirability of a protective structure or with defining the properties of an optimum structure. Rather, it will ask questions about the implications of a set of nontariff barriers for resource allocation, consumption patterns, and so on. The reader is referred to standard references in welfare analysis and international trade theory for the basic and detailed theoretical structure which underlies the descriptive and case study approach followed herein.[12]

As has already been implied, the measurement of nontariff protection is a difficult undertaking—much more difficult than that of tariffs, which are not only more identifiable but also more quantifiable. Also, we have noted that many nontariff barriers are concealed in administrative practice, and their effects are in many

cases indirect, vague, and hard to measure. What follows in succeeding chapters is an attempt to demonstrate briefly that, even
though there are difficulties in theory and measurement, protection through the use of nontariff agricultural barriers is still recog-
nizable, and deliberate discrimination against foreign production
is still identifiable. Admittedly, however, satisfying the economist's criteria with respect to welfare in every case is almost a
hopeless task.[13]

Perhaps a warning should be given to those economists and all
others who deem all government restrictions on trade as "bad."
Not all so-called nontariff barriers are evil, nor are they all equivalent to tariffs in their effects. Since the economist's case against
nontariff barriers can be overstated and confusing as to assessment
and remedy, several clarifying points need to be made.

First, as has been already pointed out, there are literally thousands of national laws and regulations which affect the movement
of agricultural products across international boundaries. Many of
these national—even supranational—laws and regulations are trade-
facilitating and trade-enhancing, being necessary to the commerce
of a modern society. Indeed, the fivefold growth in trade volume
since World War II in an increasingly economically complex and
technological world would hardly have been possible without
regulations, standards, and public direction. There is a whole range
of national statutes and regulations designed not only in the public
interest of particular nations but also in the interest of the world.
The prohibition of foods unfit for consumption and of articles
dangerous to the health of human beings, animals, or plant life
falls into this category. The enforcement of these laws and regulations can lead to confusing and misleading assessments about
economic effects of nontariff barriers.[14]

The economist is not alone in his inability to assess the impact
or alternatives in such matters. Biologists, chemists, and engineers
also are often at variance in determining risks involved with
certain government actions and policies. Industry interests and
officials who are aware of the probable consequences of laxity
are inclined to take no risks. Nontariff barriers in the regulatory
field are likely to range downward from this absolute type to
those which are much more questionable and which are simply a
method of indirect protectionism; but quantification is still a
problem.

The demand for new, processed agricultural products in industrialized countries is diversified and tends to change continuously. If conditions permit, developing countries can take advantage of the existence of these expanding outlets by resorting to appropriate marketing strategies, e.g., with new products.[15] Much is being done by *Codex Alimentarius* to make food and other standards preparatory to international shipment uniform.

The *Codex Alimentarius* Commission first met in 1963 with thirty countries represented. Today, membership has grown to over ninety countries. The objectives of the commission are, first, to develop international food standards on a worldwide, regional, or group-of-countries basis; second, to publish these standards in a food code (the *Codex Alimentarius*); and third, to record the acceptance and implementation of the standards by governments. The standards elaborated by the commission aim at ensuring the health of all consumers and the maintenance of fair practices in national and international food trade. They contain requirements which will ensure the consumer a sound, wholesome, correctly labeled product free from adulteration. In order to ensure that all concerned have a chance to register their points of view, each standard goes through a system which involves ten separate steps. There is no legal obligation upon member governments to accept a recommended standard. If they do accept it, they do so in accordance with their own established legal and administrative procedures and in respect of the distribution of all products complying with the standard, whether the products are imported or home-produced. Provision is made for three forms of acceptance:

Full acceptance: which is acceptance of the standard as it is written.

Target acceptance: which is a declaration that the standard will be given full acceptance in a specified period of time.

Acceptance with minor deviations: which broadly means that the government accepts the standard with the exception of a few minor points (which must be specified, as must the specific provisions which replace them, together with the reasons for the exceptions.)

A second clarifying point on economic assessment of laws and regulations relates to discriminatory measures which governments take that, judged by conventional economic criteria, might worsen the welfare of the country imposing the policy but improve that of the rest of the world.[16] With some nontariff distortions, such as export subsidies and certain quota systems under which quota rights are allocated to foreigners rather than to nationals, the economic case against the distortion is different from that against conventional tariffs. The reasoning by economists implies the possibility that a nation, by imposing tariffs, may gain at the expense of the rest of the world, thereby reducing world income; whereas with certain nontariff instruments such as those cited above, even though world income still is reduced, the "rest of the world"–other than the nation imposing the distortion–gains. The changed outcome in those instances between tariff and nontariff barriers gives rise to the question, With whose welfare should international arrangements be concerned?

Obviously, the problem does not terminate simply as one of measurement of aggregate incomes between one nation, the "rest of the world," and the world. Should nations be constrained from using instruments which are consciously used to reduce the welfare of their citizens? Distributional problems in "the rest of the world"–some nations gaining, others losing–will also result from nontariff national policies, and an outcome is not determinable a priori. The point remains, in this issue, as with the issue regarding regulatory policies, that not all outcomes of nontariff intervention can be judged "bad" on the basis of conventional resource allocation analysis. There are, of course, many more complex economic issues involved which will not be discussed here.

Yet another point that needs to be clarified relates to the attributes and the role of economics as a policy science. If it might be assumed that all citizens of a country are enlightened and well informed and that a general will or purpose emerges without serious protest, one might accept the notion that political decisions, including those about nontariff protection and related policies, must embody a collective utility sufficiently large to offset the loss of private utilities they obviously occasion. Tobin has asked why the preferences of individuals "should be worthy of respect only when they are expressed in the market, why the preferences of the very same individuals expressed politically should be regarded as distortions."[17] One reply to this, of course, as Ohlin points out, is that "anyone who is preoccupied with the prevalence of market failure in the economic process must be at least as impressed with 'market failure' in the political process."[18] In short, public action cannot abolish Keynes's famed "risk, uncertainty and ignorance" and cannot itself escape them. To postulate the rationality of national governmental processes is to eliminate the political element of political economy and to neglect the problem of inadequate knowledge on the part of politicians and administrators. This might be more heroic than to postulate market perfection.

Ohlin, like many others, recognizes that nations are bound to seek a degree of control over their economic destinies which will in some cases entail a sacrifice of conventional resource allocation, at least in the short run.[19] Moreover, continued trade liberalization will probably force governments to seek this control in new ways. The domain of domestic distortions through development, technology, and new industrial policies and those nontariff trade barriers relating thereto will more than likely be where government intervention will increasingly assert itself rather than as trade restrictions at national borders. Comparative advantage and the traditional concept of an effective division of labor thus become more difficult to ascertain in a changing world of sophisticated protectionist instruments, which do not lend themselves easily to codification and measurement.

Finally, because the impact of nontariff barriers is difficult to quantify and measure, they do not lend themselves easily to bargaining in a multilateral context, as have tariffs in previous rounds of GATT negotiations. Hindley speculates that the Kennedy Round success was facilitated by each government's knowledge that it could, if necessary, substitute nontariff methods of protection for the explicit tariff protection it was giving up.[20] No such facilitating reservation is possible for nontariff barriers, which probably means that future negotiations must deal with the hardest core of governmental impulses toward protectionism. The economist's objective in all this lies in trying to define a positive outcome which could satisfy economic criteria of welfare improvement (for this study, an increase in world welfare) and which would stand some chance of official acceptance. The political objective, again, is in minimizing or eliminating the political element in political economy, and in overcoming the problem of inadequate knowledge on the part of politicians and administrators.

Chapter 3.

THE EVOLUTION OF AGRICULTURAL PROTECTION FROM TARIFF TO NONTARIFF BARRIERS

Clearly, there are factors which differentiate the elements of agricultural protection in the 1970s from those which existed a hundred—or even twenty-five—years ago. Underlying the changes both in the policies of governments toward protection and in the measures taken to implement those policies are some major forces which should be recognized when analyzing the problem.

First, and perhaps most important, scientific discovery and technological change have greatly altered the production and distribution of agricultural products. The impact of technology has particularly affected the *economies of scale*—hence costs; *geographical areas of production; time, form, and function of utilities created;* and *the dominant consumer orientation of the products.*

Second, changes in forms of government and in the role which public policy plays in economic life took a radical turn after World War I, resulting in more direct intervention by the state in production and trade activities.

Third, techniques of protection were altered. Entirely new measures were invented and imposed by governments in order to cope with foreign and domestic economic disequilibria. There were, of course, other forces at work such as natural disasters and war which affected production and trade in agricultural products.

One mistake commonly made is to emphasize agricultural protection as having become important only after the formalization of the import quota, the variable levy, and the export subsidy. Various forms of protection have existed at least since the mercantilist era of the seventeenth and eighteenth centuries. One has but to study the history of Western European and United States agriculture and related governmental policies during the past hundred years to conclude that many of the problems of the present era—market surpluses, high-cost programs, low farm incomes, rural poverty, and others—are the result of the unwillingness of the agricultural sector to adjust. The failure of that sector to adjust to changed economic and political circumstances brought on attempts to insulate agriculture from outside pressures.[1]

There is also a school of thought which holds that the relatively free trade periods of the nineteenth and twentieth centuries and Great Britain's peculiar role therein are but aberrations in history and that the true state of affairs is not free trade and internationalism, but protection and nationalism. This point of view cannot be accepted without encouraging the advocacy of trade impediments for all sorts of reasons. The history of tariffs and mercantilism is largely a record of interest groups maneuvering for a privileged position while advancing high-sounding economic reasons, even patriotism, as the basis for their actions. Arguments between mercantilists and classical liberals in nineteenth-century England centered on questions of employment, living standards, national welfare, and national power; the lengthy prevalence of the liberal, free-trade position should be interpreted less as a historical accident than as a demonstration of the benefits to be gained from a policy of unfettered international commerce. Experience with tariffs in the latter part of that century, when there was a widespread increase in their use, is sufficient proof that moderate and stable tariffs, while they hamper and distort trade, do not destroy it. This is primarily because they are not compatible with the working of competitive prices and not destructive of the market mechanism.

Really dangerous tariff and other protection policies come into play when trade impediments are used primarily for reasons of state, or as instruments of economic warfare. When protection is advocated as a means of strengthening the power of the state through measures of self-sufficiency or by establishing strategic industries, or by building up trade connections which are less vulnerable in times of crisis—when national power and prestige are thus invoked—then a specialized, interdependent trading system becomes more difficult to operate. What ultimately leads to international commercial breakdown—as was the case in the demise of the nineteenth-century trading system—is the pursuit of economic policies for nationalistic goals, the use of instruments of protection for predominantly political rather than predominantly economic objectives. Nontariff measures lend themselves much more readily than tariffs to purely political objectives.

George Jones of the Institute of Agricultural Economics, Oxford University, makes the following point:

> More might be made of the growth of the size of the units controlling the protective devices rather than the growth of the devices. For instance, measures to promote both inflow and outflow of grain at the provincial level have a very long history as well as restriction on the kind of things and people that will be permitted at local markets. Both antedate the mercantilist era by a long stretch. The persistence of protective devices over a long period of time only suggests that they are in the local interest and not that they are in the international interest. It may not even prove this if the "territory" instinct is as strong as Ardrey suggests. Clearly the national avoidance of risk and national flexibility have been given as reasons for limiting trade but very often in an illogical manner. I think it is almost always the case that a degree of external dependence is safer than relying on oneself for everything—even in a war situation. One need not go quite as far as the Dutch revolutionaries who said that they increased the chances of winning their war by earning foreign exchange by selling firearms to Spain. I would rank the distinction between a search for absolute national benefits from trade as less harmful presently than a search for more benefit than other nations are getting. I think it is the latter spirit which is fouling up the works more effectively and is even encouraged by the GATT insistence on Reciprocity. Perhaps reciprocity would be O.K. with a coinage by which devices may be measured simply in terms of the net damage they inflict on other parties. Then one is simply required to put so much into the pool all round in proportion to G.N.P. and/or trade in some combination and "pay" for any new device.[2]

EARLY AGRICULTURAL PROTECTION POLICIES

Tariff structures developed and used by some countries in the nineteenth and early twentieth centuries were but more formal means of achieving essentially the same results as the variable, discriminatory, and opportunistic use of import duties of the mercantilist era. Those structures were at first simple but later became much more elaborate. Protective tariffs played a major role in preserving the feudal status of agriculture in many European countries, and adjustment processes were prevented, continually causing problems in liberalizing international trade policies. Exceptions were in Great Britain, Denmark, and the Netherlands, where liberal trade policies and progressive agricultural legislation assured a different outcome on farms and in rural areas. Britain's unique experience resulting from the enclosure movement, the industrial revolution, and the abolition of the Corn Laws in 1846 placed it in a position of world leadership with respect to trade expansion. The United States first initiated a detailed protective policy toward agriculture in the 1890s when it adopted a complete schedule of duties on farm products. These increased in level and in scope to culminate in the famous Smoot-Hawley Tariff Act of 1930. As they became involved in international commercial activities, other countries adopted the protective tariff according to the assessed needs of their agricultural sector.

In the years before 1930, chief reliance was placed on the customs tariff for agricultural protection. By the beginning of World War II, however, in many countries, and particularly in Europe, the tariff had come to be overshadowed by the newer and more directly effective methods of trade regulation such as quotas and exchange control. Nevertheless, the greater part of the trading world was still regulated by tariffs. The trade policies of the United States, the British Commonwealth, and most of Latin America were operated largely under a tariff system until World War II broke out. And even after the trade breakdown of the early 1930s, when quantitative and other restrictions became predominant, tariffs were still intimately linked with the new methods of control and stood at inordinately high levels. Moreover, though not nearly so much was heard about them after the Reciprocal Trade Treaty, the GATT, and the Kennedy Round, tariffs have through the years remained formidable barriers to agricultural trade.

With exceptions, such as those of Britain, Denmark, and the Netherlands, and that of the "free-trade interlude" after the Cobden-Chevalier Treaty of 1860, tariffs on world agricultural trade were high during the nineteenth and early twentieth centuries. Of course, since most of the trade was within Europe or between Europe and other Temperate Zone countries, it was there that the effects were most noticeable. France had substantial duties on all major agricultural products and on livestock and livestock products. Germany's protective policy was directed particularly at foreign grain with its high tariff rates of 1885 and 1887, which were raised even higher in 1902. In Italy, Belgium, and Switzerland, foreign grain, livestock, and livestock products were taxed heavily. From 1870 on, tariffs were increasingly raised on agricultural products entering Austria-Hungary, Sweden, Spain, and Portugal.

In the United States, the McKinley Tariff of 1890 assured a powerful alliance between eastern industrialists and western grain and livestock producers, and high duties on agricultural imports for more than forty years. In retrospect, the high-protection position of the American farmer during that era is difficult to rationalize because tariffs were of little value to low-cost producers in solving their price and income problems.

"Make the tariff effective for agriculture" was one of the slogans around which farmers rallied after World War I. Essentially, this plan was based on tariff protection with a concomitant purchase plan for surplus farm products. The maximum price to be paid for surpluses was to be the world price plus the tariff. High tariffs on agricultural products continued as United States policy until the 1930s, but none of the many schemes coupling tariffs with two-part price systems and export dumping were enacted during the agitation for farm legislation that lasted for a decade after World War I. It is important to note, however, that during this chaotic period in American and European agriculture the seeds were sown for those statutory and regulatory actions which in the 1930s ushered in a new era of nontariff protection and mercantilism that has been with the world ever since.

A general assessment of tariff policy and agricultural protection up until about 1930 indicates some underlying forces operating not only in Europe but also in other parts of the world. A preponderance of these were favorable to the protectionist argument. First, and perhaps most important, during the formative years of tariff construction were those forces deriving from the feudal heritage, land patternization and tenure, which were reinforced by philosophical tenets surrounding the agrarian mystique. For example, the physiocrats and J. Méline in France, Professor Adolph Wagner in Germany, and their disciples argued for special protective considerations to preserve farming and rural life. These were overriding factors in giving agricultural interests the power they needed to obtain high import duties in France, Germany, and many other countries. To be sure, the sheer size of the farm and rural population gave added weight to their political power.

Trade policy negotiators have been confounded and frustrated for a long time by those who argue for a special dispensation for agriculture based on those apparent mystical relationships between man, land, and nature; between national culture and farm tradition; and between personal identity and rural living. Fundamentally, these, along with farm structure problems, constitute a strong reason why agricultural trade problems have not been brought into the mainstream of recent trade negotiations. One may also detect in certain free-trade arguments—e.g., in Ricardo—a selective attitude in the deliberate writing off of landlords as too reactionary to make good economic agents in comparison with entrepreneurs. The implication is that "agriculture is different" and must be treated differently. No doubt, the more direct price and income objectives of national farm policies have now become the major obstacles to international trade liberalization, but agricultural fundamentalism is not yet dead in the argument for protection.

A second major force at work in early agricultural tariff formulation was the shrewd rationale used by certain industrial interests to ally themselves to farmers or groups representing the predominantly agrarian population in order to legislate high duties on all imports. This was particularly true in Germany and the United States, where in many cases the major parties being served were the industrialists, but where farmer interests appeared to be the more vociferous. In the United States, agricultural protectionist sentiment crystallized around the McKinley and Dingley legislation, when tariff levels varied between 20 and 57 percent during the period 1882–1902.[3] An alliance between industrialists and dairy and livestock groups—particularly wool growers—had skillfully fostered the proposition that the welfare of farmers, and indeed that of the country as a whole, depended on high tariffs in agriculture.

Third, tariffs supported arguments for national self-sufficiency. This was particularly true in continental Europe; and, indeed, the self-sufficiency reasoning has prevailed over the years as the basis for tariffs as well as all types of import controls. It has finally made inroads even in Britain, where during the nineteenth century tariffs were shunned in favor of cheap bread and no taxes on food during the industrial revolution.

Various attempts have been made to measure the level of tariff protection for agriculture prior to the modern era. This is not easy because of statistical weighting problems involved in translating "specific" duties to ad valorem or nominal terms of protection. Liepmann made an attempt to compare tariff levels for foodstuffs in selected European countries in selected years.[4] Tracy has extracted data from that study for expository purposes.[5] Levels of protection for the years 1913, 1927, and 1931 are presented in table 3.1.

TABLE 3.1. Average "Potential" Tariff Levels for Foodstuffs

Country		Tariff Level	
	1913	1927	1931
France	29	19	53
Germany	22	27	83
Italy	22	25	66
Belgium	26	12	24
Switzerland	15	22	42
Austria[a]	29	17	60
Sweden[b]	24	22	39
Finland	49	58	102

Sources: H. Leipmann, *Tariff Levels and the Economic Unity of Europe* (London: George Allen and Unwin, 1938); M. Tracy, *Agriculture in Western Europe: Crises and Adaptation since 1880* (London: Jonathan Cape, 1964).

Note: These figures represent the unweighted averages of duties on thirty-eight important foodstuffs, expressed as a percentage of the export prices of leading European exporting countries. Hence the results cannot be regarded as precise, and the increased incidence of specific duties reflects the decline in prices as well as increases in the duties themselves. Nevertheless, the figures indicate the relative levels of prevailing tariffs.

[a] For 1913, the figure given is for Austria-Hungary.

[b] Fruits and vegetables not included.

Even though the statistical data and the methodology of measurement used in this and similar studies leave much to be desired, it seems reasonable to conclude that in most countries with a protectionist policy before World War I rates lay between 20 and 30 percent. In the United States, many products were protected by 20 percent rates, some by more than 50 percent. By 1931, tariffs had been raised to several times their pre-World War I level in many countries, Britain had converted to protectionism, and the United States had passed a succession of tariff acts culminating in the almost prohibitive Smoot-Hawley Tariff of 1930. These high rates, coupled with the steady decline in agricultural prices on world markets during the 1920s, resulted in the anomalous situation in which tariffs on some commodities in some countries were 200 or 300 percent of their world market price.

Yet, even these high levels of tariff protection could not restore prosperity to agriculture in a world plagued by depression and unemployment. In fact, the retaliatory tactics used by countries against foreign imports only exacerbated the fundamental disequilibrium in agricultural trade that had resulted from an overexpanded industry during World War I. Yates has shown that world trade in Temperate Zone farm products was considerably lower in the mid-1930s than a decade earlier.[6] The volume of trade was up from 1913, but the value of exports for most products was below that of the pre-World War I period. (See table 3.2.)

For example, the value of world food exports in 1937 was only 85 percent of 1913 levels. In the case of fibers, the value of exports was 6 percent higher in the latter period, but the volume was 4 percent lower. Though certain agricultural economies of Europe suffered less from reduced trade than the large exporting countries, agriculture and agricultural markets everywhere were in a severe state of depression after 1930.

Attempts at international action to alleviate agricultural depression were ineffective in these recurring crises, as were the unilateral actions to raise tariffs. These attempts at cooperation, beginning as early as 1889 at the International Congress of Agriculture in Paris, included frequent efforts by the International Institute of Agriculture (founded 1905), the League of Nations, the London Economic Conference of 1933, the International Wheat Committee, the Chadbourne Sugar Agreement of 1931, and

TABLE 3.2   World Food and Fibers Exports, Selected Years

Commodity	Current Value			Unit Values[a]		Volume Index[b]	
	1913	1929	1937	1929	1937	1929	1937
	($ Millions)			(1913 = 100)		(1913 = 100)	
Cereals	1,784	2,052	1,526	107	88	107	98
Livestock prod.[c]	1,152	2,132	1,557	137	114	135	118
Coffee, tea, cocoa	553	946	653	123	79	139	149
Oilseeds & fats	751	1,109	882	92	68	161	171
Fruits & vegetables	449	872	660	105	69	185	214
Sugar	461	719	432	84	62	185	152
Other food & drink	385	626	541	--	--	--	--
Total food	5,535	8,456	6,251	113	85	136	133
Fibers	2,018	3,213	2,060	133	106	120	96

Source: Adapted from P. Lamartine Yates, *Forty Years of Foreign Trade* (London: George Allen and Unwin, 1959).

[a]Weighted average of unit values of the various items in each group.

[b]Current value deflated by indices of unit values.

[c]Including live animals.

others. Many cooperative efforts were made to restore balance to agricultural markets and to reduce tariff and other distorting trade measures. Excellent studies were made, conferences held, and admirable resolutions passed, but with little impact on national policies.

These international actions and joint efforts in the fields of monetary and trade policies during the critical periods prior to the mid-1930s seemed to have one thing in common: international agricultural trade problems had a relatively low priority and were pushed aside repeatedly and ultimately ignored as being impossible to deal with in meaningful fashion. Lessons can be learned from those experiences as well as from those of the "standstill agreements" on agricultural problems during the Dillon Round negotiations (1959–61) and the inaction on agricultural trade barriers of the Kennedy Round. That lesson is this: problems of agricultural trade and structural adjustment are important issues even in the most advanced industrial countries, and problems involving the production and marketing of agricultural products in the current content of world trade are not so different from those problems of other industrial sectors, nor can their solutions be delayed indefinitely.

STATE INTERVENTION:
THE NEW AGRICULTURAL PROTECTIONISM

Though the massive interwar intervention of the state in economic processes appeared to be entirely new at the time, the general philosophy was as old as mercantilism itself. Over most of the new systems of trade regulation which arose during the 1930s might be written Thomas Mun's seventeenth-century precept "We must ever observe this rule: to sell more to strangers yearly than we buy of theirs in value."[7] New types of intervention in international trade—and in production processes contingent to trading practices—were new only in the sense that they adapted old devices to modern monetary and administrative conditions in what was essentially a reversion to the primitive ideas and trade practices of the seventeenth century. The setting was new, but the idea of and desire for "a favorable balance of trade" was very old.

After the financial and commercial breakdown in the 1930s when the major trading countries found themselves with low agricultural prices and mounting surpluses, they reverted to the most rudimentary forms of mercantilism: credit and exchange controls (their mercantilist predecessors were concerned with precious metals), reduced imports, increased home production, and increased exports. The result was trade distortion, rising budgetary costs, and widespread misallocation of resources in agricultural production throughout the world.

Behind the visible signs of economic stress, manifested in currency depreciation, capital movement, and exchange control, were more fundamental economic disequilibria brought on by the contractions of export markets and the decline in world prices for agricultural products. Cause and effect were interrelated, and the chain of events led inevitably to more protection. The rapid fall of agricultural export prices after 1929 resulted in balance-of-payments difficulties for the heavy agricultural exporters and the agricultural debtor countries. They made strenuous efforts to meet their international obligations by increasing production and exports, at the same time reducing imports of manufactured goods. But these efforts were largely nullified by the continuing fall of agricultural prices, and the stress on capital balances led inevitably to nervous withdrawals, accentuating the stress and causing an intensification of tariff protection as well as the erection of new types of trade obstacles.

The reduction in industrial imports by debtor countries (developing countries, as they would be called today) and their strenuous export efforts led to increased passive import balances in the trade of creditor countries. Quantitative import restrictions were erected against foreign export promotion. A good example of this was the case of France. But the great bulk of cheap agricultural exports were directed at traditional free-trade countries—Britain, the Netherlands, and a few others—all of which in turn took steps to protect their domestic agriculture. In some cases, the flood of exports breached even the high tariff barriers of European industrial countries which had always protected their peasant agriculture.

Many European countries were bound by commercial treaties and conventions which had stabilized their tariff duties. This fact, coupled with the sterling devaluation in September 1931, brought further pressure on their inefficient farm production due to price reductions on exports from Commonwealth countries. For example, a French or Swiss peasant already faced with cheap Australian wheat and wool suddenly found domestic prices for these products halved in terms of francs. The costs of peasant agriculture being relatively fixed, such surplus product dumping and foreign exchange manipulation could not be offset by corresponding currency devaluation in this instance because of the lively memory of post-World War I inflation, especially in the peasant communities of Germany. Finding themselves "boxed in" by economic and political circumstances, these countries understandably turned to new, direct, more effective trade restrictions.

The new agricultural protectionism was radically different in nature and scope from the protective tariff in that it involved a philosophy which assumed a role for government of direct intervention in the production and marketing processes. Particularly affected at first were internationally traded products. A vast array of nontariff barriers supplemented tariffs in protectionist orthodoxy, and public intervention became an accepted norm for domestic agricultural adjustment.

Most of the effective trade restrictions on agricultural products that countries have adopted since the early 1930s have been but adjuncts to their domestic farm policies, which is to say that nations have not developed a separate and identifiable trade policy for farm products. Trade restrictions of a wide variety have been developed to make possible the functioning of domestic price and income policies as well as many programs which do not have specific and identifiable price and income objectives. In the latter category lies almost all the regulatory and indirect protectionism which has emerged over the years.

This new era of nontariff barriers on agricultural trade first emerged in European countries when high tariffs and monetary controls were ineffective in protecting domestic agricultural producers from foreign exporters who were prepared to sell at almost any price. Sumptuary laws, such as milling regulations, required the mixture of a fixed ratio of domestic and foreign grain in order to safeguard the market for local production. These were imposed on millers in Norway, France, and Germany in the period 1927–29, then spread through the world. These were but one of a family of so-called linked-utilization and linked-purchasing measures by which a home-produced product had to be used or purchased in conjunction with an imported product.

Import licensing systems were introduced and soon developed into quantitative import quotas as measures of trade restriction. Tariff quotas had been an integral part of commercial treaties since the mid-1920s, but the outright use of quotas on a large scale for agricultural protection occurred only after France initiated the practice in 1931. The restriction of imports by this technique spread rapidly during the depression years and is widely used today as a protective device, particularly in connection with domestic agricultural programs.

For example, import quotas have been used as an essential

counterpart of United States price support programs since 1935. Quotas on agricultural imports have also been associated with other devices such as license fees and exchange controls to protect agricultural and raw material producers and distributors from foreign competition. During that decade of chaos in world trade, the 1930s, veterinary, quarantine, and other regulations were strictly enforced. Also, an entirely new and complicated apparatus of state trading, monetary, and indirect protectionism was rapidly developed and put into practice.

Ultimately, the most significant form of protection for agriculture, which began on a large scale during the 1930s depression, derives from the direct intervention by the central government in the domestic production and marketing processes. Since that time, techniques of intervention have been applied in most countries, mainly to bolster returns to agricultural producers of individual commodities and to enable them to earn incomes higher than they would without intervention and protection. This intervention has resulted in wide-scale distortions in world prices and trade, large costs to taxpayers and consumers, and uneconomic expansion of farm production in the industrial countries, with corresponding ill effects upon associated countries. Today, supplemented and effectuated by other nontariff obstacles applied at national borders, they have replaced import taxes as the principal method of agricultural protection.

From a historical standpoint, in the period between World War I and World War II, we saw farmers and agriculturists again in the forefront arguing for protection and against adjustments in resource use in agricultural industries and the related rural sector. Economic conditions differed somewhat between the 1930s and the late nineteenth century, but the protagonists were the same. Particular national positions have changed little, but governmental agricultural and related programs and policies undertaken in the 1930s and after World War II affected international and commercial activities as the protective tariff had never done. Experiences of these and past eras give credence to the generalization that wars and depressions usually lead to increases in protection, whereas periods of peace and prosperity encourage movements toward free trade.[8] It could be observed rightly that the European Economic Community (EEC) and the Common Agricultural Policy (CAP) would hardly have achieved their current success except for the boom period in economic activity following World War II. Also it is unlikely that the United States could have followed its simultaneous policies of protection and surplus disposal of the past twenty years except in a period of exceptional economic growth, and increasing demand for–or disposal of–food and fiber.

It might seem unwarranted to draw comparisons between these confused early days of the new agricultural protectionism and the situation facing world agriculture and trade in the 1970s. Yet, there are sufficient similarities–as to both their nature and intensity–in the elements to give cause for concern. In the former situation, once the collapse of international monetary equilibrium gathered momentum, there was an interplay of cause and effect, one currency depreciation leading to another, and one country's trade restrictions provoking retaliation from others throughout the world. It was obvious that successive stages of protection could be justified in each country by its own urgent economic considerations.

What was not so obvious was that, however urgent these considerations might have seemed, they were not the fundamental causes, but instead the consequences, of the breakdown in the international economy. The real causes were deeper and lay in the gradual hardening of national economic policies until flexible adjustment became impossible. How far is the world down that same road today, despite current levels of prosperity and despite the institutional and political changes that have been made in order to stabilize monetary and trade conditions and to prevent a recurrence of catastrophic protectionism? There is certainly cause for concern in that governments have been slow to comprehend the need for flexibility in their national agricultural policies and have recently even shown tendencies toward thwarting readjustment in their agricultural sectors. Furthermore, nontariff barriers of many types appear to have emerged as an extremely formidable problem in liberalizing world trade in agricultural products.

PROGRESSION TOWARD NEOMERCANTILISM
IN AGRICULTURAL TRADE

The thirty-year period from the mid-1930s to the mid-1960s generally was characterized in agriculture by attempts on the part of governments to raise and stabilize returns to the commercial sector, to become more self-sufficient in basic crop and livestock sectors, and to develop their agriculture in an exchange-saving way so as not to be susceptible to the wild swings of world commodity markets. These attempts, which required ever increasing involvement by governments in agricultural production and trade, had their genesis in, or were predicated upon (1) the economic breakdown following World War I and the failure of tariffs to generate economic uplift for the farmer; (2) the failure of earlier nontariff measures to raise incomes; (3) the reasoning by agrarian fundamentalists that if only agriculture could be stimulated, other sectors of a national economy would respond with a "take-off" due to multiplier effects; and (4) war preparation for self-sufficiency reasons, or the effects of war. Agricultural and trade policies in Britain, Europe, the United States, and elsewhere underwent further change as they diverted their efforts from protective tariffs to direct governmental intervention in the agricultural production and marketing processes. Tariff structures were reinforced in many countries by new levies and administrative techniques. New devices to support prices and incomes were introduced and effectuated by a wide variety of administrative devices. Entirely new regulatory and administrative barriers to trade arose during the early days of this period, some of which subsided or became dormant after World War II when the first flush of expanding trade pushed them into the background.

The great reversal of commercial policy by Great Britain began during this period. It abandoned free trade in 1931 and adopted emergency protection measures which were replaced in 1932 by the Import Duties Act. This act has remained essentially the basic instrument of British tariff policy. What happened in Great Britain is illustrative of the trend toward state intervention and control throughout the world. The lasting economic effects of measures undertaken, along with the abandonment of the gold standard, the restrictions imposed in international lending, bilateral treaty negotiations, clearing and payment agreements, and a long list of state interventions in various fields of international economic relations—as well as in agricultural production and marketing— were to be felt from that time forward.[9]

The pattern of crisis and intervention was generally the same in all countries, but particularly in Europe from the 1930s on.

Agricultural protection by tariffs gave way to a variety of new, more effective nontariff devices which, for the most part, insulated domestic markets from foreign competition. Such restrictive and autarchic measures by one country were taken at the expense of others; the international market stagnated and the depression was prolonged by domestic economic policies which led to retaliatory and defensive strategies. The need for protection was thus perpetuated by actions in the domestic sphere, which governed actions at country borders and on the international scene. Behind the highly protective restrictions of most European countries, agriculture was encouraged to expand. Various countries used a variety of measures to deal with marketing problems thus created, but no consistent agricultural policy was developed to deal with structural maladjustment in agriculture. Hence, after World War II high price supports and other interventionist techniques were necessary to maintain incomes for uneconomic producing units. The merits of a free-trade policy will not be debated in this context, but it is obvious that protectionism failed because it insulated farming and agricultural industries from economic forces which could have induced changes; and it diverted attention from the need for more constructive programs.

In general, therefore, it can be asserted that effective agricultural protectionism increased after large-scale government interventions and with the advent of nontariff barriers. This increased protection came about in Europe because of a lack of structural development and a failure of the agricultural sector to adjust to changing economic circumstances. Ojala declares:

It is probably true to say that in most of continental Europe, agriculture emerged from the industrial transformation of Europe up to the Second World War still relatively insulated not only from external factors but also from the internal modernization of the European economies.[10]

After a century of relative shelter from outside forces making for change, post-World War II agricultural adjustment in Europe lagged behind the exigencies of the time and used nontariff protective devices to maintain farm incomes.

Exacerbating the adjustment and incomes problem in Europe and the United States were the increased production brought about by advanced science and technology and the slow growth in effective—commercial—demand for agricultural output. Thus the factors which farming desperately needed to adjust to became largely internal, in contrast to the previous century of experience, when the challenge came from outside competition and was answered with tariff protection. The general response to this need for adjustment was high price supports, which further stimulated output, imbalanced supply and demand on domestic markets even more, but did facilitate modernization. In this situation, Europe, with little or no supply control procedure, instituted measures at national borders, that is, import controls and export subsidies. These were necessary in order to perpetuate the high-price policies which followed. With a large number of wealthy countries in Europe subsidizing their agriculture either at home and/or in export markets, the external impact became one of the dominant factors in world markets.[11]

Clearly then, as European recovery from World War II proceeded, substantial increases in agricultural production were not reflected in trade. Though many trade restrictions had been removed in the industrial and other sectors, and though some progress had been made in removing quantitative agricultural barriers between European countries, a large portion of their production and trade of agricultural products remained subject to state intervention and control. In general, as shown in table 3.3, between the end of World War II and the early 1960s there was a marked increase in agricultural protection.

The study from which this table is taken calculated an "equivalent tariff" based on the suggestions of the Haberler Panel in 1958 which decided that the best way to measure the degree of total protection given to any line of agricultural production in any country by the combination of all protective devices used in that country would be to measure the percentage change by which the price (including any subsidy) received by the domestic producer exceeded the price at which the product was available from foreign suppliers or could be sold to foreign consumers.[12]

National methods for protecting agriculture were viewed as a combination of the following: (1) devices which directly discourage imports (import duties, quantitative restrictions, state trading, multiple exchange rates); (2) devices which encourage exports (export subsidies, multiple exchange rates); and (3) devices which directly encourage domestic production (price supports, deficiency payments). All these are reflected in measuring

TABLE 3.3 Changes in Degree of Protection, 1950-61

Country and Period	Wheat	Barley (all)	Beef	Pork	Eggs	Milk
Denmark:						
1950/51–1952/53	-9	9	3^a	3^a	-4^a	-3^a
1956/57–1958/59	2	8	-4^a	0^a	-3^a	9^a
1959–61	9	7	-3^a	-3^a	-4^a	35^a
France:						
1950/51–1952/53	7^a	––	––	28	––	18
1956/57–1958/59	20^a	5^a	-10^a	––	4	34^a
1959–61	17^a	21^a	29^a	3^a	19	46^a
Italy:						
1950/51–1952/53	13^b	-11	––	38	45	46
1956/57–1958/59	27^b	26	40	23	32	55
1959–61	37	28	41	23	39	62
Netherlands:						
1950/51–1952/53	-28	6	-8^a	8^a	-9^a	-6^a
1956/57–1958/59	12	16	-9^a	-4^a	1^a	32^a
1959–61	21	26	-12^a	-7^a	0^a	45^a
United Kingdom:						
1950/51–1952/53	16	9	40	36	38	36
1956/57–1958/59	9	24	42	24	34	61
1959–61	3	24	36	17	36	62
West Germany:						
1950/51–1952/53	7	10	34	24	19	18
1956/57–1958/59	29	36	45	23	32	36
1959–61	31	38	41	24	38	39

Source: U.S. Department of Agriculture, *Measures of the Degree and Cost of Economic Protection of Agriculture in Selected Countries,* Technical Bulletin no. 1384 (Washington, D.C., 1967), table 17, p. 21.

[a] Export values.

[b] Soft wheat.

an equivalent tariff, and in the degrees of protection shown in the table.

During this period, the degree of protection increased in France and West Germany for nearly all commodities, while for Denmark,

Italy, and the Netherlands, such increases were confined mainly to grain and milk. In the United Kingdom little change was observed in the overall degree of protection, as increases in one agricultural sector tended to be offset by decreases in another.

It is important to stress again at this point that the new protectionism and the neomercantilist tendencies in world agricultural trade are not simply a matter of trade barriers at national borders in the traditional sense. It is more a question of national agricultural policies—even monetary and fiscal policies—buttressed by internal and external administrative intervention and the social, economic, and political setting of the agricultural policies in particular. The locus of governmental intervention has shifted generally from overt trade interventions to operations within domestic economies. With this shift, the situation of world trade in Temperate Zone agricultural products has been deteriorating progressively despite appearances and temporary reprieves. An array of national and regional policies, buttressed on the one side by restrictions on imports and on the other by incentives to exports, is slowly closing available commercial markets to exporters. Our analysis will now turn to selective governmental actions illustrating this tendency.

Chapter 4.

TYPES OF NONTARIFF INTERFERENCES

As noted earlier, nontariff barriers began to supplant tariffs as the principal means of agricultural protection in the early 1930s, when tariffs were unable to prevent the effects of dumping surpluses on world markets. Domestic agricultural support schemes were part of overall programs to improve incomes in agriculture, which required protective measures in order that the schemes might work effectively. Many new techniques to restrict trade were instituted during this era.

Not all of these techniques involved import-restricting measures. Some export-increasing schemes were added to, or combined with, import nontariff interferences to make this one of the most protective eras of world history. What is embraced here and in the more elaborative Chapter 6 is the broad concept of nontariff trade interferences; hence the chapter title, "Types of Nontariff Interferences," to draw attention to that fact. Even so, major emphasis will be on restrictions, particularly on imports.

In 1947, when the General Agreement on Tariffs and Trade was drawn up, a series of provisions were written in principally to reduce tariffs, but also to avoid the frustration of tariff concessions through the use of nontariff measures. A variety of topics, including those which relate to agriculture—tariff and nontariff— are covered by this code of good behavior. GATT provisions are for the most part brief, dealing mainly in the principles to be followed, principles whose validity for nontariff barriers has been demonstrated despite trade developments over the years and in the face of multilateral reexaminations from time to time, such as that which has taken place under the Trade Expansion Program. The limited results of Kennedy Round negotiations in the agricultural sector are frequently attributed to their failure to come to grips with the nontariff question. Furthermore, it is asserted generally that a discussion of the question was hampered by a lack of precise knowledge about the subject.

In this chapter we shall give attention to efforts made by GATT and others to come to grips with the nature of nontariff barriers, particularly efforts throwing more light on the subject so that negotiations might proceed. First, this involves outlining the principal types of nontariff measures used in the agricultural sector which are suspected of interfering with the free flow of trade, irrespective of whether these are applied in conformity with GATT rules. After presenting this description of the major categories of measures, they are related to selected countries in which they are used. Finally, there is a brief discussion on the frequency of application of nontariff barriers and how they impinge on the broad product groups in agricultural trade.

TAXONOMY OF NONTARIFF BARRIERS

In recent years, there have been various attempts to identify, classify, and tabularize in some quantitative sense governmental measures which affect agricultural production, imports, and exports. The basic inventory made by GATT after the Kennedy Round consisted of over eight hundred items,[1] agricultural and nonagricultural, but other agencies, such as the United States Department of Agriculture, have done subclassificatory and identification work, as will become evident later. In the agricultural field, the GATT classification process was not limited to measures taken at national borders, since domestic programs, most of which relate to production and supply, often have a powerful effect on possibilities of market access by foreign distributors. The items were arranged in five general categories:

Section 1. Government participation in trade, including:
    (a) production subsidies;
    (b) export subsidies;
    (c) countervailing duties;
    (d) government procurement and restrictive business and union practices;
    (e) state-trading enterprises in market-economy countries.

Section 2. Customs and administrative entry procedures, including:
    (a) customs valuation;

(b) anti-dumping practices;
(c) customs classification;
(d) formalities connected with importation.

Section 3. Industrial, health, and safety standards, and packaging, labeling, and marking regulations.

Section 4. Specific limitations on imports and exports, including:
(a) licensing arrangements;
(b) quantitative restrictions including embargoes;
(c) bilateral agreements;
(d) voluntary restraints;
(e) motion picture restrictions;
(f) minimum prices on textile imports.

Section 5. Restraints on imports and exports by the price mechanism, including:
(a) prior deposits;
(b) administrative and statistical duties;
(c) restrictions on foreign wines and spirits;
(d) discriminatory taxes on motor cars;
(e) special duties on imports;
(f) credit restrictions for importers;
(g) variable levies;
(h) border taxes.

Even though it is becoming increasingly evident that analysis and measurement of agricultural trade barriers must go beyond national borders and treat the entire range of production and distribution problems, only a limited number of barriers will be treated in this study and their implications will be described for only a selected number of trading countries. Most of the analysis will center on the basic categories described as follows:

Quantitative Restrictions: These are devices which limit the amount of imports and exports of a product; they would include quotas, embargoes, and restrictive licensing. Probably the most familiar nontariff barrier, it is used on a wide number of products. The size of the quota (or the number of licenses issued) is the sole determinant of the degree of restriction created. With the exception of complete embargoes, quantitative restrictions usually involve the use of import or export licenses, although sometimes no quota is set and the limitation derives from restrictive licensing. Tariff quotas—a device whereby imports above a given level pay a higher duty—are also included under quantitative restrictions.

Licensing Requirements: As noted above, the existence of licensing requirements often entails import and export quantitative restrictions. In that sense, the terms may be used almost interchangeably. In some countries, imports of all, or nearly all, agricultural products are subject to licensing requirements. In those cases such restrictions need not be treated on a product-by-product basis but should be dealt with as a whole system. Increasingly, in a world short of agricultural products and raw materials, export licensing and control are coming into play. Licensing may also be restrictive in that it places an additional administrative and/or financial burden on the importer or exporter and may cause substantial delays between contracting and delivery dates; it may be only a nuisance (if freely granted) or a strong deterrent. Furthermore, on the import side, the requirement for a surety deposit, often including a provision to confiscate such deposits if shipments are not received in a specified time period, can place a substantial burden on an importer.

Variable Levy: This term is used in a broad sense to include those devices which impose a variable charge on imports. It may be applied in lieu of or in addition to the tariff. The basis for the variability of the charge differs by country and by product. Most often it is related to a minimum import price; in other cases, other criteria are used, such as the level of domestic prices. While generally associated with the European Community, the variable levy originated in Sweden and, as broadly defined here, is practiced by many other countries. It is generally connected with an internal price support scheme and is most frequently applied on imports of grain. The use of the variable levy provides a greater level of protection against international price competition than can be provided by a tariff; its tendency is to reduce external competitors to the position of residual suppliers.

Export Subsidies: Not all nontariff trade interferences come on the import side. A variety of schemes have been used to dispose of excess agricultural supplies generated by high support prices, mostly in industrialized countries. Even though they give us the *appearance* of being a by-product or afterthought of farm price programs, export subsidies in the form of direct price payments have, in effect, been a convenient tool, available as an integral part of national systems of trade interferences. Subsidization of transportation, usually in the form of a requirement that agricultural exports be shipped in national bottoms, is another type of subsidy. Also in the same category are favorable purchase terms, low-interest loans for purchases of farm products, and related subsidies. Export subsidies and promotion schemes are an invidious form of nontariff interference because they are often coupled with forms of import control and domestic supply-demand distortion. The dairy industry is one example of an industry which has simultaneously used all such nontariff protective devices.

Minimum Import Price: This device is almost always combined with some form of variable levy or supplementary charge, for which it acts as a trigger.

Supplementary Charge: This category normally includes all those charges (except variable levies) which are applied in addition to the regular tariff: surcharges, special import taxes, etc.

Import Calendar: These are restrictions on entry which apply only during certain periods of the year, generally when domestic production is marketed. The restriction may be either a complete prohibition, or a limitation on quantity, and is usually associated with fresh fruits and vegetables.

Conditional Imports: This barrier derives from a system whereby permission to import is made contingent in some way upon the sale of the domestic crop. The extent to which it restricts trade depends on the size and importance of domestic production.

State Trading: Importation by government or by a government-authorized agency results in varying degrees of restriction or discrimination, depending on the degree of control on price and consumption and the extent to which sources of supply are influenced by so-called nonmarket factors.

Mixing Regulations: These require the manufacturer to use a prescribed proportion of domestic products. In some cases, permission to import is withheld until the requirements are met; in others, mixing regulations work in conjunction with the tariff schedule. Failure to meet the requirements results in the imposition of a higher tariff rate. This device is generally associated with grain and tobacco products.

Health and Sanitary Regulations: All countries maintain health and sanitary regulations on imports and domestic products which, if properly applied, cannot be considered as nontariff barriers. The fundamental international trade problem is that each country sets its own standards, and these vary greatly. The determination of whether a regulation is reasonable or is being properly applied requires technical knowledge and is often controversial. Also, knowledge of such regulations in the trade policy field is generally skimpy and usually develops as a result of some special trade problem. Such regulations are considered to be trade restrictions if they are obviously unreasonable, if they are applied against imports in a discriminatory manner vis-à-vis domestic products, or, most important, if they pose special problems for world trade. They particularly affect trade in livestock, meat, and fruit and vegetables.

Marketing Standards and Labeling: This category includes those standards or specifications (other than sanitary and health regulations) imposed on domestic and imported products in the interest of quality control, consumer protection, etc. The situation with regard to marketing standards and labeling is much the same as with health and sanitary regulations. They abound in all countries and qualify for inclusion as barriers only if the considerations specified under health and sanitary restrictions apply. In the EEC, health and sanitary regulations and marketing standards are, for the most part, still administered by member states, although they are eventually to be administered on a Community-wide basis.

Bilateral Agreements: These are agreements between countries providing for the purchase or exchange of specific commodities or for special concessions to facilitate imports. They restrict trade from other countries in the sense that they tend to isolate the commodities negotiated from the realm of free market forces. Because information about such agreements is often not readily available, it is difficult to identify their trade impact. Bilateral agreements are particularly important in the trade of those countries with substantial nonconvertible currency dealings.

NONTARIFF BARRIER CLASSIFICATION
IN SELECTED COUNTRIES

After the basic inventory of nontariff measures was made in the GATT, the next process was to examine and to discuss each case in detail, giving the countries which maintain them a chance to explain the rationale behind their application. As would be expected, a variety of reasons—economic, social, political, strategic, health, safety, and moral—was given for the imposition of statutory and regulatory measures. Moreover, "not unexpectedly, there was a tendency in many cases to explain that the trade effects of the measures were small. Also, not surprisingly, many were not convinced."[2] Therefore, it is understandable that the countries involved made no initial attempt to reach accord on the quantitative effect of these restrictions. Assessment of trade effects of various measures must, of course, be undertaken by individual governments before negotiations can be concluded about their removal.

An Agricultural Committee was set up in GATT after the Kennedy Round to search for mutually acceptable solutions to nontariff barriers in both agriculture and other industries. All along, agricultural problems and nontariff barriers within the agricultural sector had been underestimated by most negotiators as a source of trade conflict. This became even more evident as each country defended special features of its agriculture in the committee discussions aimed at progress toward trade liberalization.

It was a recurrence of the same problem theme of agricultural maladjustment and protection from international competition that was born in the nineteenth century and that had been exacerbated in the 1930s by depression and in the 1950s by surpluses. Agricultural production problems were reflected in the international trade of agricultural products. Both production and marketing problems, as well as those of socioeconomic adjustment, continued to cause considerable difficulties for many countries, including those developing ones where agricultural output is efficient and cheap.

The GATT Agricultural Committee, therefore, encountered many difficulties in carrying out its task. Documentation and problem identification took more than two years, during which time the basic inventory was made of measures affecting agricultural imports (including processed products) of the major trading countries.[3] That inventory included tariffs, quantitative restrictions, variable levies and other special changes, health and sanitary regulations, and various other nontariff barriers to trade. This inventorying and cross-classification involved a vast amount of time and paperwork, as any visitor to the GATT offices can testify. The inventory is kept up to date and could, during the future trade negotiations, provide a concrete basis for progress in trade liberalization.

In the case of import restrictions, detailed summaries of data prepared by GATT cover those countries for which information on all types of restrictive measures is available. In the case of tariffs, the information is presented in the form of four ad valorem incidences for each country and for each Brussels Nomenclature heading. In the case of quantitative restrictions (including centralized trading), summaries indicate the type of restrictions in force. For variable levies and other special changes, summaries show for each country, and for each four-figure heading, the simple and weighted averages of the incidences. In the case of health and sanitary regulations, a succinct tabulation has been constructed with extensive notes as to country and regulation.

Out of these vast and detailed summaries one is able to derive generalized summaries of import restrictions by country and by general product category. Such a classification has been prepared for nontariff restrictions in table 4.1. Quantitative barriers and related licensing procedures dominate in this particular table, which has a variety of country types. Note, for example, the dairy products category listed in the first column. Only five countries out of the twenty-four listed do not report some form of quantitative restriction or licensing. And of the five, health, state trading, or other nontariff barriers are reported in three. Other nontariff barriers may be generally observed by studying the table more closely.

Even though no attempt is made in the GATT to interpret the results of the original classifications and summaries, nor by this writer to interpret results in table 4.1 and other such subsummaries,

TABLE 4.1 Summary Inventory of Agricultural Nontariff Barriers of Selected Countries, 1969

Abbreviations

BA	Bilateral Agreements	MP	Minimum Price
H & S	Health and Sanitary Regulations	Prohib	Prohibited
H Reg	Health Reg	QR's	Quantitative Restrictions
Imp Cal	Import Calendar	ST	State Trading
Lic	Licenses	Sup Ch	Supplemental Charge
Mix Reg	Mixing Regulations	VL	Variable Levy

Country	Dairy Products	Grains	Livestock & Meat	Fruits & Vegetables	Vegetable Oils & Oilseeds	Tobacco	Cotton
Australia	H & S	Prohib	Prohib	H & S	H & S VL	Mix Reg	Imp Cal
Austria	MP Sup Ch QR's Lic QR's	MP Sup Ch ST QR's	MP Sup Ch H & S	QR's Imp Cal Quotas	---	ST	---
Brazil	Sup Ch	ST BA QR's	---	Sup Ch	Sup Ch	---	---
Canada	Lic	Lic ST	---	QR's	---	---	---

TABLE 4.1 Continued

Country	Dairy Products	Grains	Livestock & Meat	Fruits & Vegetables	Vegetable Oils & Oilseeds	Tobacco	Cotton
Chile	ST Sup Ch	ST Sup Ch BA Advance Deposit	—	—	Advance Deposit	—	—
Denmark	Lic	MP Sup Ch Lic	Quotas Lic H & S	Lic Quotas Imp Cal	—	—	—
European Community	VL Lic	VL Lic	VL Lic QR's	Imp Cal QR's Lic MP Sup Ch	VL Lic	QR's ST	—
Finland	VL Lic	Lic ST	VL Lic	Lic ST	VL Lic	ST	—
Greece	—	Lic ST	—	Lic	—	ST Lic	Sup Ch
Ireland	QR's	QR's	QR's	Imp Cal	—	QR's	—

Country	Dairy Products	Grains	Livestock & Meat	Fruits & Vegetables	Vegetable Oils & Oilseeds	Tobacco	Cotton
Israel	Lic ST	Lic ST	Lic	Lic	Lic	Lic	Lic
Jamaica	Lic	Lic	—	Lic	Lic	Lic	—
Japan	QR's ST	ST	QR's	QR's	QR's	ST	—
Korea	Lic	Lic	Lic	Lic H & S	Lic	ST	—
New Zealand	—	ST H & S	H & S	BA ST	H & S	MP	—
Norway	QR's	ST	QR's	QR's Imp Cal ST	ST	—	—
Peru	Lic Sup Ch	Lic Sup Ch	Prohib Lic Sup Ch	Prohib Lic Sup Ch	Sup Ch Prohib Lic	Sup Ch Prohib Lic	—
Portugal	QR's	QR's	QR's ST	—	QR's	ST	QR's
South Africa	Lic QR's	Lic QR's ST	Lic	Lic ST	—	BA Lic	Lic QR's

TABLE 4.1 *Continued*

Country	Dairy Products	Grains	Livestock & Meat	Fruits & Vegetables	Vegetable Oils & Oilseeds	Tobacco	Cotton
Spain	ST Lic	ST VL Lic	ST H & S VL Lic	Lic	QR's Lic VL ST	ST	ST
Sweden	MP VL Lic	MP VL	MP VL H & S Lic	MP VL Imp Cal ST	ST VL	—	—
Switzerland	ST QR's Sup Ch	Mix Reg Sup Ch ST	Sup Ch QR's	Imp Cal QR's	Sup Ch	—	—
United Kingdom	QR's	MP Sup Ch	QR's	QR's	—	QR's BA	—
United States	QR's	QR's on Wheat & Wheat Flour	Auto Imp Control once a certain level is attained H Reg (Wholesome Meat Act)	QR's on peanuts, sugar	—	—	QR's

Source: Developed from information given in various Foreign Agricultural Service publications.

the reduced form of these materials assists one in appreciating the nature and location of certain import restrictions. In fact, the GATT warns repeatedly of the danger of assessing degrees of protection from the "raw" classification. For example, it is often impossible to make a direct comparison between the ad valorem incidence of tariffs and variable levies. The protective effect of a tariff of 30 percent ad valorem is, for example, not necessarily the same as the protective effect of a variable levy with an ad valorem equivalent of 30 percent. In any case, a straight comparison of the ad valorem equivalents of tariffs and levies in various countries is not significant, since the levy is usually the only protective device used at the frontier, whereas tariffs are often reinforced by quantitative restrictions.

This fact is brought out in the GATT tabulations, which also deal with quantitative restrictions. Another point to be borne in mind is that the type of quantitative restriction and variable levy used in different countries varies considerably. In some cases levies are, in practice, varied infrequently and are thus similar in effect to a tariff, while others vary frequently and effectively equalize internal and world market prices. The fact that two types of levy have the same ad valorem incidence would not necessarily mean that they have the same effect.

Table 4.2 shows another way of presenting the extent and general nature of nontariff barriers applying to imports of agricultural and other primary commodities for the leading industrial countries. This table, adapted from UNCTAD material, involves not only an explanation of the general nature of the restraint at country borders, but also certain types of explicit government intervention in domestic markets.

These summaries and similar materials, along with research being done in individual countries, will assist greatly in understanding the nature of the problem and will benefit those who are dealing with the removal of restrictions and with trade liberalization. The Foreign Agricultural Service (FAS), USDA, for example, published a series of circulars in 1972–73 on its trade with selected European countries and Japan. These circulars dealt with import control devices by country and recent changes in nontariff barriers and tariffs. They also tabularized U.S. exports to the countries in question for a seven-year period, and types of nontariff barriers of those countries by commodity description and tariff number.

TABLE 4.2 Nontariff Barriers to Imports of Agricultural Commodities into Major Industrial Countries, 1971

Commodities	European Economic Community		Japan		United Kingdom		United States	
	A	B	A	B	A	B	A	B
Food, Beverages, and Tobacco								
Wheat	CMA	Se	QM	S	—	Sd	Q	Se
Rice	CMA	Se	QM	S	—	—	—	Se
Barley	CMA	Se	QM	S	—	Sd	—	Se
Maize	CMA	Se	—	—	—	—	—	Se
Sugar	CMA	Se	Q	S	Q	S	Q[a]	S
Beef and veal	CMA	Se	—	—	—	Sd	Q[a]	—
Pigmeat	CMA	Se	M	S	q	Sd	Q[a]	—
Mutton and lamb	q[b] m[b]	—	—	—	—	Sd	Q	—
Poultry	CMA	Se	—	—	—	Sd	—	—
Eggs	CMA	Se	—	O	—	Sd	—	—
Butter and milk	CMA	Se	QM	Sd	Q	S	Q	Se
Fish	CMA	—	q	—	—	S	—	—
Citrus fruit	Q[b]	Se	q	—	q	—	—	—
Bananas	CMA	—	—	—	Q	—	—	—
Wine	CMA m[b]	S	—	—	—	—	—	—
Tobacco	CMAm[b]	Se	M	S	—	—	—	Se
Oilseeds, Oils, and Fats								
Soybeans and oil	—	—	—	Sd	—	—	—	Se
Groundnuts and oil	—	—	—	—	—	—	q	Se
Cottonseed and oil	—	—	—	—	—	—	—	S
Rapeseed and oil	CMA	S	—	Sd	—	—	—	—

62

Commodities	European Economic Community		Japan		United Kingdom		United States	
	A	B	A	B	A	B	A	B
Linseed and oil	CMA	S	—	—	—	—	—	S
Sunflower seed and oil	CMA	S	—	—	—	—	—	—
Olive oil	CMA	Sd	—	—	—	—	—	S
Castor seed and oil	—	—	q	—	—	—	—	—
Fish meal	—	—	—	—	—	—	—	—
Agricultural Raw Materials								
Cotton	—	—	—	—	—	—	Q	Se
Wool	—	—	—	—	—	S	—	Sd
Jute and bagging	q^b	—	—	—	q	—	—	—

Sources: UNCTAD, *Commodity Problems and Policies: Access to Markets. A Report by the UNCTAD Secretariat.* TD/115, Santiago, Chile, January 22, 1972, table A; EEC Commission, *Fourth General Report on the Activities of the Communities, 1970* (Brussels, February 1971); Great Britain, Ministry of Agriculture, Fisheries and Food, *Annual Review and Determination of Guarantees, 1971* (London: H.M. Stationery Office, March 1971); Commission on International Trade and Investment Policy, *United States International Economic Policy in an Interdependent World* (Washington, D.C.: U.S. Government Printing Office, 1971); GATT documents prepared in connection with the work of the Agriculture Committee and the Committee on Trade and Development.

Note: Column A shows the general nature of the restraint at the frontier, a small letter indicating that the measure is applicable to only part of the item in question: M,m = state trading or trading by an authorized monopoly; Q,q = quota restrictions; CMA = commodity falling under Common Market arrangements.

Column B indicates the general nature of explicit official intervention in domestic markets, not including direct or indirect subsidies of inputs of the primary sector or fiscal privileges accorded to that sector: O = organization of the domestic market without official price fixation; S = price supported or production subsidy paid; Sd = price guaranteed by deficiency payment; Se = support accompanied by provision for export subsidy.

^a Contingency quotas on beef and veal and mutton, authorized by legislation (not so far applied), accompanied by restraints by supplying countries.

^b Certain member states only.

APPLICATION AND IMPINGEMENT
OF NONTARIFF BARRIERS

A noticeable aspect in the current discussion of nontariff barriers in agricultural trade is the lack of "hard" evidence about the manner in which the statutory and regulatory restrictions are applied, the degree to which trade is impeded by their application, and the magnitude of protection to particular commodities or commodity groups afforded by them. The GATT work of inventorying and classification is clearly preparatory to the next stage of exploring possible ways in which barriers arising from agricultural measures can be dealt with. That stage has been underway in GATT for some time but clearly does not involve measurement and commitment on the part of participatory governments.

Another striking aspect of the nontariff deliberations (as well as those dealing with customs duties) is that such evidence as exists pertains to violations or infringements in developed, as opposed to developing, countries.[4] This, of course, is understandable because of the magnitude and importance of trade in the developed countries and the dominating nature of that trade on economic growth and welfare in developing countries.

Tables 4.3 and 4.4 are illustrative of these aspects of the nontariff barrier problem. The import restrictions shown in table 4.3 are those which are applied in individual developed market countries on products of export interest to developing countries. UNCTAD, which generated the information for these tables, has not taken the additional step of calculating scientifically the effective rate of protection in various countries, either for tariffs or for nontariff measures. Table 4.4 does, however, give a general idea of the "visibility" of the relative impact of nontariff barriers on developing countries after tariffs had been reduced on certain processed agricultural products. Processed meats, processed cereal products, fruits, and vegetables have a high frequency of restriction, and in the case of meats, fruits, and vegetables, high trade values are involved. The nontariff restrictions covered by these tabulations include all those types described earlier in this chapter; the most frequently used of these are import quotas and licensing.

Table 4.3 shows that the use of nontariff barriers varies widely among developed countries. This reflects not only the competitive position of the countries involved in world trade but also the degree of reliance in the various countries on regulatory mechanisms

TABLE 4.3   Frequency of Selected Import Restrictions in Developed Countries

Importing Country	Number of Products Affected by the Restrictions	Frequency of Application of Restrictions[a]
France	88	140
Federal Republic of Germany	40	54
Italy	33	38
Benelux	25	27
Denmark	26	29
Finland	26	33
Austria	22	37
Norway	20	26
United Kingdom	17	19
Sweden	17	17
Switzerland	13	24
Japan	34	34
Ireland	21	21
United States	15	17
Canada	11	11
Australia	4	4
Total Products Affected	130[b]	531

Source: UNCTAD, *Commodity Problems and Policies,* table A-1.

[a] Each particular type of restriction is counted once for each country applying it to a particular product or group of products; more than one type of restriction may be applied to a product in a given country.

[b] About 50 percent of these products are affected by restrictions applied in more than one country.

in the trade process. France, for example, clearly uses nontariff techniques to regulate its international trade to a greater degree than Canada or Australia. Again, one must be warned that summaries and frequency charts are not measures of effective protection. They are indicators, however, of the potential harrassing—as well as restrictive—nature of the nontariff measures in countries where they exist.

Fortunately, the international organizations are all becoming more involved in the measurement of agricultural protection

TABLE 4.4   Frequency of Nontariff Import Restrictions
Applied by Product Group

Product Group	Imports by Developed Market Economy Countries, 1968[a]	Frequency of Restrictions[b]
	(Millions of Dollars)	(Percent)
BTN Chapters 1–24		
Processed meat products	114.6	21.4
Processed cereal products and preparations	16.4	24.6
Processed fruit products	118.7	22.5
Processed vegetable products and edible preparations	61.5	12.5
Sugar, sugar derivatives, and chocolates	4.4	7.9
Beverages and alcohols	96.0	7.9
Tobacco manufactures	2.1	1.8
Other products	0.3	1.4
Total	414.1	100.0

Source: UNCTAD, TD/120/Supp. 1, January 31, 1972.

[a] Based on those countries which maintained restrictions recorded in 1971.

[b] Each particular type of restriction is counted once for each country applying it to a particular product or group of products; more than one type of restriction may be applied to a product in a given country.

occurring at the border of a country and of those domestic means a country uses to restrict the free flow of trade.[5]

The Food and Agriculture Organization (FAO) and the OECD, in addition to GATT and UNCTAD, are currently researching the techniques of agricultural protection. These efforts, coupled with a large number of national and private studies, should assure the world of more and better information on the subject than has existed in the past.

STATE TRADING AS A NONTARIFF BARRIER

The large grain purchases by the Soviet Union in 1972, the partial cancellation of U.S. grain sales to the Soviet Union in 1974, and the increasing importance of the People's Republic of China as an agricultural importer have focused attention on appropriate methods of dealing with exports to and imports from planned economies. Problems involved in exporting agricultural products to them should not be minimized if, as many experts believe, those countries continue to purchase large quantities of grain from the market economies.

Planned and centrally controlled economies like those of the USSR and China have a considerable degree of monopsony power in agricultural markets. This power presents great problems to major grain exporters such as the United States with its private traders and even to Australia and Canada with their state marketing agencies. Marketing monopsony in the case of the Soviet Union is exacerbated by the year-to-year variability in its grain production, which accounts for a large fraction of world grain production variability.

How to accommodate to such monopsonies in the likelihood of their continued purchase of farm products, especially when monopsony is reinforced by natural variation in supplies in the purchasing countries, presents a large problem to farmers and the marketing structures of market-oriented economies. One reaction to such uncertainty would be the "natural" response, or unilateral control of supplies—in this case, exports. Such a response would, if perfected, create the essential elements of a state-controlled oligopoly-oligopsony situation which might be even more unstable than several situations since World War II when the Soviets entered the world grain market. Certainly there would be grave dangers to farmers and to the agricultural marketing structures of market-oriented economies if they turned toward monopoly techniques in response.

Problems created by state trading and related monopoly-monopsony conditions of demand and supply in world trade of agricultural products can be solved partially through better information, especially about total world supplies. Improved information and the rational decisions which might flow therefrom are to be preferred to the confrontation of buyers and sellers acting in ignorance. The alternative of shared information on matters relevant to potential imports and exports is discussed in a recent publication of the United States Department of Agriculture.[6] This general alternative was further explored at the Rome World Food Conference in late 1974.

A large part of the advantage of monopolist and monopsonist in international trading consists of having a monopoly on information and using it skillfully. In the 1972 grain purchase, the USSR used its monopoly on information skillfully; so this one purchase set the tone for destabilizing skepticism and reaction in subsequent trading: witness the confusion surrounding the 1974 Soviet grain purchase from the United States and its cancellation. It is not clear that such secrecy was in the long-term interests of the Soviet Union because now any seller who may be approached becomes suspicious and wary. Such may be the general case in state-controlled trading situations.

Finally, because of the tendency of modern economies toward control brought about by the concentration of decision-making power in administrative machinery (Chapter 2), there is danger of essentially economic decisions turning more toward purely political considerations. Market factors in such cases become dominated by extramarket factors. And nontariff barriers in their most complex, regulatory forms exist and flourish in the guessing game of administrative bureaucracy.

Chapter 5.

QUANTITATIVE AND RELATED NONTARIFF BARRIERS IN AGRICULTURAL TRADE

It was pointed out above that the use of quantitative restrictions, while not new as trade impediments, has accelerated greatly since the Great Depression of the 1930s. Until that time, import quotas came almost always in the form of tariff quotas instead of absolute forms or were limited to emergencies such as World War I, when they were used to restrict imports to conserve foreign exchange or shipping. The distinctive era of government intervention in agriculture and trade which began in the 1930s changed all this. For the last forty years, import quotas, along with other quantitative restrictions, have been coupled with a variety of instruments —including the price mechanism—to implement protective agricultural policies. This chapter reviews selected instances in which quotas and related instruments have been used in agriculture to carry out domestic policies whose purpose was to raise domestic prices, and, by so doing, to improve and stabilize incomes over those which might have prevailed in unrestrained world competition. First, however, a few introductory remarks must be made about quotas themselves.

Quotas almost invariably mean restrictions on imports formulated in terms of maximum quantities of specified commodities permitted for import per unit period. Quantities are usually expressed as absolute numbers of physical units, although sometimes they are specified in value terms. Trade agreements which include quota provisions usually state the size of the quota allotted to particular countries in terms of a percentage of total imports from the countries in question. Sometimes they are stated simply in absolute terms. Quotas may be global, that is, without geographic allocation, but more often they are allocated among exporting countries.

Quantitative restrictions, including quotas, may take on a

variety of other attributes. As already implied, they may combine with specified minimum rates of duty to form "tariff quotas," additional imports being admitted without limitation subject to payment of higher rates of duty. Technically speaking, therefore, the tariff quota is merely a device for differential tariff treatment of various quantities of the same product.

Quotas vary as to point of application, most being applied directly to importers (or to exporters in the country of origin), but some are applied to processors (for example, mixing regulations are restrictions on the maximum amount of foreign grain which may be used in domestic flour or feed formulas). Furthermore, when quotas are granted to other countries, they may differ as to discriminatory arrangement. Guaranteed quotas or purchase agreements, where the importing country agrees to buy a stated minimum quantity during a specified period, are much more discriminatory in practice than "permissive" marketing grants where the exporters in the countries issued grants are unrestricted in their trading practices.

More recently there has been an increase in those cases where importing countries have persuaded or coerced exporting countries to police quantitative restrictions. Voluntary restraint agreements, as they are commonly known, have as one of their motives to shift from the importing country the onerous task of allocating quotas to particular importers. In other cases, the administrative branch of government in charge of such matters may be reluctant to use statutory authority, or it may hesitate to proceed with the job of applying quotas among importers by time period, etc. Furthermore, there may in fact be certain administrative and economic advantages to having quotas applied in exporting countries.

For example, when the export trade is more concentrated than the import trade, quotas can be much more effectively policed against evasion, and shipments can be better adjusted to variable market conditions in the importing country. Needless to say, one central economic question in the administration of such voluntary agreements is how to distribute the *margin* which results from the difference between the prices in importing and exporting countries. Because exploration of this question would take us too far afield here, the reader is referred to special texts on international trade theory.[1] It should be remembered that forcing voluntary quotas on exporting countries forces their governments to become more interventional in their behavior and outlook, and causes the corruption of civil servants that usually follows when they are put into the position of dispensing valuable rights.

It is important to distinguish between quantitative restrictions and other nontariff barriers as they relate to agricultural policy. However, it should be remembered that quantitative restrictions almost always entail licensing requirements and, in some cases, are coupled with foreign exchange controls. Without doubt, however, quotas compose by far the most important set of instruments available to governments for the restriction of world trade in agricultural products and for discrimination in that trade between markets. They are particularly important in developing countries where governments by their use influence the allocation of resources. Even more significant, if one classifies the variable levy system of the European Common Agricultural Policy as a form of import quota, as is the case in this study, the importance of that instrument in agricultural policy deliberations becomes more understandable. Most EEC variable levy items are also subject to licensing. The validity of these licenses, which are freely granted, is generally limited in time. Moreover, the licenses also contain certain stipulations concerning the quantity of the product in question.

Very recently, especially during the period following the precipitous events of 1972, governments have used quantitative and other measures to limit exports of farm products. In appearance, export subsidies and promotion devices used by many countries in the past are opposite to quantitative restrictions; the effects of all these actions are often similar. An examination of the nature and effects of these export control actions will be undertaken later in this chapter.

SECTION 22: ANALYSIS OF A QUANTITATIVE BARRIER

Section 22 was added to the United States Agricultural Adjustment Act of 1933 by Public Law 320, Seventy-fourth Congress, approved August 24, 1935. Amended several times and supplemented by trade agreement legislation, Section 22 authorizes the president to restrict the importation of commodities by the imposition of fees or quotas, if such importation tends to render ineffective or materially interferes with programs of the United

States Department of Agriculture which relate to agricultural commodities. It requires the Tariff Commission on direction of the president to conduct an immediate investigation, including a public hearing, and to make a report and recommendation to the president.[2]

The scope of the original legislation was expanded by the Trade Agreements Extension Act of 1951, under which no trade agreement or other international agreement can be applied in a manner inconsistent with requirements found in Section 22. The Trade Expansion Act of 1962 also makes that exception. One clause of Title II of this act reads as follows: "Nothing contained in this Act shall be construed to affect in any way the provisions of Section 22 of the Agricultural Adjustment Act, or to apply to any import restriction heretofore or hereafter imposed under this Section."

Section 22 special procedures, to be used in emergencies due to product perishability, were first introduced with the Trade Agreements Extension Act of 1951. The secretary of agriculture reports the emergency to the president and to the Tariff Commission, and the commission must make an immediate investigation and make appropriate recommendations to the president. The commission's report to the president and the president's decisions must be made not more than twenty-five calendar days after the case is submitted to the Tariff Commission. The president, if he believes it necessary, however, may make a decision before getting the commission's report.

This possible emergency action was clarified by Section 104 of the Trade Agreements Extension Act of 1953 and is now incorporated in Section 22 legislation. The president may take immediate action without awaiting the recommendation of the Tariff Commission whenever the secretary of agriculture reports to him with regard to any article that requires emergency treatment. Such action by the president may continue in effect pending his receipt of the report and recommendation of the commission on the Section 22 investigation and his action thereon. Strangely enough, the emergency clause was never used until the cheddar cheese action of 1966, and ironically, in that case a quota increase was recommended by the secretary.

Three specific guidelines are given the president in acting on these recommendations: (1) he may impose fees not in excess of 50 percent ad valorem; (2) he may not reduce the importation or warehouse withdrawal to less than 50 percent of a representative period; and (3) he may, in designating any article or articles, describe them by physical qualities, value, use, or any other attribute.

All actions under Section 22 are initiated in the Department of Agriculture, with primary responsibility assigned to the administrator of the Foreign Agricultural Service. It is here that preliminary investigations and actions are usually initiated. There have been more than fifty investigations, many of which have been devoted to studies and reports on cotton and wheat. One would naturally expect this because it is in these products that the stakes are highest. That is, price support and control programs have intervened more significantly there. More recently, however, dairy products, particularly cheeses, have provided the most activity.

Import controls under Section 22 were in effect as of June 1973 for four groups of commodities: cotton and cotton products, wheat and wheat products, specified dairy products, and peanuts. Cotton and wheat controls have been in effect for many years: cotton since 1939, wheat since 1941. The others were instituted more recently.[3]

Since Section 22 was enacted, import controls have been imposed on eleven different commodities or groups of commodities. All or a part of nine of these commodities or groups of commodities have been removed from import controls. Details on commodities or groups of commodities under Section 22 control at one time or another, and those now under control, may be obtained from the Foreign Agricultural Service, USDA.

Section 22 controls are of a continuing nature; that is, they continue automatically until modified or terminated by the president. Certain other details apply to the various commodity programs, but time and space preclude their discussion here.

APPRAISAL OF THE PROGRAM

Several points about Section 22 should be clarified. First, the legislation of which the section is a part deals with policy in the field of agricultural prices and incomes and has always been deemed "in the public interest" domestically. In other words, Section 22 is not the legislation of primary leverage erected directly as a protective instrument. Second, under Section 22 there is no authority to excuse importers from complying with other legislation and regulations of the United States. In other words, if there are tariffs, fees, regulations as to health, etc., all these must be complied with as well as the quota. Examples are U.S. tariffs on cheeses, peanuts, wheat, and other products. Third, though Section 22 and similar legislation give the Executive Office of the United States a dominant hand in policy making, it is to the credit of this country that trade policies are debated in the open for all to see. Restriction can be invoked only after full and complete hearings before the Tariff Commission, and testimony is welcomed from everyone, even foreign exporting interests.

The president, the secretary of agriculture, and the Tariff Commission are obligated to perform duties set forth by law. These duties have been performed well. The mechanics for hearing and for acting on a complaint are sound and operate in an orderly and efficient manner.

If one must criticize Section 22 and related programs which curb imports, it should be on the basis of their efficiency once they have become operative. The major brunt of the criticism should be borne by the original plan inherent in agricultural price support legislation; that is, attempts by the United States to justify and make economically feasible a program which raises domestic prices above world prices for large segments of its agricultural industry without seriously disrupting domestic resource utilization and historical international production and trade patterns. While Section 22 is a logical part of the original Agricultural Adjustment Act (AAA), it is surprising that it was not utilized before September 1939, more than four years after it was passed. In the succeeding decades, administrators, especially those at the intermediate level in the Department of Agriculture, seem to have been prudent in their sifting of requests, in their confrontation with the issues, and in their administration of the entire program.

Imports could not help but be attracted by the price programs which were part of the AAA, the Marketing Agreement Act of 1937, and other programs. The various detailed investigations by the Tariff Commission and the many hearings on Section 22 by the secretary of agriculture will attest to the fact that this device is well known to United States agricultural interests, and that it has been utilized in fulfilling the original objectives of the price program.

It is possible to argue the economics of decisions made by the above three federal offices. Many times, the decisions by administrative personnel and advisory boards on foreign trade matters have been arbitrary, and only time will determine their ultimate effects. The secretary of agriculture has a particularly wide range of authority within which he can operate. The motivation is toward effectuating a piece of legislation; yet the administrators and even the president are limited as to what they can initiate under the law. In passing, it might be added that while administrators of Section 22 have been prudent, the president has likewise been prudent in the use of his authority under Section 22. He has used the executive power with considerable restraint; i.e., he has decided not to act in many instances.

It is not possible to be so generous when Section 22 and related programs are appraised in light of overall U.S. agricultural and trade policies. The principal paradox arises from the inconsistency between domestic agriculture programs and what is desirable in the politics of international trade—domestic surpluses accumulated as a result of price supports, for example. This has resulted in both overt and subtle attempts to insulate the U.S. market against foreign competitors. These actions by the United States are the practices which this country has been urging other nations to abandon in the interest of expanding multilateral trade.

The 1966 cheddar cheese case provides a specific example. The decision by Secretary Freeman in the case was hotly debated. It appears that the U.S. dairy industry was infuriated after the quota on cheddar was raised for the remainder of 1966 and after the proposal was made by the secretary of agriculture to the president that the annual quota be increased. How could quota policy be blamed for the plight of the dairy industry at a time when (1) there were virtually no stocks of cheeses, butter, and skim milk powder; (2) milk production in the United States was down for the second year, with the likelihood of a third annual decline; (3) domestic and foreign relief had been curtailed; (4) there had been no direct milk product purchases by the secretary for some time; (5) essentially all controls remained the same as in previous years; and (6) a tight market prevailed, i.e., prices were well above support levels?

SECTION 22 AND THE GATT

Even though Section 22 was first applied in 1939, it did not become ominous as a protective measure until 1951 when the United States Congress required the imposition of quotas on imports that threatened to interfere with domestic farm programs, *irrespective of any U.S. international obligation.* More moderate and liberal import quotas were introduced in 1953; but at the insistence of the United States, exceptional treatment was given in the GATT to quantitative import restrictions when they are coupled with domestic supply control measures (Article XI 2 (c) (i)). In 1955, the United States asked for and obtained a GATT waiver allowing it to use import quotas or fees to the extent that Section 22 requires their imposition to prevent material interference with U.S. agricultural programs. This waiver reserved all compensation rights of other contracting parties of GATT with regard to any impairment of concessions obtained by them from the United States.

The U.S. position on agricultural trade liberalization has been compromised by the waiver and related trade restrictions. During the Kennedy Round negotiations, legislation was being enacted in Washington which could be used to control meat imports and trade in sugar, and maintain control of trade in manufactured dairy products and peanuts. Moreover, the substantial export subsidy programs were maintained. As Johnson says, "While farm groups and legislators from farm areas strongly supported reductions in barriers to trade in farm products, they had little appreciation of what changes had to be made in domestic policies to facilitate a liberal trade policy."[4]

Certain circumstances have prevented the United States' position from being completely undermined by the Section 22 waiver in the GATT. The quasi-judicial procedures of Section 22 have limited recourse to protective action. Furthermore, there are provisions for the suspension, termination, or modification of quotas or fees if and when changed circumstances permit (1974 increases in cheese quotas and temporary suspension of the wheat quota verified this). Finally, in addition to the liberalization of some old quotas, there has also been a reduction in Section 22 quotas over the years.[5] Recent price and trade conditions for agricultural products have also helped in lifting the onus from trade barriers, but it should be remembered that Section 22, like its counterparts in other countries, is an integral part of a mechanism by which effective protection can be administered for domestic agriculture. Also, the relative arbitrariness of Section 22, which permits action regardless of any trade agreement or other international contract, brings into focus the nature of contradictions between trade and agricultural policies.

POLITICAL ECONOMY OF SECTION 22
AND THE QUANTITATIVE RESTRICTIONS

The import quota introduced along with other nontariff barriers in the early 1930s threw a different light on tariffs and other political instruments as protective measures, and Section 22 was no exception. If a country has some idea of the shape and level of supply and demand curves for a given commodity, and if these curves are not particularly inelastic, there are few differences among many of the economic effects which result from the imposition of a tariff or a quota. If the quota is set at the volume of imports which would result from the imposition of a given tariff, the protective effect will be the same in either case, and so will consumption and redistribution effects.

Economic theory provides us with comparisons between the effects of tariffs and quotas.[6] Both tend toward higher internal prices, reduced overall consumption, limited imports, and increased domestic production.

The revenue effect of the two is another matter, however. Governments collect duties resulting from tariffs. Under a quota policy, domestic prices are higher than without quotas, and the organizational structure of importers and exporters will dictate who receives the "rent" surplus. There are many ramifications of the revenue effect, especially where governments follow a system of import licensing. The closer a situation approaches that of bilateral monopoly, the more theoretically indeterminate a particular situation becomes.

Quantitative controls and tariffs differ in other ways, primarily in the manner in which the quota is set. Tariffs, of course, place no quantitative limits on imports. Quotas are allocated by arbitrary and fixed formulas among competing countries, many times in a discriminatory manner. Historical cost-price conditions are often ignored in attempts to change the situation, as was the case with sugar.

Economists endeavoring to analyze the economic effects and incidence of import quotas and attendant devices often forget their most important characteristic—administrative flexibility. Tariff duties are stable over time, as a rule, and tariff acts—even those relating to peril points, escape clauses, and the like—take time to change. Not so with quotas. They are temporary by nature and subject to administrative discretion. Tariffs are usually imposed at a sensitive point of the price mechanism and their effects are diffused among the variables affecting supply and demand. They can be imposed at sufficiently high levels to keep a commodity out of a country; but circumstances may prevail which allow imports to continue, even at high tariff levels, since the effects of the duty may be borne by the foreign exporter or can be passed on to the initial consumer.

This situation exists with respect to the most important case in quota theory: the highly inelastic supply of exporting countries. In this case, a tariff will neither materially increase the price in the importing country nor reduce the volume of imports. However, while the tariff improves the terms of trade and gains revenue for the importing government by taxing the foreigner, political circumstances among producers at home often dictate a different "solution." Quotas have provided this solution.

Figure 5.1 illustrates this case. We are assuming a closed system in which total supply and demand conditions for a particular commodity are represented by importing country M and exporting country X. In this situation, no reasonable tariff will raise and redistribute incomes among producers in country M. A quota which halved imports, on the other hand, would clearly raise prices from OP to OP'. If country X does nothing about this quota, the export price there will drop to something like P''. Hence, the quota in country M is likely to be followed by a stabilization scheme in country X.

This case is the theoretical norm in agriculture. Schemes abound all over the world for guaranteeing a "fair price" to domestic producers. In many countries, policies of price raising and income support to farmers would be defeated by free imports or any reasonable tariff rate. Hence the widespread use of quotas and other restrictions to reduce the quantitative impact of foreign competition to a tolerable amount.

PRICE PER UNIT IN MONEY

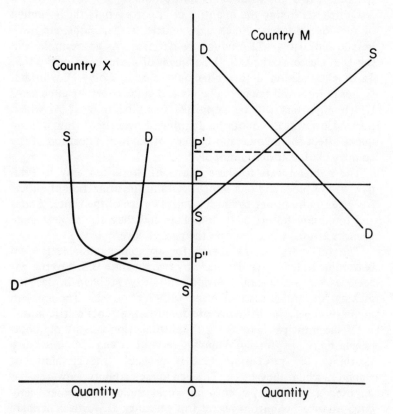

FIGURE 5.1. Imposition of Quotas in Partial Equilibrium in Face of Inelastic Supply. From Charles R. Kindleberger, *International Economics,* rev. ed. (Homewood, Ill.: Richard D. Irwin, © 1958), p. 238.

Then there is the case where the quota is used to protect industry and to redistribute incomes because of a lack of knowledge of supply curves in exporting countries. Governments appear unwilling to tolerate an unrestricted policy of importation in the modern world when both foreign governments and suppliers practice all forms of price discrimination and dumping in order to increase revenues or to rid themselves of a domestic problem.

Though the quota gives an element of certainty in economic affairs, especially in cases of inelastic and unknown foreign supply, and though it has advantages over the tariff in its administrative flexibility, it is not without its own problems. We shall list only a few of these. Fixing the quantity of imports is only the beginning of such questions as: Which units (cattle, bushels, tons, etc.) will be allowed? How will products be defined? (As an example, will the U.S. Customs, the U.S. Department of Agriculture, or the U.S. Tariff Commission define blue-mold cheese, Colby, Edam, and Gouda?) How will the quota be divided globally among exporters? Which importers will be permitted to utilize quotas? At which ports? How will the quota be distributed over time? How will the quota affect the income and balance of payments position of the country? Will it foster monopoly?

The right answers to these questions, while not easy to find, have been found, and one thing is certain: the utilization of quotas has given more power to the Executive Office of the United States and to administrators of trade policy; and they also subject trade to more arbitrary decisions on the part of government.

The difficulty of the search for economic rationale is even better illustrated in reports made by two separate U.S. government agencies on the so-called divided-authority problem in decision making concerning cases involved with Section 22.[7] The problem in question was the difficulty of administering quota restrictions.

Of the principal reasons for the introduction and use of quotas —inelasticity in foreign supply, certainty, and administrative flexibility—the most important is probably the certainty, or stability, which they bring. This economic certainty, however, has imposed a considerable cost on world trade. Yet, under many circumstances, countries regard this certainty as worth their share of the cost.

The economic indeterminacy of our era has magnified the politics of economic questions to a level greater than at any other time in the last two centuries. (This is why the term *neomercantilism* is used in describing certain trade policies.) This indeterminacy has thrown upon those who have the power a responsibility to decide a range wherein price and output shall fall. With all the ramifications of such a decision, how is it possible to say what the "correct" economic choice for the president is when he is presented with a Section 22 decision on, say, cheddar cheese, which affects hundreds of U.S. producers, thousands of U.S. consumers, and relations with countries such as Canada, Denmark, and Italy? International politics aside, this development empha-sizes the power struggle between organized economic groups.

THE VARIABLE LEVY

In contradistinction to tariffs and tarifflike measures (e.g., import surcharges, multiple-exchange rates, and advanced deposits on imports), quantitative restrictions break the link between domestic and world prices. These restrictions reduce the volume of imports into a country, not by artificially raising the cost of importing—as is the case with tariffs—but by placing direct limits on the quantity (or value) of imports that may enter the domestic market, irre-spective of prices.[8] This is pointed out in an analysis of existing quantitative and other import restrictions in selected developed market-economy countries on products of export interest to the developing countries. There is no built-in measure of the rate of nominal protection in the case of such quantitative restrictions.

In the case of a variable levy system, such as exists in the Com-mon Agricultural Policy, the domestic support price and/or a minimum import price is usually fixed and independent of the world price. This assumption of independence becomes more difficult to justify in those instances, as in the CAP, where supplies produced domestically have become a relatively large part of world supplies and/or a large part of domestic consumption, and where the intervention in domestic markets results in the neces-sity of dumping excess supplies on world markets. The amount of the margin at any given time is visible in the variable levy itself. Theoretically, a variable levy has the advantage of at least accru-ing to the government as revenue part of the margin of nominal protection. However, in cases where there is simultaneous, or mixed, application of both tariff and quantitative restriction, the protective role of the tariff becomes redundant—as will be demon-strated later—except as double insurance against the possibility that the quota system may break down.

The variable levy is the most important single element in a farm policy system (perhaps a better label would be group of commod-ity arrangements), the basic objectives of which are quite laudable and surprisingly similar to those of the Agricultural Adjustment Act and subsequent legislation of the United States, and to the philosophy underlying much other farm legislation in industrialized countries.[9] Just as the original Agricultural Adjustment Act of the United States was found to be inoperable vis-à-vis world markets without an instrument such as Section 22 to limit imports, so the Common Agricultural Policy would be inoperable without an instrument such as the variable levy to enforce limits on imports, which in some important cases—as will be shown later—takes on the attributes of absolute quotas. The variable levy, therefore, was the instrument around which an agricultural customs union was formed and by which a common external tariff on certain commodities could be presented to non-EEC countries.

The European countries can and do, of course, use other measures to restrict and regulate trade among themselves, EEC members, and the Third World. But it is the variable levy about which so much discussion has arisen with respect to agricultural protection in Europe. Free intra-European trade was its raison d'être; it isolated the agricultural sector from world market fluctuations, allowing domestic objectives to be pursued without fear of interruptions. The variable levy in farm policy has been compared to the flexible exchange rate in domestic monetary policy, with both said to be grasps for independence.[10] Though this analogy is not altogether correct—because in the case of the levy some absolute limit to flexibility in imports may be reached more rapidly than in the case of money supplies—it illustrates the point of increasing isolation and self-sufficiency within the European Customs Union.

In the context of the CAP, the variable levy was lowered progressively between members, and varied against *imports* from Third World countries according to the relation between the EEC support prices and world market prices. It is buttressed by two other instruments to give practical expression to a well-rounded commercial agricultural policy, namely, support buying and export subsidies. Such proceeds as come from the levy are used to help cover costs of market intervention, to make Community products competitive in world markets, and to make grants for structural reform in agriculture. In actual operation, levy proceeds have covered less than half of the CAP support costs.

In the international market, as already intimated, the variable levy of the CAP and its auxiliaries operates similarly to the policy instruments of the United States. Earlier it was shown that if Section 22 did not place quotas on certain commodities, foreign supplies would disrupt the workings of the price support operations and make domestic programs inoperable. The same can be said of the variable levy vis-à-vis the CAP, though the degree of price assurance provided by the regulations differs considerably from product to product. In order to demonstrate this, we must compare certain relevant price and trade policy instruments of the EEC and the United States.[11]

1. *EEC target prices* are theoretical, fixed, with the purported objective of ensuring reasonable prices to consumers and reasonable incomes to producers, as well as to promote harmonious development of international trade. For some commodities, guide prices are fixed instead of target prices, but these are similar in intent.

   U.S. parity prices, tied to a historical base period, are also theoretical. If met, they give agricultural commodities a dollar value pegged to the cost of articles farmers buy. Income is a subsumed objective and parity is part of legislation intended to balance supplies with demand, promote international trade, and ensure stable supplies to consumers. In effect, parity has become a principal objective of U.S. farm policy for all intents and purposes.

2. *EEC threshold prices* are minimum prices at which imports can enter the EEC. If trade prices on the world market are below threshold prices, a (variable) levy is imposed to the extent of the difference. Imports entering at the threshold price should sell at around the target price on internal markets because the two are linked by hypothetical transport costs.

   There is no exact U.S. equivalent to the threshold price, since operation of its farm programs is not contingent on import levies. On the contrary, parity prices are calculated and commodities are supported through the price mechanism by the secretary of agriculture, contingent upon farmers' acceptance of domestic supply controls. Regional equivalents of parity are set, taking into consideration transport costs and quality differentials.

3. *EEC intervention prices* are guaranteed prices at which EEC governments will undertake support buying of certain commodities if necessary. They range from 40 percent of the targetlike price for some fruits and vegetables to 95 percent of sugar and

less than 90 percent for grains. The intervention price represents a floor to the market.

U.S. level of parity is the particular level at which the secretary of agriculture is obligated to step in and buy, or to absorb, a commodity, should the price of the commodity fall to it. It is in essence the same as the intervention price in that it sets the price floor for the domestic market.

We are now in a position to describe how the variable levy approaches a quota in operation, and functions as an equivalent of Section 22. The variable levy, operating at the threshold, keeps the target price from being undermined, which is similar to what Section 22 does for the parity price.

The variable levy does not function as an exact equivalent to Section 22 because the quotas under Section 22 prevent interference with the domestic (U.S.) support price. The variable levy not only prevents such interference but also gives an additional margin of preference or protection to the domestic (EEC) producer. This margin is at the maximum the difference between the threshold price and the intervention price. The variable levy mechanism differs with regard to various commodity groups, the most typical and representative being that for grains.

It is important here to point out that it is the target price (through the threshold price) that largely determines the magnitude of the levy. See area *BC* in figure 5.2.

The variable levy of CAP must, of necessity, *act like* a quota, its magnitude depending on (1) the relative decrease in the world price and/or (2) the relative increase in European prices. As the spread between the two widens, the levy increases, and vice versa. To repeat, it is the *spread* between threshold price and world price, c.i.f. European ports, which dictates the relative degree to which the variable levy acts like a quota. The nominal levels of either one or the other, therefore, are not sufficient to demonstrate its quota nature.[12]

For policy considerations, some have dubbed this spread the "reasonable discrepancy" between threshold and world prices. Further evidence for this brief analysis might be adduced from theoretical constructs, where under monopolistic conditions of commodity exports from foreign countries it becomes increasingly "profitable" to exporters to have the world price edge up to the

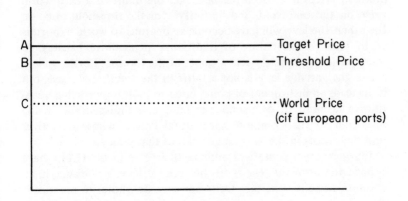

FIGURE 5.2. CAP Price Concepts

EEC threshold price. In order to protect domestic producers, under such conditions threshold prices—and even intervention prices—must necessarily be pushed higher and higher year after year. It might be noted that collusion among exporters to EEC can possibly result if some sort of explicit quota is not arranged by EEC governments, since exporters may prefer to collude and divide the marginal profit rather than pay the levy. Only so much of the product, e.g., cereals, sugar, beef, milk, is likely to be licensed for importation in any event. Collusion is not likely to happen, however, as long as a commodity is widely traded and so long as importing firms and governments are privileged to go into the foreign market for supplies—both conditions which are fulfilled in the case of the grain trade.

To those who might object to thinking of the variable levy in terms of a quota, it should be pointed out that as world prices c.i.f. European ports decline and approach zero—the threshold price remaining constant—the variable levy approaches the threshold price and reaches its absolute functional limit of embargoing foreign agricultural products. On the other hand, as target prices—which is to say threshold prices—are raised relative to world prices, a similar effect takes place and the levy again acts more and more like a quota. (The latter has been more prominent in recent years.) In both circumstances, of course, long before the absolute limits in prices have been reached, i.e., the limits of a zero world price on the one hand, and "infinity" for the threshold price on the other, the levy will have become so onerous to world exporters as to take on the nature of traditional quantitative barriers. In fact, the levy implicitly sets a quota at the threshold price. In any event, the variable levy is not a tariff in the traditional sense, but is, instead, an instrument of policy used to limit imports in a quantitative fashion. It, or a similar technique, is indispensable in the operation of the Common Agricultural Policy, whose objectives find their roots in the long-range goals of that policy.

European representatives arguing their case in the GATT have applied the term *sui generis* to the variable levy. To be sure, in an absolute sense it is neither tariff nor specific quota. In practice it acts like both. But with respect to its ex post application, i.e., *after* target prices have been set by the commission, it must, by necessity, act like a quota when certain price conditions prevail.

The use of a variable levy to attain agricultural development and adjustment over time is not in itself inconsistent with the principle of international comparative advantage. In order not to be unduly protective, however, the average height of the levy must be adjusted regularly in the light of world supply conditions so that other countries can expand exports to the protected area as their competitive positions improve. This has not been the case with the CAP because world prices for agricultural products, except for the 1972–75 experience, did not rise over time as its designers envisioned, and because prices in Common Market countries have been kept disproportionately high. Because there have been serious consequences for certain products, such as grains and dairy products, the variable levy system constitutes a most difficult problem for European agricultural and trade policy. Weaknesses were even more demonstrably apparent after the enlargement of EEC occurred.

As a counterpart to the variable levy, export subsidies are paid to facilitate the disposal of EEC surplus agricultural products on world markets. Generally speaking, the subsidy makes up the difference between world prices and those prevailing in the EEC. Products are accumulated through support buying (at intervention prices) and subsidized for export by receipts from the variable levy, other tariffs, and direct payments from EEC member countries. In practice, export subsidies have been paid for practically all CAP products. Agricultural export subsidies in the EEC may be compared somewhat to Section 32 of the United States Agricultural Adjustment Act of 1933, which allocated 30 percent of all customs revenue for the purpose, among other things, of subsidizing exports of farm products. It is an interesting as well as an instructive exercise in agricultural trade policy analysis to compare the instruments used by the advanced industrial countries which seemingly become inevitable once a general policy of agricultural protection is determined.

The general similarity of instruments used in the United States and Europe becomes more apparent as the analysis proceeds. Their general effects also are similar in nature, though not always in *degree,* because of the strong emphasis on self-sufficiency in Europe of agricultural programs. (Costs are high because programs tend to ignore domestic supply considerations.) This particular difference has led some economists to postulate that both the variable levy and quotas have the same tendencies toward external insensitivity, but that the levy is apt to respond more quickly to changes in internal conditions. Admittedly, there is a point to be made in this regard: the administrative apparatus constructed around a policy of quotas is quite inflexible, and only the most radically changed circumstances in domestic or world demand and supply considerations seem to be able to affect it. For example, the invoking and repeal of quotas by the United States on meats in 1971 and the doubling of quotas on cheeses by President Nixon in April 1973 and January 1974 was done only after critical shortages in supply had developed domestically.

There is a further similarity between the CAP and U.S. price support policy: many of the costs of both are either hidden and/or difficult to calculate in a direct sense. Recently, there has been an increasing tendency on the part of both the United States and the EEC to move to other forms of assistance—such as structural adjustment in agriculture, and regional or rural development—in order to justify high price supports and protection for commercial agriculture and to take political pressure off the demand for reduced agricultural budgets.

Measurement of the increases in protection brought on by the Common Agricultural Policy have been suggested by converting total charges of the variable levy system at the EEC border into ad valorem equivalents.[13] For live animals, protection rose from

14 percent in 1959 to 49 percent in 1968; for meat, from 19 to 52 percent; for dairy produce, from 19 to 137 percent. Though not shown separately, butter alone increased from 30 to 350 percent. In cereals, protection rose five times, from around 14 percent, pre-CAP, to 72 percent, post-CAP.

Various government intervention measures, other than the variable levy, do not figure in the above measures; these include other quantitative import restrictions, programs to stimulate production, and export restitution, which buttress the variable levy system and add to the protective nature of the Common Agricultural Policy. Tariff protection alone—including the variable levy—for agricultural products in the EEC has been estimated to be about triple what it was prior to the CAP. Malmgren has compared the levels of tariffs and other import charges in agriculture for selected countries after the conclusion of the Kennedy Round of tariff negotiations.[14] Table 5.1, taken from that study, presents this comparison and suggests the high tariff protection in the EEC which resulted from the variable levy system.

Variable levies of EEC agricultural products can be expressed in ad valorem equivalents insofar as the admitted volume of imports is concerned. Done for recent years by UNCTAD, the results are shown in table 5.2. As can be seen, the current margins of (nominal) protection for the principal commodities are very substantial. Butter, sugar, and soft wheat receive considerable protection and are perennially the most costly to both consumers and taxpayers. As table 5.2 does not present data for oilseeds, it is of interest that the Secretariat of the EEC estimated the Community price of this commodity group as being double the world market price in 1967–68.[15]

EXPORT INTERFERENCES

Beginning increasingly in 1972, agricultural exporting nations turned to export controls and related export-limiting devices to prevent surging world prices from pushing up domestic consumer and producer prices of grain and other food products. Such devices are not a novelty in world trade, for in earlier times emphasis was placed on domestic employment or sagging world prices as reasons for limiting agricultural and raw material exports. The effects of the U.S. cancellation of soybean contracts in 1973,

TABLE 5.1   Post-Kennedy Round Level of Import Protection
for Agriculture in Selected Countries, 1967

Country	Import Protection Percent Ad Valorem Equivalent
Austria	16
Denmark	6
EEC	33
Japan	9
Norway	2
Sweden	3
Switzerland	9
United Kingdom	7
United States	4

Source: H. B. Malmgren, *Trade Wars or Trade Negotiations: Nontariff Barriers and Economic Peacekeeping* (Washington, D.C.: Atlantic Council of the U.S., 1970), p. 40. Estimated unpublished data in the world trade and tariff computer from tabulations developed by the Office of the Special Representative for Trade Negotiations, Executive Office of the President, Washington, D.C.

Note: Weighted by 1964 imports and including incidence of protection afforded by tariffs or other direct charges such as the variable import levy in the Common Market. The impact of quantitative restrictions, such as quotas and other similar restrictive measures, is a separate problem, with Japan maintaining the most.

followed by the delay and partial cancellation of a grain sale to the USSR in October 1974, though given great publicity at the time, were but examples of one country interfering with its export trade for internal political ends. Limiting exports for many reasons are: Australia and Canada through their wheat and grain boards; the EEC through export levies, licensing, and embargoes; and other countries by a variety of devices (e.g., Argentinian and Brazilian export controls on beef, Thailand's on corn, and others too numerous to mention here).

A considerable part of the large increase in international grain prices between 1972 and 1974 was due to export-limiting interferences as a number of large consumers did not permit their

TABLE 5.2   Ad Valorem Tariff Equivalents of Variable Levies
in the EEC, 1967-71

Commodities	1967-68	1968-69	1969-70	1970-71
		(in percentages)		
Soft wheat	90.7	95.4	114.4	89.3
Durum wheat	62.6	67.9	80.9	82.0
Rye	68.9	79.3	78.0	72.4
Barley	62.5	97.0	102.9	46.0
Oats	54.4	84.3	76.9	42.4
Maize	65.5	77.9	59.1	40.8
Sorghum	61.0	86.0	66.8	49.2
Rice, husked or polished, excluding broken	18.0	38.1	85.5	110.2
Rice, broken	0	18.5	46.9	60.4
Sugar, raw	--	232.4	169.2	110.0
Sugar, white	--	329.3	252.8	155.3
Olive Oil	24.1	14.1	6.5	4.5[b]
Pigmeat	43.7	71.0	76.0	53.3
Eggs in the shell	34.2	52.0	53.2	37.2
Chicken, eviscerated	22.9	30.6	29.9	23.5
Turkeys, eviscerated	23.8	32.5	33.2	26.0
Butter	--	526.2	535.8	214.2
Fat cattle (excluding calves)[a]	--	43.3	22.4	20.7
Calves[a]	--	2.6	0	1.1

Source: UNCTAD, *Commodity Problems and Policies,* Table A-3 of that publication was calculated from EEC, *Marches Agricoles, Prix,* various issues.

Note: As a rule, figures shown represent yearly averages of levies imposed, expressed as percentages of average c.i.f. prices of imports to which levies applied during the year. The yearly averages relate to the period August 1–July 31, except for rice (September 1–August 31), sugar (July 1–June 30), and olive oil (November 1–October 31).

[a] Excluding ad valorem tariff of 16 percent for live animals. (For beef and veal, an ad valorem tariff of 20 percent—to which variable levies are added—is applied.)

[b] Average for first ten months of the year.

domestic prices to adjust to changing world supply-demand relationships and monetary conditions. For example, because of the combined effects of the dollar devaluation and the variable import levies of the European Economic Community, the increase in U.S. export prices for wheat from about $60 per ton in 1971-72 to $130 per ton in early 1973 had no effect on the consumer or producer in EEC. When wheat prices increased even further, EEC imposed export levies and licensing procedures to discourage sales of domestic wheat in foreign markets. Grain prices in local currencies, as a result, increased by no more than 10 percent between 1971 and early 1974 in the Original Six, except for Italy. In the summer of 1974, export levies on grains were increased substantially. Export levies for soft wheat were raised from unit of account (u.a.) 40 per ton to u.a. 60 per ton (U.S. $50.37 and U.S. $75.55 per ton, respectively) and for barley, more than 100 (U.S. $18.89 to U.S. $44.07). Reasons given for these drastic increases were strongly higher world market price levels and reduced 1974 production prospects for feed grains in the United States. Thus, during a period when dollar prices for grain were doubling and trebling in world markets, grain within the EEC (except for its nine members) became relatively cheaper. The same nationalistic approach to grain sales has been followed in Japan and the Soviet Union.

When such drastic export-limiting measures are taken, either by major consumers or by major producers of a large internationally traded product, such action forces the rest of the world to adjust or retaliate. In the case of the European action on grain, virtually all the required price adjustments were imposed on the major grain exporters and a number of developing countries which rely heavily on food imports. Whether the U.S. actions to cancel soybean and grain contracts were "forced" because of these required adjustments makes for good economic argument. Suffice it to say there is little doubt that, if conditions approximating free trade had prevailed in grains and other foods over the past few years, price increases would have been significantly smaller than they have in fact been.[16]

At the opposite extreme in the export control question is the situation in which a country (or countries) limits exports because of depressed world markets in hope of increasing gross receipts for its production and/or stocks. Tropical products such as coffee and cocoa have been subject to international commodity agreements using supply control as the fulcrum to reach an economic objective.[17] Export taxes for revenue and supply control purposes are another common form of export intervention in internationally traded products.

Note should be made of the generic case against export controls in international trade. Just as such controls are questionable as an economic tool to provide help to a sick industry with weak international markets—the normal case in the past—export controls also are a poor way to fight inflation. They present very special dangers in the kind of world which existed in the 1972–74 period. Such controls affect the international value of the currency of the country imposing the controls. For example, if U.S. grain can't be purchased by foreign traders, dollars become less valuable. In a world of floating exchange rates, that loss in value is soon reflected in what a dollar can buy and has an inflationary impact in the United States.

A corollary to this result of export control is that the ability of the restricting country to buy in foreign markets diminishes in real terms. This, in turn, has an impact on the economies of weaker nations dependent on the export market. Major export restrictions of foodstuffs by the United States and other countries in the 1970s crisis, added to the price increases and export limitation by the oil producers' cartel, threatened to precipitate a downward spiral in world trade and a consequent slowdown of major proportions in real economic activity. World currencies and financial markets were dangerously near the breaking point, and some countries, such as Britain and Italy, already in bad shape, were menaced by further economic dislocation.

A more serious risk in restricting exports of vital commodities in world trade is that such restrictions inevitably distort patterns of world trade. Attempts to relieve price pressures domestically by restricting exports soon interfere with trade patterns in commodities like grains, dairy products, beef, and many other products. In a country such as the United States with a large national economy, an important international currency, and major farm exports (at the 1973 rate of more than U.S. $20 billion), any notable limitation on those exports will distort trade patterns.

The ultimate danger, as was pointed out in Chapter 3, is that the world could return to the conditions of the 1930s when international trade had collapsed. The effect is the same whether trade is strangled by competitive import barriers, as it was during the Great Depression, or by competitive export barriers, which was the threat during the mid-1970s.[18]

Finally, trade regulation by way of export interferences, whatever their economic motivation, cannot be limited to exports alone. Cause and effect are highly interrelated in a world where more than U.S. $500 billion in product value is being exported by the nations of that world. Export control will, through the chain of events, lead inevitably to other forms of protection, even to the nontariff barrier import restrictions which have been the central theme of this study. The time to curtail or reduce protectionism and to liberalize trade is *before* trade barriers come into being and are institutionalized.

OTHER QUANTITATIVE RESTRICTIONS

Though Section 22 and the variable levy compose the authority for the most pervasive quantitative restrictions in the United States and Europe, there are other CAP as well as quantitative nontariff barriers in particular nations which restrict trade. There is also a vast array of quotas and related obstacles to trade in other industrial countries such as Japan and in the developing world. Some of the most obvious of these additional cases of quantitative restrictions will be described here to further illustrate the problem.[19]

The principal *exception* to the general GATT prohibition of quantitative restrictions relates to those imposed for balance-of-payments reasons. Developing countries have used, and will probably continue to use, such control procedures. Certain industrialized countries have, however, used quantitative controls and the exception until quite recently when they turned to other methods such as prior deposits and import surcharges supplemented by assistance to exports. A special problem in this respect exists for certain countries such as Japan, a very rigorous practitioner of quantitative import quota restrictions which discriminate against its suppliers.

Despite liberalizations in its import policies in the early 1960s, Japan's restrictions remained virtually intact from 1964 to 1969, with quota restrictions applied to 174 items, only 43 of which the

Japanese claimed as falling within the national security and public health and morals provisions of GATT.[20] Since 1969, Japan has made further modifications in its trade restrictions, reducing the number of categories under quota from about 120 to 34, almost half of them agricultural.[21] Fresh fruits, vegetable oils, live animals, and selected processed products came in for liberalization.[22] In October 1972, Japan announced a five-point program to help restore equilibrium in its balance of payments and trade. One major point called for expanding imports through such means as larger allocations for items under quotas, improvement in the generalized preference scheme for developing countries, and improved import financing and procedures.

Though a decade of liberalization has reduced agricultural protection in quantitative as well as in other nontariff barrier categories, many quota and related restrictions remain in Japan. Licensing procedures, to which all imported products are subject, are applied especially to products under quota. Although information on the quota is not officially released, it can usually be obtained on an unofficial basis. In sum, the recent actions by the Japanese government still leave much to be desired with respect to quantitative barriers and related matters. Japan not only still maintains quota restrictions on many products it supports, but there are other protective devices with strict procedural requirements, the cumulative effect of which is to inhibit trade while making it possible for the government to influence importers to switch to domestic products.

Emphasis should be given to the constraining nature of quotas when combined with the use of other instruments and procedures such as discretionary import licensing. Governments can administer licenses in a way which creates additional barriers to imports. Delays often occur in the issuance of licenses; cash deposits or other financial constraints may be imposed as prerequisites to their issuance; they may be issued only to certain companies, or for imports from certain countries which will assure that quotas will not be fully utilized. Hence, it is not enough to talk about the restricting features of import quotas without bringing into focus the entire set of administrative controls which accompany quotas, such as import licenses, prior deposits, import calendars, credit restrictions, and other administrative or supplementary charges.

While Japan is not alone in using administrative controls to inhibit imports, it is unique in the manner and extent to which the techniques have been an endemic feature of domestic economic organization and a mechanism of economic policy supported by a strong historical, cultural, and political national consensus which adds effectiveness to a state-controlled monopsony. The system epitomizes aspects of the administrative nontariff trade barriers described in Chapter 6.

The so-called administrative guidance system deserves particular comment. Government bureaucracy exerts its influence over business forms through administrative signaling and suggestion.

In the trade field, numerous joint government-business associations are the conduits through which signals are passed from protection-minded firms to government and from government to prospective importers. Concentration of most import transactions in the hands of a relatively small number of large trading firms enhances the effectiveness of the system.[23]

When a bureaucratic administrative mechanism is coupled with a vast array of items under quantitative restriction, the possibility of a high degree of protection of domestic production arises. Japan has, indeed, liberalized its quantitative barriers since 1968, as table 5.3 demonstrates. Yet, as seen in Section II of that table, there is a large list of items still under restriction. The next decade should determine whether administrative as well as statutory aspects of the quantitative nontariff barrier mechanism for Japanese agricultural imports will be operated so as to further reduce protection.

TABLE 5.3   Japan's Quantitative Restrictions on Agricultural Products, 1968-72

I. Items Liberalized since 1968:

April 1970

Dried dates; fruit flavors; instant coffee; fruit flour; gluten and gluten flour; malt sugar.

September 1970

Lemon juice; margarine; shortening; manioc for feed; flour, meal, and potato flakes; tapioca, sago, and other starches; residues of manioc, sweet potato, sago, other.

January 1971

Fresh grapes; cake mixes; macaroni, spaghetti, noodles; puffed rice, corn flakes, and similar products.

June 1971

Fresh grapefruit,[a] soybean oilcake and meal; rapeseed meal; vegetable oils,[a] including soybean, safflower, corn, and cottonseed (except for mayonnaise); peanuts for oil extraction; rapeseed; sausages; live horses,[a] bases for beverages, nonalcoholic; fresh apples,[b] frozen pineapples; limes, grapes, and apples, provisionally preserved; black tea; grain sorghum, other than for feed; lemonade and spa water.

October 1971

Live cattle,[a] live swine,[a] pork,[a] instant potatoes; canned corn; confectionery products; cookies, biscuits, and crackers; manioc, arrowroot, sweet potatoes, other, and their flour and meals; molasses; sugar and chocolate confectionery; chocolate food preparations; flavored or colored sugars, syrups, and molasses; nectar; certain peppermint oil.

April 1972

Ham and bacon,[a] salted meat and edible offals; refined beet and cane sugar,[a] tomato puree and paste; certain mixed feeds,[a] rock candy.

II. Items Still under Restriction:

Beef; certain prepared meat items; processed cheese; dried peas; other pulses (navy, pinto, great northern, lima); oranges; tangerines; wheat, rice, barley flour, and groats; peanuts, other than for oil extraction; dates, denatured; grape, malt milk sugar; sugar syrup, carmel, artificial honey; fruit puree, pastes, pulps; canned pineapple; roasted peanuts; fruit juices (lemon liberalized); tomato juice; tomato ketchup and sauce; mixed seasonings; ice cream powder, prepared milk powder for infants, and other preparations mainly consisting of milk; also food preparations based on rice or wheat; malt.

Source: USDA, Foreign Agricultural Service, "Nontariff Barriers Affecting Trade in Agricultural Products—Japan," *Agricultural Trade Policy*, FAS circular ATP-2-72, June 1972.

[a]Tariff rates increased when quotas removed.

[b]Imports from the United States still restricted for health and sanitary reasons.

For balance-of-payments or exchange control, developing countries, and even certain industrialized countries, maintain import quota systems on certain products or groups of products from particular countries or trade areas. The GATT recognized this as a legitimate reason for a country to impose quantitative restrictions and made exceptions to their use for such purposes.[24] Many developing countries, such as India, for example, maintain pervasive quantitative devices, including licensing, exchange controls, quotas, and even embargoes on all commercial agricultural imports. What is not so well publicized are the various quotas maintained by certain industrialized countries ostensibly for exchange or other preferential reasons.

Illustrative of these quotas are those which the United Kingdom established after World War II on products from certain areas when the dollar was in short supply. These were imposed on bananas, cigars, and fresh and processed citrus from dollar-area countries. These items are imported freely from all other sources, and since the dollar is no longer in short supply in the United Kingdom, these quotas are discriminatory in favor of nondollar-area suppliers.

More specifically, citrus illustrates the quota idea and how quantitative measures, once they become institutionalized, are difficult to eliminate even though their economic justification has long since passed. Until 1958, U.S. citrus was purchased in the United Kingdom under U.S. government-assisted programs (PL-480, etc.) on an intermittent basis. In that year, the United Kingdom established dollar-area quotas, first for fresh lemons and lemon juice; and on June 30, 1958, the following dollar-area quotas were established:

Commodity	c.i.f. Value	Period
All fresh citrus	1,050,000	July 1–June[a]
Canned grapefruit	450,000	June 1–September 30
All fruit juice	300,000	June 1–September 30

[a]Fresh grapefruit limited to April 1–September 30.

Various liberalizing measures were taken on these and other dollar-area quotas from 1959 to 1972 with respect to amount of quota, timing, and composition, but as of this writing most of them remain and affect the United States and a number of Latin American countries. The United Kingdom argues that the dollar-area quotas on citrus and other products, the total trade value of which sometimes runs as high as $60 million, are preserved to assist Caribbean Commonwealth countries. Countering this argument, the United States points out that U.K. imports of citrus from the Caribbean have been steadily diminishing, and in any event, the real beneficiaries of the quotas are Third World countries which have an unrestricted access to the U.K. market.[25]

This example from a relatively minor trade item demonstrates how complicated the process of quantitatively limiting the trade process can become. The initial justification for the quotas—balance-of-payments problems in the United Kingdom—has not been particularly valid since the 1950s. The quotas are in contravention of Articles XI and XIII of the GATT and have been the subject of numerous complaints by the exporting country—the United States. Such quota ceilings thwart cooperative marketing agreements between producers in the exporting country (United States) and distributors in the importing country (United Kingdom), thus denying consumers in the latter price benefits which might otherwise be enjoyed. These particular quotas have not all been removed, and a precedent has been established for the continuation of discriminatory treatment of United States products for the United Kingdom within the EEC.

Finally, quotas, when they are small, sometimes remain unfilled because of factors relating to economies of scale. In the case of grapefruit, shipments from the United States to the United Kingdom are not economic unless in large volume, and such volume is discouraged and prevented by quotas. Large importers and exporters who negotiate trade deals often find the quota is exhausted, thus leaving an unfilled demand.

Quotas of the nature described above are directly related to preferential arrangements and, unlike customs unions and free-trade areas, are not sanctioned by the GATT. Preferences run contrary to one of the most fundamental principles of the GATT: nondiscriminatory treatment. The proposals now being considered for the extension of preferential access by the developed countries to the less developed are being justified as an exception warranted to assist the development of infant industries in the latter, and would require a waiver under the GATT to be permissible.

Relating the preferential arrangements principle to the specific illustration of the U.K. dollar-area quota example, one questions whether the Caribbean Commonwealth countries have a genuine trade interest which would be adversely affected by withdrawal of dollar-area quotas. The West Indies already faces unrestricted competition from Israel, Spain, and South Africa for the U.S. citrus juice market; from Israel, Cyprus, and South Africa for the fresh grapefruit market; and from the Netherlands for the cigar market. Data show that the West Indian share of the U.S. citrus juice market dropped from 36.6 percent in 1964–65 to 17 percent in 1969–70, while for fresh grapefruit its share dropped from 8 percent to 2½ percent during the same period. The West Indian share of the cigar market dropped from 17 percent in 1964 to 3 percent in 1970.[26]

Since the United Kingdom is one of the world's largest net importers of agricultural commodities, its past policy on quantitative restrictions is obviously of great interest even though it has now largely adopted the CAP. In addition to the quotas described above, the United Kingdom maintained restrictions on a variety of other products. It exercised control over the bacon market through voluntary export restraints agreed to by major suppliers and through a direct prohibition of imports of whole hams other than in airtight containers. It also controlled imports of butter and cheese by quota in order to safeguard the pricing and marketing system for fluid milk. Sugar was imported under quota arrangements which discriminated in favor of Commonwealth suppliers. A Hops Marketing Board fixed quotas for importation from sources other than the Commonwealth and Ireland. The United Kingdom also used seasonal quotas to restrict importation of fresh apples and pears.

It would be misleading to end this treatment of quantitative restrictions with the implication that most of the barriers have been covered and that the only violators are Europe, Japan, and the United States. For example, bilateral quotas, state trading, and export quotas have not been discussed, nor have "voluntary" agreements such as the U.S. Meat Import Act of 1964 and the various agreements on cotton textile imports. Market sharing, commodity agreements, and other arrangements have a certain appeal from the point of view of international equity but in no way affect the basic characteristic of a quota system, which is an attempt to sever the link between domestic prices and those which exist on world markets.

Quotas and related quantitative restrictions are important in the trade policies of developed countries whose dominant exports are agricultural products (e.g., Australia, Argentina, Canada, New Zealand) and of countries in the developing stages (e.g., Brazil, India), not to mention the countries of Eastern Europe, where all commerce is controlled by a state trading mechanism. Research into the particular situation of each of these groups or of particular countries would carry us far beyond the scope of this book and will have to wait for more extensive study.

Chapter 6.

NONTARIFF AGRICULTURAL BARRIERS
IN SELECTED MAJOR
TRADING COUNTRIES

This chapter is composed of illustrations of nontariff trade barriers arising from the commercial and agricultural policies of selected developed countries. Major emphasis is placed on the principle and not on factual illustration. That is reserved for Chapter 7. In the case of the United Kingdom and the Common Market, the two are left separate, as data were gathered on the United Kingdom prior to 1975. The United States Farm Act of 1977 is not sufficiently different in price support principle from 1976 data to warrant reworking.

One of the most complete pragmatic studies of the nontariff trade barrier question from a U.S. viewpoint was completed in 1974 by the U.S. Tariff Commission for the Senate Committee on Finance. This study covers nontariff charges on imports such as variable levies, border adjustment taxes, and a variety of other charges. It also includes all types of quantitative restrictions and similar specific limitations on trade as well as a variety of other restrictive controls of the nontariff genre.[1]

THE UNITED STATES

Nontariff barriers began to supplant tariffs as the principal means of agricultural protection in the United States during the early 1930s, when domestic farm programs were inaugurated in the Agricultural Adjustment Act of 1933. As can be seen from table 6.1, U.S. general tariff levels were progressively lowered between 1934 and 1967. The actual decrease in tariffs measured by average ad valorem equivalent was from 47 percent in 1934 to 7.8 percent at the end of the Kennedy Round in 1967. From the standpoint of effective protection, however, these figures on nominal tariff rates can be misleading.

TABLE 6.1 U.S. Tariff Reductions, 1934-67

Legislation	Size (%) of Reductions Authorized	Maximum Reduction Authorized on Basis of Actual Use of Tariff-Cutting Authority			Actual Change in Average Ad Valorem Equivalent (%)	
		Authorized Reduction in Tariff Level (%)		Average "Percentage Point" Reduction Authorized		
		From	To		From	To
934 Act	50 percent (of 1934 rates)	47.0	23.5	23.5	47.0	28.0
945 Act	50 percent (of 1945 rates)	28.0	14.0	14.0	28.0	12.0
955 Act	15 percent (of 1955 rates, over 3 years)	12.0	10.2	1.8	12.0	11.0
958 Act (Dillon Round)	20 percent (of 1958 rates, over 4 years)	11.0	8.8	2.2	11.0	12.0
962 Act (Kennedy Round)	50 percent (of 1962 rates, over 5 years)	12.0	6.0	6.0	12.0	7.8[a]

Source: *Congressional Record* (Washington, D.C.: U.S. Government Printing Office), June 21, 1968, p. E5718.
[a] Assuming no change in price levels.

U.S. domestic production and supply, internal demand, and imports and exports during the past forty years have been subjected to a variety of programs and administrative measures to achieve policy goals. Attempts to raise domestic farm prices and incomes while shielding the agricultural sector from outside competition by various import barriers today constitute the basic elements of agricultural protection in the United States and most other industrial countries. The U.S. experience has in one sense been unique, however, in that, under most commodity programs to which import controls were attached, domestic production restrictions were applied in order to reduce program costs. Programs in other countries seldom included restrictions on output or on the supply side.

When reading the brief inventory of U.S. nontariff barriers that follows, one must appreciate the temporary nature of such nontariff compilations. For operating purposes, it is necessary that governments and trading firms keep a day-by-day account of program or administrative changes. Also, one must caution that such items as the Meat Import Act, U.S. sugar legislation, and the Long-Term Textile Agreement are subjects sufficiently important for major analytical treatment in themselves. Nevertheless, this inventory is illustrative of the variety of trade obstacles, even though the nature and degree of protection which result from their existence and administration cannot be determined without closer scrutiny.

This inventory[2] represents U.S. practices that other countries have called to the attention of the GATT as the most commonly mentioned impediments to their trade. The United States, in like fashion, also submitted an inventory of foreign nontariff barriers affecting U.S. exports. The inventories of seventy countries, including the United States, were submitted to the GATT as part of a comprehensive GATT-wide inventory. The list of restrictions omits items not particularly relevant to trade in agricultural products, and does not include, among other things, voluntary export controls imposed by foreign governments to avoid disruption of the U.S. market, state and local governmental measures, and private practices.

Quantitative Restrictions

Presidential authority to impose quotas or fees on imports of agricultural commodities. Such restrictions are now in effect on wheat and wheat flour, cotton, peanuts, and several dairy products.

Presidential authority to limit imports for national security reasons, currently applied only to petroleum shipments.

Sugar quota which reserves 65 percent of the national market to domestic producers.

The Meat Import Act's provision for automatic import controls once a certain level (not yet reached) is attained.

A tariff rate quota on brooms, whereby all imports in excess of a stipulated number are assessed at higher rates of duty.

A ban on purchases of foreign-built containers by U.S. flag vessels if the vessels' operations are governed by operating differential subsidy contracts.

A provision that vessels engaged in U.S. coastal trade must be U.S.-built and U.S.-manned.

Under a provision of the Long-Term Cotton Textile Agreement, the United States controls imports of cotton textiles under separate bilateral agreements with twenty-four countries, accounting for more than 80 percent of U.S. cotton textile imports.

Imports of ermine, fox, kolinsky, marten, mink, muskrat, and weasel furskins produced in the USSR or Mainland China are banned.

Valuation Practices

The U.S. system of customs valuation provides nine different methods of establishing the value of articles, the two most frequently used of which employ free-on-board (f.o.b.) values. Other countries contend that the complexity of U.S. valuation provisions is in itself a barrier to trade, and some have proposed adoption of the Brussels definition of value, which is the landed cost-including-freight (c.i.f.) value.

The American Selling Price System, whereby imported benzenoid chemicals, some rubber footwear, clams, and certain wool knit gloves have duties assessed on the value of competing U.S. products rather than the value of the imported article.

Valuation of certain products on old system of appraisement

rather than the method established in the Customs Simplification Act of 1956.

Other Customs and Administrative Entry Procedures

Special customs invoice used to report entries valued at more than $500 requests some data which foreign suppliers consider unnecessary and burdensome.

Tariff schedules of the United States vary from the Brussels Tariff Nomenclature, which is used by more than one hundred countries, including all our major trading partners except Canada. Among other things, foreigners say that the U.S. tariff schedules classify items so that many parts are no longer listed with the product to which they belong.

Special dumping duties may be imposed under the Anti-dumping Act of 1921, which by law takes precedence in case of conflict over the International Dumping Code, to which the United States adheres.

U.S. countervailing duty practice does not provide for the injury requirement called for by GATT.

Certificates of origin are required for importation of commodities into the United States when goods of Communist Chinese, North Korean, or Vietnamese origin may be involved.

U.S. practice does not fully conform to the provisions of the international convention to facilitate imports of samples. The convention limits deposits on samples to the amount of import duties plus 10 percent, whereas the United States requires a deposit of double the estimated duties. (U.S. rules are being revised to bring them into line with the convention.)

Government Procurement Policy

The Buy American Act of 1933 requires the federal government to buy only domestic materials unless (a) they are not available, (b) their purchase would not be in the public interest, or (c) the cost would be unreasonable. Unreasonable is defined as more than 6 percent higher than the foreign bid. Another 6 percent is added if the material will be produced in a depressed area or by a small business. The Defense Department currently applies a 50 percent differential due to balance-of-payments problems.

The Department of Defense cannot buy any article of food, clothing, cotton, wool, silk, or spun silk yarn for cartridge cloth, or synthetic and coated synthetic materials which has not been produced in the United States.

Health and Other Standards

Certain provisions of the Quarantine and Food and Drug Law, the Wholesome Meat Act, and the Agricultural Marketing Agreement Act have been viewed as trade barriers by foreign suppliers.

The Fair Packaging and Labeling Act of 1966 prescribes the manner in which certain consumer commodities are to be packaged and labeled. (This law also applies equally to domestic and imported products).

The name of the country of origin must be marked in a conspicuous place on all products coming into this country. Exceptions are permitted, but in such cases the container must be marked.

Other Nontariff Practices

Escape clause actions allow the president to increase duties or otherwise restrict imports of items found to be injuring or threatening to injure a domestic industry.

Imports of bottled distilled spirits are assessed as though they were 100 proof, so that in effect a bottle of 86 proof Scotch is assessed for an additional 14 proof.

Corporations that conduct all of their business in the Western Hemisphere and derive 95 percent of their gross income from outside the United States are eligible for certain tax rebates.

The Internal Revenue Service classifies sparkling cider as a sparkling wine. The law sets 0.277 grams of carbon dioxide per 100 milliliters as the upper limit for still wines, and sparkling cider generally has more than 0.4 grams per 100 milliliters. (This law applies with equal force to foreign and domestic products.)

Other U.S. Nontariff Agricultural Barriers

These are but examples. In order to understand their potential restrictive nature, it is neither necessary to describe in detail each of the statutory and regulatory items shown in the above inventory nor to trace their administration through the channels of trade. Suffice it to say that, in addition to these, other means of trade interference do exist and are used by the United States, such as the export subsidy, the Export Control Act of 1949 as amended, the excise tax, the tariff quota, bilateral and state trading agreements, monetary arrangements, national security provisions, and others, as well as outright embargoes. No attempt will be made to describe or to analyze all these measures.

The first large-scale effort at government intervention in agricultural product distribution was the path-breaking United States Agricultural Marketing Act of 1929. That act had domestic and foreign ramifications. It provided large-scale loans to cooperatives (with a view to their achieving virtual marketing monopolies) for propping up prices which were falling to disastrous levels. Conditions were such that the experiment failed, in part because of the open-ended nature of the purchase plan by the cooperatives, continued depression, and excess production in agriculture. From this effort the United States went on to pass an enormous amount of agricultural legislation during the 1930s, some of which constitutes the basis for programs existing there today. U.S. programs and experiments provided models which have been followed in one way or another by many other countries. Most significant of all were the price support and loan program, marketing agreements, and related legislation which pegged agricultural prices at levels higher than the world market, then protected producers from world competition. The program was assured of working by quotas and other forms of trade restrictions. This principle underlies much of the agricultural nontariff protection in the industrial countries today.

In the course of time, U.S. price and income supports and import quotas were supplemented by production controls and export subsidies. Even so, overproduction resulted through the years. Therefore, counterbalancing and demand-inducing legislation has been a part of the programs. Section 32 of the Agricultural Adjustment Act of 1933 allocated up to 30 percent of all customs revenues of the United States for the purpose, among other things, of subsidizing the exports of farm products. When a variety of control techniques failed to stem farm production in the early 1950s, the United States resorted to massive export programs through Public Law 480, based on grants, soft loans to recipient countries, and other trading devices, supplemented by export subsidies. The subsidy constituted, in some cases, a large percentage of the world price of the commodities exported.

As of the early 1970s, the United States operated a variety of export programs, some concessional, some commercial. Concessional programs consist principally of long-term sales on favorable terms and grant-type arrangements, and the soft-terms sales for local currency are being replaced. While concessional sales accounted for approximately 15 percent of U.S. exports, they were of great importance for some commodities. In 1971, for example, more than a third of the wheat, a fourth of the cotton, half the rice, more than 40 percent of the soybean oil, and nearly 90 percent of the nonfat dry milk were exported under this program.

Commercial and quasi-commercial export programs involve less subsidy but, nevertheless, do involve costs to the U.S. government and ultimately must involve control programs and protection for agricultural producers. The USDA Commodity Credit Corporation (CCC) extends short-term credit (six months to three years) to foreign importers at interest rates normally higher than the cost of money to the government, yet low enough to be attractive to most countries which qualify for such credit. What were barter programs in the earlier days of Public Law 480 are now consummated under what could be described as "payments arrangements." Under such arrangements, dollars generated by agricultural exports are transferred to U.S. government agencies to purchase abroad goods and services for which the agencies would otherwise spend appropriated dollars. Subsidization arises out of this program in that barter contractors are given a payment of 1 or 2 percent as an inducement to participate and are eligible to obtain credit from the CCC at $6\frac{1}{8}$ percent interest on money equal to the value of commodities exported.[3]

Another type of commercial aid was the cash subsidy made to exporters which enabled them to meet day-to-day foreign competition in world markets. These payments were made on wheat and flour, rice, and tobacco. Finally, the CCC-owned commodities acquired through price support or direct purchase programs were available to private commercial firms for export. For example, the United States–USSR grain deal of 1972 involved substantial government-owned stocks, a cash subsidy, a favorable interest rate, and a subsidy to U.S. shipping.

The 1973 Agriculture and Consumer Protection Act changed much of the older legislation, which is still in effect. It changed the thrust from restricting production to encouraging production and attempted to make farmers' income maintenance dependent on the marketplaces, both foreign and domestic, rather than on the U.S. Treasury.

The 1973 act, in effect for the years 1974 through 1977, provides for target prices and deficiency payments for wheat, feed grains, and cotton, with a payment limitation of $20,000 per person. (Rice was added in 1975 with a payment limitation of $55,000 per person.) These target prices are based on costs of production and have been sufficiently low that no deficiency payments have been made during most of the time the 1973 act has been in effect, since market prices have stayed above target prices. Some deficiency payments were made in 1976, mostly for wheat. The act set loan rates at lower levels vis-à-vis market prices than in prior legislation, and the secretary of agriculture was given greater discretionary authority. Payments to producers were authorized if natural disasters prevented them from planting or harvesting, if production fell below two-thirds of a normal crop of wheat, feed grains, cotton, or rice.

Acreage allotments were maintained but were used only to determine disaster and deficiency payments, not to restrict production, as they had been used in previous programs. The 1973 act also retains provisions for cropland set-asides, additional diverted acres, and farm-conserving base acres. These were not put into effect. Wheat and cotton marketing quotas were suspended through 1977. Marketing quotas are currently in effect for extra-long staple cotton, peanuts, and most kinds of tobacco.

Other major provisions of the 1973 act are: (1) the Public Law 480 and food stamp programs were extended for four years; (2) dairy price supports and Class 1 base plans for wool and mohair were continued; (3) a disaster reserve of wheat, feed grains, and soybeans was put into effect; (4) annual cost of production studies were required for wheat, feed grains, cotton, and dairy products; (5) most sections of the 1973 act continued existing programs with moderate changes.

The 1973 act did not attempt to cover everything. Many older programs remained in effect, including those for peanuts, tobacco, and extra-long staple tobacco (and rice until 1975). Legislation for export controls in situations of short supply is provided by the Export Administration Act, and exports of surplus can be handled by PL 480 and trade agreements, among other things.

Conditions in U.S. agricultural production and trade changed considerably during the five-year period ending in 1976, but the changes were in terms of magnitude, not in the nature of fundamental programs and policies themselves. All the basic farm and trade legislation and regulatory activities were still in the making, as was the case in most other developed countries. The basic strategies were still around despite several years of "storm" in world production and distribution.

Table 6.2 presents specific program measures taken by the United States as of 1976 to support prices and incomes of selected crop and livestock products. Included are domestic price supports and other payments, and production controls. Contrary to the situation in the past, export subsidies do not exist. Table 6.3 pre-. sents information on U.S. controls—both tariff and nontariff—for agricultural products. Not included in either table are the various indirect subsidies such as conservation payments, subsidized credit, and others. As will be noted, the export subsidies which played a significant role up until 1972 vanished under the impact of higher prices for grain and other agricultural products in world markets. Nominal tariff rates exist for all grain, dairy products, oilseeds, and meats. The rates on tobacco and sugar are more significant. Of the nontariff barriers, highly effective quotas exist for sugar, peanuts, dairy products, and wheat.[4]

The principal objective of this tabulation of support mechanisms and the inventory of nontariff barriers presented earlier is to illustrate the diversity of the instruments of protection available to legislators and administrators of farm programs. Measuring the effectiveness of this protection is another matter, and rectifying imbalances in international trade caused by them yet another.

THE UNITED KINGDOM AND COMMONWEALTH
NONTARIFF AGRICULTURAL BARRIERS

Beginning in the 1930s, nontariff barriers superseded tariffs at a rapid rate and on a large scale in Europe in order to maintain and increase protection for the agricultural sectors. When the flood of low-priced surplus agricultural exports lapped over tariff barriers—

TABLE 6.2 U.S. Government Activities Affecting Production and Marketing of Selected Agricultural Commodities

Product	Unit	Support Prices $ Loan Rate	Support Prices $ Target Price	Other Payments Applicable, 1976 Disaster and Fed. Crop Ins.	Other Payments Applicable, 1976 Gov't. Purchase	Controls Applicable to 1976 Production	Controls Applicable to 1976 Marketing	Other
Wheat	Bu.	1.50	2.29	X	X	None	None	CCC sales policy per bu. $2.63
Corn	Bu.	1.25	1.57	X	X	None	None	CCC sales policy per bu. $1.81
Grain sorghum	Bu.	1.19	1.49	X	X	None	None	CCC sales policy per bu. $1.71
Barley	Bu.	1.02	1.28	X	X	None	None	CCC sales policy per bu. $1.47
Oats	Bu.	0.60	0	X	X	None	None	CCC sales policy per bu. $0.87
Rye	Bu.	1.00	0	X	X	None	None	CCC sales policy per bu. $1.45
Rice	CWT	6.00	8.00	X	X	None	None	Rice Production Act of 1975 Nat'l allotment = 1.8 mil. acres Payment limitation per person = $55,000
Dairy Milk (3.5%)	CWT	8.13	0		X	None	Quota	CCC also purchases by competitive bids to fulfill nonsupport price programs
Butter Grade A NY Cheddar cheese	Lb.	0.8775	0		X	None	Quota	
Grade A Nonfat Dry	Lb.	0.9050	0		X	None	Quota	
Milk	Lb.	0.6240	0		X	None	Quota	

TABLE 6.2 *Continued*

Product	Unit	Support Prices $ Loan Rate	Support Prices $ Target Price	Other Payments Applicable, 1976 Disaster and Fed. Crop Ins.	Other Payments Applicable, 1976 Gov't. Purchase	Controls Applicable to 1976 Production	Controls Applicable to 1976 Marketing	Other
Soybeans	Bu.	2.50	0	X	X	None	None	CCC resale policy = market price but not less than $3.62 per bu.
Peanuts	Short ton	414.00	0	X	X	None	Quota	Nat'l. acreage allotment = 1.6 mil. acres; CCC minimum sales policy = 100% of loan
Tobacco								
FC 11-14	Lb.	1.060	0			Acreage allotments	Poundage quota	Level
B 31	Lb.	1.093	0			Acreage allotments	Poundage quota	
VFC 21	Lb.	0.741	0			Acreage allotments	Poundage quota	
KTFC 22-23	Lb.	0.741	0			Acreage allotments	Poundage quota	
DAC 35-36	Lb.	0.659	0			Acreage allotments	Poundage quota	
VSC 37	Lb.	0.659	0			Acreage allotments	Poundage quota	
CB 51-52	Lb.	0.756	0			Acreage allotments	Poundage quota	
CF & B 42-44	Lb.	0.546	0			Acreage allotments	Poundage quota	
PR 46	Lb.	0.567	0			Acreage allotments	Poundage quota	

| Product | Unit | Support Prices | | Other Payments Applicable, 1976 | | Controls Applicable to 1976 | | Other |
		$ Loan Rate	$ Target Price	Disaster and Fed. Crop Ins.	Gov't Purchase	Production	Marketing	
Wool								
Shorn	Lb.	0	0.720			None	None	Payments to producers based on the percentage needed to bring the average return received by all producers up to the support level. This percentage is applied to each producer's proceeds from the sale of wool. Pulled wool is supported by payment on sales of unshorn lambs. 1976 shorn wool payment rate was 61.1%, or $61.10 for each $100.00 of marketings.
Pulled	Lb.	0	0.720			None	None	
Mohair	Lb.	0	0.820			None	None	Same procedure as for shorn wool. No incentive payments, since 1976 market prices were above the support price.
Sugar	CWT	0	0				Import duty of $1.87	

TABLE 6.2 *Continued*

| Product | Unit | Support Prices | | Other Payments Applicable, 1976 | Gov't | Controls Applicable to 1976 | | |
		$ Loan Rate	$ Target Price	Disaster and Fed. Crop Ins.	Purchase	Production	Marketing	Other
Fresh, chilled, or frozen cattle, goat, and sheepmeat							Import quotas limited to 1.233 mil. lbs. Prohibited imports of foreign beef processed in foreign trade zones, including Puerto Rico, from Oct. 26 for remainder of 1976.	
Bees	Hives	0	0	X				Beekeepers Indemnity Payment Program pays beekeepers for hives seriously damaged or killed by insecticides used in crop production.

Source: Compiled from information provided by the Agricultural Stabilization and Conservation Service, USDA.

TABLE 6.3 U.S. Import Controls on Agricultural Products, 1976

Products	Tariff	NTB
Wheat	21¢ per bu. of 60 lbs.	Quota suspended 1/26/74
Feedgrains		
Corn, other than for seed	25¢ per bu. of 56 lbs.	None
Grain, sorghum	0.4¢ per lb.	None
Barley	7.5¢ per bu. of 48 lbs.	None
Oats	7¢ per bu. of 32 lbs.	None
Rye	6¢ per bu. of 56 lbs.	None
Rice		None
Unmilled: Paddy or rough	1.25¢ per lb.	
Brown rice	1.5¢ per lb.	
Milled: Bran removed	2.5¢ per lb.	
Broken	0.3125¢ per lb.	
Dairy Products		
Milk	Containing over 1% but not over 5.5% butterfat, for not over 3,000,000 gallons entered in any calendar year, 2¢ per gal.; other, 6.5¢ per gal.	Quota
Butter	When entered during the period from Nov. 1, in any year, to the following Mar. 31, inclusive: for not over 50,000,000 pounds, 7¢ per lb.; other, 14¢ per lb. When entered during the period from Apr. 1 to Jul. 15, inclusive, in any year: for not over 5,000,000 pounds, 7¢ per lb.; other, 14¢ per lb. When entered during the period from Jul. 16 to Oct. 31, inclusive, in any year: for not over 5,000,000 pounds, 7¢ per lb.; other, 14¢ per lb.	Quota

TABLE 6.3 *Continued*

Products	Tariff	NTB
Cheddar Cheese: Not processed	15% ad val.	Quota
Processed	20% ad val.	
Nonfat dry milk	1.5¢ per lb.	Quota
Oilseeds		
Soybeans	1¢ per lb.	None
Cottonseed	1/3¢ per lb.	None
Peanuts: Not shelled	4.25¢ per lb.	Quota
Shelled	7¢ per lb.	
Meat, fresh, chilled, or frozen		
Beef	3¢ per lb.	Quota
Veal	3¢ per lb.	Quota
Swine	0.5¢ per lb.	None
Poultry	Birds, whole or which have been plucked only: chickens, ducks, geese, and guineas, 3¢ per lb.; turkeys, 8.5¢ per lb.; other, 2.5¢ per lb. Birds which have been plucked, beheaded, and eviscerated but not cut into pieces: chickens, 5¢ per lb.; turkeys, valued under 40¢ per pound, 5¢ per lb., valued 40 or more cents per pound, 12.5% ad val.; other, 5¢ per lb. Other (cut into pieces), 10¢ per lb.	None
Tobacco		
Burley	12.75¢ per lb.	None

Products	Tariff	NTB
Flue-cured	12.75¢ per lb.	None
Other	Not stemmed, 16.1¢ per lb.; stemmed, 23¢ per lb.	None
Sugar	Sugar beets and sugar cane: in their natural state, sugar beets, 80¢ per short ton, sugar cane, $2.50 per short ton. In other forms suitable for the commercial extraction of sugar, 0.5¢ per lb. of total sugars Sugars, syrups, and molasses, derived from sugar cane or sugar beets: principally of crystalline structure or in dry amorphous form, 0.6625¢ per lb. less 0.009375¢ per lb. for each degree under 100 degrees but not less than 0.428125¢ per lb.[b] Not principally of crystalline structure and not in dry amorphous form, containing soluble nonsugar solids equal to 6% or less by weight of the total soluble solids, dutiable on total sugars at the rate per lb. applicable under Item 155.20 to sugar testing 100 degrees. Other, 2.9¢ per gal.	a

Source: USDA, Foreign Agricultural Service.

[a]The United States International Trade Commission has recently recommended to the president that he should impose new quotas on imports of sugar.

[b]Presidential Proclamation 4463, September 21, 1976, 41 F.R. 41681, as amended by Presidential Proclamation 4466, October 4, 1976, 41 F.R. 44031, effective date September 21, 1976, modified this duty to 1.9875¢ per lb. less 0.028125¢ per lb. for each degree under 100 degrees but not less than 1.284375¢ per lb. This new duty applied to all shipments of sugar except those exported to the United States before 12:01 a.m. (U.S. Eastern Daylight Saving Time), September 21, 1976, and entered for consumption on or before November 8, 1976.

however high they were, and notwithstanding existing commercial treaties—all countries took additional measures to protect themselves. Even Great Britain, Denmark, and the Netherlands, historic bastions of free trade, shifted to protectionist policies, following other European nations into a variety of nontariff measures to accomplish policy objectives.

Because of its unique history as a free-trade country, it was inevitable that protection of and intervention in agriculture by Great Britain would follow a different direction during the economic crises of the 1930s and thereafter. It abandoned free trade in 1931 and adopted emergency protection measures, which were replaced in 1932 by the Import Duties Act. This act remained essentially the basic instrument of the British tariff for forty years. An ad valorem duty of 10 percent was imposed, but certain major agricultural products were exempted, including wheat, corn, meat, livestock, and wool. Imperial preferences were established for the Dominions through the Ottawa Agreements of 1932. Despite all these and other measures, little benefit accrued to British agriculture, which was still exposed to the pressure of competition from the Empire as well as imports from low-cost foreign producers who paid low duties. A policy of cheap food which had prevailed for nearly a century was difficult to change.

For these and other reasons, Great Britain did not follow what could be called a deliberate policy toward controlling agricultural production and marketing during the 1930s. Instead, a series of measures were applied, commodity by commodity, to assist agricultural producers and producer groups. These involved subsidies, import restrictions, marketing schemes, and various combinations of these measures. Thus, for wheat and sugar beets, assistance was given by subsidy alone; for milk, by a marketing scheme and by subsidy; for bacon, potatoes, and hops, by marketing schemes combined with import control; for eggs, by voluntary restrictions applied by exporting countries.

The marketing schemes introduced by official parliamentary acts of 1931 and 1933, like the United States Marketing Act of 1937 and various types of statutory and regulatory acts instituted by other countries, attempted to deal with the supply function in agriculture in order to raise incomes to farmers and make minimum prices work. Britain, like other countries, found that supporting prices was a hazardous undertaking without some form of supply regulation. Hence, legislation to permit producers to vote binding minimum and maximum prices on themselves had to be followed by legislation to regulate imports so that the effects of marketing schemes would not be dissipated. If a marketing scheme was voted by producer groups, as was the case for milk, bacon, potatoes, and hops, the government could regulate quantities sold by registered producers and could regulate imports. This was necessary to make schemes operate in such a way as not to be too expensive to consumers. Thus, the element of protection in these schemes consisted of raising domestic prices through constraints on local supplies, buttressed by import controls once the domestic supply control operation got underway.

Britain entered a variety of bilateral agreements with several countries during the 1930s, all of which took into consideration its pledges and concessions to the Dominions and the programs for its domestic farm producers. These agreements involved guaranteed maximum duties on products from Denmark and Argentina, and duty-free or duty-reducing concessions on a wide range of products from the United States. Specific clauses in some of these agreements, however, guarded the right to impose quotas should imports interfere with domestic marketing schemes.

The shift from free trade to protectionism during this chaotic period, along with a further shift to self-sufficiency after World War II, did not take place without controversy. During the 1930s, arguments for protection in agriculture had centered on increasing employment in domestic agriculture and equity considerations which would give farm producers protection equivalent to that of industry. After World War II, arguments for subsidization of agriculture and backing for protective measures were based on the dual considerations of self-sufficiency and balance of payments. One argument held that comparative advantage had shifted against British industry and that the country would be unable to finance large food imports. Coupled with this was the fear that food prices would rise relatively faster than those of manufactures, thus exacerbating balance-of-payments problems. The calculated shift in agricultural policy in Britain from free trade to market intervention and modified protection is demonstrated by the fact that it now produces more than 50 percent of its food requirements (two-thirds of Temperate Zone products), compared to about 30 percent before World War II.

The distinguishing feature of British agricultural policy since World War II has been its deficiency payments system. In brief, it allows agricultural prices to be determined by the free operation of the market, yet enables a minimum price to be guaranteed to producers. Direct payments are made to producers on specified commodity amounts. This is a convenient method of providing a means for reconciling support for farmers with free entry for food imports, but it would be a mistake to label the system as nonprotective. Josling has shown that the terms-of-trade effect of producer subsidies of this type, given the low price elasticities which exist for foodstuffs in general, restricts trade volume almost as effectively as an import quota or tariff.[5]

In 1964, a system of minimum import prices for grains, to be supported by variable import levies if import prices were not observed, was negotiated with four suppliers. Then in 1968, the British government announced that it would continue until 1972–73 its policy of selective expansion of agriculture and that priority would continue to be given to wheat, barley, beef, and pork.[6] The government in 1970 announced its intention to introduce as soon as possible interim levy schemes for beef, veal, mutton, lamb, and milk products other than butter and cheese. The existing scheme was modified at that time. This change signified higher market prices for agricultural commodities and consequential savings in government payments, but with higher prices for consumers.

On January 1, 1973, Britain entered the European Economic Community; and on February 1 the Common Agricultural Policy was applied, with a period of five years allowed for harmonization to CAP rules and regulations. One of the far-reaching implications of this move will be the change in access for present overseas suppliers to the U.K. market, which is still a major outlet for a number of Temperate Zone agricultural products.[7]

Currently, therefore, the United Kingdom is in a five-year period of transition to the CAP system of variable import levies and other policy techniques. In the meantime, the principal nontariff barriers consist of a minimum import price system, quota restrictions and prohibitions, and certain health, sanitary, and quality controls. Table 6.4 presents a selected list of the United Kingdom's nontariff restrictions.

TABLE 6.4 Selected U.K. Nontariff Trade Barriers

Tariff Number	Commodity Description	Type of Restrictions[a]	Remarks
Ex 01.02 Ex 02.01 Ex 02.06	Fat cattle and fresh, chilled, or frozen beef and veal, including offals	VL, SDI, ST, LI, QR, TDA	Hoof-and-mouth disease controls
02.02 02.03	Poultry meats and offals	VL, SDI	
Ex 02.06 Ex 16.02	Whole hams other than in air-tight containers	VL, SDI	
04.01	Fresh milk and cream	VL, SDI, LI, QR	
Ex 04.02	Milk and cream, preserved, concentrated, or sweetened	VL, SDI, LI, TDA	
04.03	Butter	VL, SDI, LI, TDA	
Ex 04.04	Cheese	VL, SDI, LI, TDA	
Ex 04.05	Eggs	VL, SDI	
Ex 08.01	Bananas	QR	
Ex 08.02	Fresh grapefruit	VA	
Ex 08.06	Fresh apples and pears	MPR, TDA	
Ex 10.01	Wheat and meslin	VL, SDI, LI, TDA	
Ex 12.03	Clover and grass seeds	TDA	

TABLE 6.4 *Continued*

Tariff Number	Commodity Description	Type of Restrictions[a]	Remarks
12.06	Hop cones and lupulin	QR, TDA	Discretionary licensing except from the Commonwealth. An annual determination is made of import needs and licenses are issued accordingly.
Ex 16.01	Sausages	VL, SDI	
Ex 16.02	Other prepared or preserved pork or poultry products	VL, SDI	
17.01	Beet sugar and cane sugar	VL, SDI, LI, TDA	
Ex 20.05	Fruit jams and jellies	VL	
Ex 20.07	Grapefruit and orange juice, except frozen concentrates;	VL	
	Apples, black currants, and pear juice and syrup	VL	
Ex 23.07	Animal feedstuffs containing more than 80 percent weight of milk solids	VL, SDI, LI	

Source: USDA, Foreign Agricultural Service.

[a]VL = variable levy; SDI = special duties on imports; ST = standards; LI = licensing; QR = quantitative restrictions; TDA = trade-diverting aids; VA = valuation; MPR = minimum price regulations.

Minimum import prices exist for fat cattle, beef, and veal; milk powders and preserved or condensed milk and cream (including animal feed containing milk solids); poultry meat; eggs; wheat; barley; oats; corn; grain; sorghum; cereal flour; and meals and bran. A target price is established for each of these products and then a minimum price is established high enough that imports cannot enter the market at substantially less than the target price. Variable levies are used in most cases to ensure that the import price does not fall below the established minimum. This system of support is a move away from direct deficiency payments and will make possible a smoother transfer to Common Agricultural Policy.

Rigid quotas exist for only a few products—apples, pears, and potatoes—but there are certain limitations on imports for foreign exchange reasons (discussed in Chapter 5) and market-sharing arrangements on other imports. For wheat, butter, cheese, and bacon the United Kingdom has moved toward market-sharing and quantitative regulation. In the case of bacon imports, it allocates a minimum quantity plus a reserve amount between suppliers, including domestic producers, to maintain a reasonable price. For butter, import quotas have been allotted to overseas suppliers based on agreements on how to divide the market. Quotas on butter and cheese safeguard the pricing and marketing system for fluid milk. A quota arrangement through the Commonwealth Sugar Agreement has protected Commonwealth suppliers by fixing quantities of sugar to be imported into the United Kingdom, at price levels which are negotiated every three years.

Health, sanitary, and quality control legislation and regulations in the United Kingdom, even though not entirely typical of all countries, are illustrative of this type of nontariff barrier. Disease control measures are used to protect the domestic livestock industry. Imports of pork and pork products from countries in which hog cholera exists are prohibited. Fat cattle, beef, and veal imports are subject to rigorous licensing requirements in order to control hoof-and-mouth disease. In addition, red meat imports are subject to a regulation prohibiting additives which maintain color.[8] Strict quarantine, inspection, and licensing conditions are maintained on shipments of live horses.

Licensing is strictly required on dead poultry and offals when packaged separately, and licenses are issued only for poultry which can be shown to be free of Newcastle disease. Other import requirements apply to dressed poultry and offals.

Among the controls on quality are those which require clover and grass seeds to be licensed, so that imports meet minimum standards and are appropriate for U.K. soil and climate. The trade policy of the United Kingdom had a dominating influence on the Commonwealth nations until quite recently. Though minimal treatment will be given the subject, it should be pointed out that the Dominions and other Commonwealth countries, particularly those in the Temperate Zone, have taken individual actions with protective domestic measures. These actions were taken in order to ensure against their vulnerability to world price fluctuations and also to counter protective measures in other countries.

Canada, whose principal agricultural export is wheat, established a Wheat Board as early as 1935. As a trading monopoly, the board has dominated Canada's international trade policy. Some products, notably grains and dairy products, are subject to import permits. Approximately half of Canada's agricultural imports come in duty free, while tariffs on the remainder average about 8 percent. In the early 1970s some export subsidies were paid on dairy products.

Agricultural marketing boards in Australia, New Zealand, and the Union of South Africa provide the best examples of government intervention in agriculture and its cooperation with producers to raise incomes. Agricultural exports provide better than half of Australia's foreign earnings and more than 90 percent of New Zealand's Governmental marketing boards provide assistance in organizing governmental or quasi-governmental marketing schemes for individual commodities—usually those with a substantial export market. Their ultimate object is export supply control and market stabilization. In the 1930s, export subsidies or their equivalent were common in a number of countries: Argentina bought market surpluses from farmers and sold them on world markets at a loss; Australia subsidized wheat exports directly after 1938; South Africa began subsidizing sugar and foodstuffs exports in 1931 and later subsidized beef and mutton; New Zealand began export subsidies on dairy products in 1936.

Many marketing boards now exist in these countries, but the six most important with respect to export control are those dealing with deciduous and citrus fruits in the Union of South Africa; dairy products, apples, and pears in New Zealand; and dairy products and meat in Australia. (The Australian Wheat Board is a government monopoly, as in the Canadian case.) All of these boards have export monopoly powers except the wheat board of Australia, which has powers of export licensing. The "balanced development" policies of Australia have resulted in support measures and protection for farmers from competition, even though low domestic production costs and high foreign transport costs would not seem to warrant this.

The Dominions and Commonwealth countries faced certain trade adjustments during Britain's entry into the EEC and during its adaptation to the Common Agricultural Policy. New Zealand, for example, has been finding its way into new agricultural trade patterns in the Pacific and elsewhere and may gradually be eased away from the captive market it had in the United Kingdom. Other countries which have enjoyed this economic association through preferential agreements will, no doubt, also be increasingly affected. Moreover, trade relationships between Britain and the United States which have existed for over a century will likely undergo further changes when the full impact of the CAP is felt. For Britain, these shifting arrangements might be compared in importance to those momentous decisions surrounding the abolition of the Corn Laws and other events which gave to that country a unique trade policy during the industrial revolution.

NONTARIFF AGRICULTURAL BARRIERS:
WESTERN EUROPE

The protective devices initiated by European governments during the depressed period of the 1930s constituted the bulk of statutory and regulatory trade restrictions in agriculture until the Common Agriculture Policy was implemented. Quantitative restrictions and licensing, export subsidies, preferential agreements, bilateral agreements, mixing regulations, and state trading, along with health and sanitary regulations, supplemented a rather formidable tariff on agricultural products. And even the CAP did not succeed in abolishing many of the restrictions used by individual countries. It is sometimes forgotten in the polemics surrounding the EC variable levy system that this merely replaced a host of other nontariff restrictions; also, that the variable levy existed as a nontariff instrument in several European countries before it was adopted by the Community in 1962. This, among other reasons, is why we have treated the variable levy as a nontariff barrier in the fashion shown in a previous chapter. Indeed, it is perhaps the most notable nontariff barrier of all.

Direct state involvement in agriculture in continental Europe is a phenomenon which seems to have had its genesis in (1) the breakdown of trade after World War II and the failure of the tariff to generate an economic uplift to the farmer; (2) the failure of certain nontariff devices in the agricultural sector; and (3) the ancient reasoning that if only agriculture could be stimulated, other sectors of a national economy would receive the multiplier effects of such stimulus. As has been shown, policies in the United States, Britain, and elsewhere underwent a basic change, and these economies diverted their efforts from protective tariffs to direct government intervention in the production and marketing processes after the breakdown of world trade in the early 1930s. In Europe the same tendencies prevailed: the drives for self-sufficiency in food and production for foreign-exchange-saving reasons dominated all other agricultural policies. Tariff structures were reinforced by a series of new measures in France, Germany, Italy, and other European countries to protect agriculture from outside competition and to support prices and incomes with a variety of administrative and regulatory techniques. Such old issues as the social value of agrarian life and community structure once again became bases in the argument for agricultural protection. In such depressed conditions, many devices like quotas, exchange controls, export subsidies, etc., were introduced in the expectation that they would be only temporary and could be relaxed or removed when economic conditions returned to normal. The opposite happened: not only were these measures reinforced during the 1930s, but a variety of other domestic support measures were added. The entire arsenal of protective devices and arguments formed the basis of post-World War II policies, which eventually culminated, in part, in the EEC Common Agricultural Policy.

France offers a clear example of a policy which progressed from tariffs to nontariffs to more pervasive measures of intervention in order to protect its agriculture from competitive prices and the economic vagaries of the world market. Import quotas, mixing regulations, and related nontariff barriers replaced high tariffs as the first line of defense when the latter became an ineffective means of protection in the early 1930s. However, these first-line defense mechanisms were themselves replaced by direct supportive measures when import controls were no longer adequate to maintain domestic prices. This was particularly the case with wheat. Progressive state intervention in the market between 1933 and 1939 was justified on the basis of the important role which agriculture played in the economy of France, as well as the necessity of maintaining social balance in the countryside. Experiences of the 1930s left a permanent impression on French agrarian policy; there were those who thought French agriculture would have ceased to exist had the government not intervened as boldly with its protective measures between the wars.[9]

Post-World War II agricultural and trade policies have consisted principally of a series of plans involving campaigns to modernize French agriculture and to raise its productivity, the ultimate aim being to increase gross output and, in the process, to improve its competitive position in world markets and to increase agricultural exports. Faced with limited growth in demand for foodstuffs domestically, France looked increasingly for preferential agreements abroad, namely, with Germany and Britain, to dispose of her surplus production. Thus, one can understand why sponsors of French agricultural policy during these years were later some of the principal proponents of the EEC Common Agricultural Policy.

Agricultural and trade policies in Germany and Italy during the 1930s were dominated by the strict regulations of the National Socialist governments. In Germany, control of price levels and volume of imports was enforced on all important commodities by state boards beginning in 1933; these boards could buy and sell on the domestic market as well as operate buffer stocks. Imports were severely limited during the next several years. Italy's attempt to protect and stimulate its agriculture is typified by its dealings in wheat. High import duties and low prices meant that tariffs were no longer effective, and nontariff barriers in the form of milling ratios and other measures were introduced. A full state wheat monopoly instituted in the mid-1930s required growers to deliver wheat at fixed prices, and imports were controlled directly by organizations responsible to the Ministry of Agriculture.

After World War II, agricultural and trade policies in West Germany were dominated by attempts to deal with problems of farm structure and fragmentation. Strict control of imports through import boards has helped maintain domestic prices above both world market levels and those in other European countries. In part because of its protectionist policies, German agriculture, despite government assistance toward structural reform, remains highly vulnerable to increased competition from within and from without the European Economic Community. In Italy, when soft wheat and rice production began to outrun demand in the mid-1950s, export subsidies and other measures to regulate markets were imposed.

The pattern of crisis and intervention was generally the same in all Western European countries from the 1930s on; agricultural protection by tariffs gave way to a variety of new, more effective nontariff devices which, for the most part, insulated domestic markets from foreign competition. Such restrictive and autarchic measures by one country were at the expense of others; the international market was stagnated; and the depression, prolonged by domestic economic policies, led to retaliatory and defensive strategies. The need for protection was thus perpetuated by actions in the domestic sphere, which governed actions at country borders and on the international scene.

In short, behind the highly protective restrictions of most European countries (and other countries), agriculture was encouraged to expand. Various countries used a variety of measures to deal with marketing problems thus created, but no consistent agricultural policy was developed to deal with structural maladjustment in agriculture. Hence, after World War II high price supports and other interventionist techniques were necessary to maintain incomes for uneconomic producing units. The merits of a free-trade policy will not be debated in this context, but it is obvious that protectionism failed because it insulated farming and the agricultural industries from economic forces which could have induced changes; and it diverted attention from the need for more constructive programs.

As European recovery from World War II proceeded, substantial increases in agricultural production were recorded, but the trade situation was less satisfactory. Though many trade restrictions were removed in industrial and other sectors, and though some progress was made in removing quantitative agricultural barriers between European countries, since the mid-1950s a large portion of their production and trade of agricultural products has remained subject to state intervention and control. In general, as shown in Chapter 3, table 3.3, between the end of World War II and the early 1960s there was a marked increase in agricultural protection.

At the beginning of the 1970s, and before the 1973 expansion of the Common Market, a large percentage of the value of agricultural production in the member countries was subject to the support and import protection of the Common Agricultural Policy. Illustrative of CAP protection in agriculture are the measures and levels of prices vis-a-vis the world levels shown in table 6.5 for 1969. Target prices, intervention prices, export subsidies, and import controls formed a vast array of barriers to freer movement of agricultural products. Though prices, production, and trade conditions have, indeed, changed during the interim, the protectionist principle embodied in the CAP remains the same. Current price figures can be obtained from the CAP headquarters in Brussels, Belgium.

It should be noted, however, that since 1972, protection of EC agriculture has diminished. Even so, the real question remains: Is this a permanent trend toward lower protection for European agriculture? Doubters will certainly point to the reimposition of beef import duties in September 1973, a return to variable levies in November 1973, and a long series of restrictive import measures on beef in early 1974 as signaling a reversal of the move toward more open markets in CAP countries.

Under the CAP, the most important nontariff barrier is the variable import levy, analyzed in an earlier chapter. The levy, except for the beef sector, replaced both tariff and certain nontariff protection. There are, however, still other CAP nontariff barriers and, in addition, particular national nontariff barriers against imports. There are also certain agricultural products subject to fixed tariffs, duties on which range from 5 to 25 percent.

A wide range of nontariff barriers supplementary to the variable levy make Western Europe one of the most highly protected markets in the world for agricultural imports.[10] Compensatory taxes, import licenses, quality standards, and a variety of subsidies

TABLE 6.5 Measures Taken by the European Community Which Affect Agriculture and Trade, 1969

Product	Target Price	Intervention Price (Support)	Production Control	Export Subsidy	Import Controls Levy or Duty	Nontariff Barriers
Wheat	Hard $3.40/bu. Soft $2.89/bu.	$3.00/bu. $2.84/bu.	None	$1.28/bu. ($1.52 to Japan)	$1.33/bu. (62%) $1.34/bu. (88%)	Licensing
Feedgrains						
Corn	$2.41/bu.	$2.03/bu.		$1.02/bu.	$1.17/bu. (84%)	
Sorghums	Est. $2.31/bu.			$1.06/bu.	$1.11/bu. (70%)	
Barley	$2.08/bu.	$1.98/bu.	None	$1.04/bu. ($1.22 to Japan)	$1.04/bu. (97%)	Licensing
Oats						
Rye	$2.48/bu.	$2.32/bu.			$1.16/bu. (84%)	
Rice	$8.56/cwt.		None	Depends on domestic price levels	$1.19/cwt. (17%)	
Dairy products						
Milk	$4.68/cwt	78.9¢/lb.		60.3¢/lb.	73.1¢/lb. (100%)	Quotas (Germany)
Butter		56.7¢/lb.	None	19.5¢/lb.	46.8¢/lb. (162%)	
Cheese	Food—	18.8¢/lb.		9.1¢/lb.	21.8¢/lb. (220%)	Quotas (France)
Nonfat	Feed—	14.4¢/lb.		5.3¢/lb.	19.1¢/lb. (190%)	
Oilseeds						
Soybeans			None	N/A	4.6¢/lb. (100%) (Soybeans and cottonseed bound free)	Quotas (Italy) [3]
Cottonseed	Rapeseed 9.2¢/lb.	8.9¢/lb.				

TABLE 6.5 Continued

Product	Target Price	Intervention Price	Production Control	Export Subsidy	Import Controls Levy or Duty	Nontariff Barriers
Meat (fresh, chilled, frozen)						
Beef	Beef 31¢/lb.		None	None	10¢/lb. (74%)	
Veal	Veal 42¢/lb.		None		3.8¢/lb. (39%)	
Pork		33¢/lb.		Pork products (ham and lard)	10.3¢/lb. (31%)	
Poultry			None	7.4¢/lb.	11.03¢/lb.	
Tobacco						
Burley	CAP not completed	Monopoly controls in France and Italy	Monopoly controls in France and Italy		(23%)	Monopoly in France and Italy, Quotas (France) Mixing regulations (Germany) Licensing
Sugar	10.16¢/lb. (white sugar)	9.65¢/lb.	Quotas	Subsidy on exported products containing sugar and on base products	7.8¢/lb. (338%)	

Source: USDA, Foreign Agricultural Service.

are used to reduce the market for imports and to improve outlets for domestic production.[11]

A so-called reference price, based on European Community market prices, is used to calculate compensatory taxes for various products. Imports found to be selling at less than the reference price may be subject to an offsetting tax which may vary seasonally, as in the case of fresh fruits and vegetables. It applies to fresh apples, cherries, grapes, lemons, oranges, peaches, pears, plums, tomatoes, wine, and other minor products. Fats and oils regulations provide for the imposition of certain types of compensatory taxes on many imported oilseeds and oilseed products as well as marine or vegetable oils, in relation to their substitution in the Community market and subject to conditions surrounding their export. For example, imports of marine or vegetable oils may be subject to a compensatory tax if the European Community finds evidence that such products receive a subsidy from the exporting country.

Import licenses, as in most countries, are used widely as a regulatory instrument in the EC import control system. They are required for all imports of grain, rice, olive oil, sugar, dairy products, frozen beef and veal, and wine, and for imports of processed fruits and vegetables containing added sugar when the importer requests the levy to be fixed in advance.

In addition to the foregoing devices which affect imports directly, there are a number of subsidy measures which make domestic products more competitive by reducing prices in local markets. Also, there are many administrative rules and regulations which act as barriers to agricultural imports. Among these in the individual countries (not the EC itself as such) are health and sanitary regulations.

For example, in Belgium, imports of beef in cuts must weigh at least ten kilograms each, whether boned or deboned. In France, a country which traditionally has had stringent health, sanitary, and administrative procedures, imports of honey must be accompanied by a certificate indicating that it was produced within an area free of nocema, a disease which exists in France. In Germany, a very restrictive food law and a number of other regulations are more restrictive than Community requirements for some imported agricultural products. Also in Germany, metric size packaging regulations limit fruit and vegetable juices to only five container sizes and contain additional labeling requirements. In Italy, there is a general prohibition on fruit imports, although there are a few exceptions. Pesticide residue restrictions represent a potentially serious nontariff trade barrier.

In recent years, no important liberalization of nontariff barriers has been made by the European Community as such. Nor have the individual member states, with the exception of the Netherlands, reduced nontariff barriers. To be sure, the EC has reduced tariffs on certain commodities to the countries with which it has negotiated preferential trade agreements, but few reductions have been made to nonpreferred suppliers. Coupled with sharp increases in the level of protection on many products, especially grains and rice, nontariff trade barriers in Western Europe constitute formidable obstacles to a more liberal trade policy in agricultural products.

NONTARIFF AGRICULTURAL BARRIERS: JAPAN

Since Japan is one of the world's largest importers of agricultural products—almost U.S. $4.5 billion in 1976—other nations observe its trade policy with great interest. Emphasizing Japan's role in world trade and trade negotiations was the meeting in Tokyo in September 1973 of the council of GATT ministers which brought together ministers representing about one hundred countries. It had been preceded by considerable discussion in Geneva and will be followed by negotiation by the GATT nations in Geneva. The text of the Tokyo Declaration on the scope, participation, and aims of the negotiations is in Appendix B.

Brief consideration has already been given in the previous chapter to the principal Japanese nontariff agricultural trade barrier—the quantitative restriction. What remains to be discussed are aspects of Japan's overall trade policy toward agriculture, which is greatly affected—as is the case with the policies of other developed countries—by its own domestic agricultural policy, nontariff barriers included.

There is no history in Japan of attitudes toward agricultural protection comparable to that which exists in Western Europe and the United States. As a market for farm products, it was of relatively small importance before World War II and its domestic farm policy and agricultural trade policy was of little concern to others. The period of economic rehabilitation (1946–54) following the war, and radical land reform wrought unprecedented changes in Japanese agriculture. Along with rapid growth in the manufacturing and service sectors, the roles of agriculture and agricultural trade have changed drastically in Japan since then. In 1955, Japan took membership in the GATT. Tariff rates on many agricultural products have been reduced or eliminated and bound by Japan under the auspices of the GATT. With respect to its trade with the United States, its largest supplier, the products involved include cotton, hides and skins, inedible tallow, lemons, raisins, and almonds, in addition to the important products of feed grains and soybeans. Tariffs have also been lowered on products from other countries.

Since 1961, Japan has carried out a step-by-step liberalization of imports, including the removal of many nontariff impediments. Many quotas have been removed or enlarged.[12] These actions toward trade liberalization have stimulated an expansion in agricultural imports. Self-sufficiency ratios, except in the case of rice, have tended to fall, and some measures indicate that Japanese self-sufficiency in 1971 was only 53 percent, compared to 78 percent in 1960.[13] While details of Japan's rapidly changing total trade policy cannot be chronicled here, the far-reaching trade measures enacted by the Japanese cabinet on October 20, 1972,[14] have already been compromised by production and trade conditions surrounding the world agricultural disorder of 1973–74, especially through Japan's resort to a prohibition in June 1974 on beef imports for the remainder of the year to protect domestic beef producers.

It can be seen, therefore, that despite a healthy move toward trade liberalization, Japanese nontariff barriers still constitute a potentially formidable wall of restrictions constructed around the quota system described in Chapter 5. The Foreign Agricultural Service, USDA, has documented most of these and the following information is extracted directly from one of its publications.[15]

Licensing. All imports into Japan are subject to licensing requirements under one of three systems: the Automatic Approval (AA), the Automatic Import Quota (AIQ), or the Import Quota (IQ). Most Japanese imports are licensed under the AA system, with licenses issued freely by certain banks authorized by the government.

The AIQ system differs from the AA in that licenses are issued freely by the Ministry of International Trade and Industry (MITI) and not by banks. On February 1, 1972, the Japanese government transferred all items on the AIQ list to the AA system but did not abolish AIQ. Because it was not eliminated, items removed from the IQ system may be transferred to the AIQ rather than the AA system.

The IQ system is the most restrictive of Japan's licensing procedures. To import items enumerated in the IQ list, importers must apply to MITI for licenses, which are issued only in limited quantities. The amount of the quota is not usually officially announced, although it is generally obtainable on an unofficial basis.

State Trading. Under the state trading regime, imports can be made only by authorized government trading agencies. This system applies mainly to agricultural goods such as wheat, barley, and rice, most of which are major trade items. Tobacco is imported solely by the Japan Monopoly Corporation, which controls domestic acreage as well. Japan's state trading system also covers several milk products, including butter. While it may serve to protect domestic producers, this system also makes it possible for Japan to limit or expand imports of state-traded items from any one country should it suit the "national interest."

Quarantine, Food Additives, and Testing Regulations. Generally based on the need to protect domestic agriculture from the threat of foreign diseases and pests or to ensure that consumers receive wholesome foods, the Japanese government maintains a number of health and sanitary regulations governing imports of agricultural products. However, not all of these measures appear to be fully defensible for the following reasons.

Japan has a quarantine prohibition against imports of in-shell peanuts from a number of countries because of the possible entry of burrowing nematode. One reason given for the maintenance of this restriction is to protect the domestic citrus industry from the nematode, although a definite link between the two plants has not been established.

The International Seed Testing Association (ISTA), of which Japan is a member, has established standard procedures for testing seeds moving in local and international commerce. Because Japan applies more stringent tolerances than those established by ISTA for traces of ergot in forage seed imports, these shipments are sometimes rejected even though the seller has complied with ISTA procedures and rules. Ergot is already present in Japan, so there would not appear to be a valid phytosanitary reason for maintaining these stricter tolerances.

Without prior notification, Japanese officials in June 1971 began analyzing all imports of poultry meat for salmonella virus, although there is no evidence that the same tests are applied to domestic poultry. Nor does Japan allow sorbate on imported dried prunes, although it is accepted on many domestically produced foods.

The Japanese government has not yet approved a host of food additives and preservatives for certain products, even though they may have been proved safe by international testing. Experience has shown that the Japanese government prefers to consider applications for approval of these additives and preservatives on an individual basis. Their response to new items generally has been quite slow.

Chapter 7.

NONTARIFF BARRIERS AFFECTING INTERNATIONAL TRADE IN RED MEAT ANIMALS AND RED MEATS: A CASE STUDY

The preceding chapters of this study have presented a general analysis of nontariff barriers and the problems they introduce to the formulation of a liberal trade policy for agricultural products. This chapter has as its purpose the specific factual illustration of nontariff trade barriers in a commodity sector.[1] The legislative and administrative rules and regulations—the principles—are here given meaning with particular data and quantitative materials. The chapter focuses on nontariff barriers currently employed to influence trade in live red meat animals and red meats. This category was chosen as a case study because of the magnitude and the diversity of control to which these products are subject under present nontariff systems. Other commodity sectors in agriculture also have significant problems with nontariff barriers.

The growing disequilibrium of the international red meat market after 1974 adds to the importance of studying nontariff barriers in this sector. Red meat production is accelerating while short-term consumption is apparently slackening because of high meat prices, present spiraling inflation, and the resultant change in consumer budget allocations. This deviation from a ten-year trend toward growing consumption of red meat products is pressuring governments to seek means to correct the disequilibrium in their domestic red meat trade.

The lengthy buildup of cattle numbers in the industrial countries appears to be the major factor in the expansion of beef supplies and lower cattle prices. Herds were built up and marketings restricted in response to expectations of world beef shortages and continued increasing levels of consumption. Then came the 1973–74 stabilization of herds—and possible decreases in some countries—with a concomitant expansion of marketings. Coupled with economic slowdown in personal income growth and significantly higher grain prices, these marketings put a severe squeeze on cattle prices. Grain-fed cattle prices in the United States fell and producer prices throughout the world became relatively depressed.

With the forecast of growing meat supplies, many countries are actively seeking markets to expand exports. The threat of the dumping of these surpluses on the international market prompted a number of countermeasures by major importing countries to control imports in order to protect domestic livestock producers. In June 1974, Japan invoked a complete ban on red meat imports for the rest of that year. Subsequently, import quota allocations were reinstated, but, as of late 1976, the Japanese government was asking importers to delay entries of beef.

Similarly, the European Community invoked a ban on red meat imports from third countries (countries other than members of EC) while at the same time establishing in December 1973, for the first time, an export subsidy program to reduce the Community's growing stockpile of beef. Beset by general economic problems, several of the EC countries have gone beyond the restrictive import measures normally taken when such a situation develops. Italy began this move in late February 1974, embargoing further imports of fresh and chilled beef supplies from non-EC countries, only to be followed by France, Belgium, and Luxembourg. These actions then forced the EC to set up an import licensing system for fresh and chilled beef imports similar to the one already in existence for frozen beef. Import license embargoes in the four countries were removed in April but were replaced by other measures to prop up live cattle prices, including:

April 1. A 12 percent increase in the orientation price on live cattle to 96.50 u.a. per kilogram.

April 30. Issuance of beef import licenses was suspended for seven days.

May 1. A 25 percent increase in the export subsidy on fresh, chilled, and frozen beef. Also, introduction in Italy of an advance deposit system covering beef imports, which first required a deposition of 50 percent of the imported products' value but reduced this to 25 percent on June 4.

May 2. Full import levies again became applicable on young calves and certain frozen beef for processing.

May 7. Issuance of import licenses became conditional upon the importers' purchasing equal amounts of frozen beef from intervention stocks at reduced prices. Also, the period of validity for licenses for frozen beef imports was reduced.

May 9. Import levies on frozen beef were nearly doubled, primarily because of increasing the coefficient used in calculating the levy. Import levies on other beef were raised 16 percent on May 6.

June 12. Sales prices to importers for intervention-purchased beef were lowered; approximately 17,000 metric tons of intervention beef purchased in 1973 was allowed to be exported at 10–20 percent off the purchase price; intervention agencies were given subsidy to debone or process beef purchased to aid in storage; and export refunds on beef were raised from 38 to 56 u.a. per 100 kilograms and other European countries were added to the list of eligible export recipients, whereas previously the subsidy had applied only to Mediterranean countries.

June 27. Imports of live cattle from other European countries were banned until July 12.[2]

This demonstrates the complexities of nontariff trade barriers legislation and regulation activity which has been the theme of this study. As of January 1977, there were only three programs that allowed imports of beef and veal from countries outside the EC. The first is the GATT quota. The second involves import arrangements that permit various developing countries to export beef to the EC at reduced levies. The third program for imports is the jumelage-linked sales program which was introduced in January 1976 and was scheduled to end March 31, 1977. Under this program, an importer purchased bone-in frozen beef from intervention stocks before being granted an import license for an equivalent amount of imported beef or live slaughter cattle over 660 pounds.

During this same general period, government action in Canada and the United States was being demanded by cattle organizations to protect domestic producers. Canada moved unilaterally in August 1974 to place quotas on cattle and beef imports from the United States, which retaliated with quotas on Canadian cattle and beef in November 1974. With the removal of Canadian import quotas on U.S. beef and veal and U.S. retaliatory quotas on imports of beef and veal on January 1, 1976, the border was reopened in two-way trade in all categories of live animals and red meat. Canadian import quotas on slaughter cattle and U.S. retaliatory quotas on cattle, hogs, and pork were removed in August 1975. However, the border has not opened quite as widely to U.S. animals moving north as in the period prior to 1974. U.S. slaughter cattle can be exported to Canada only if they are accompanied by a DES certificate and, as of October 27, 1975, U.S. feeder cattle were subject to more stringent testing procedures imposed by Canada for bluetongue and anaplasmosis.

The Meat Import Law, PL 88-482, was again activated in the United States in 1976. The president, on October 9, imposed quotas on imports of fresh, chilled, or frozen beef, veal, mutton, and goat meat to limit 1976 imports to 1,233 million pounds (product weight). The action was taken as a result of continued large shipments of beef from Canada caused by the substitution of cheaper Australian and New Zealand manufacturing beef in the Canadian market. For the year 1977, Australia agreed to limit its beef and veal exports to Canada to about half the 1976 shipments, an action which corresponds to its restraints on exports to the U.S. market. The U.S. Department of Agriculture also issued a regulation under Section 2(e) of the law denying entry of meat into the customs territory of the United States from foreign-trade zones and trust territories or possessions for the balance of 1976.

In chaotic circumstances like those which existed in the cattle industry during the period 1974–76, there is always a clamor for protection and retaliation. Thus, as supply-demand pressures build up around the world, policies to impede international trade in red meats and red meat animals return to prominence. The nontariff interferences (including export subsidies) which have already been brought into play and which could well increase in this industry in the immediate future, are indicative of the potential restrictions and devices which could again become rampant, given the proper circumstances and the apathetic world attitude toward trade liberalization.

INTERNATIONAL COMMERCE IN RED MEATS

International trade in red meats has developed into one of the major commercial enterprises of world commodity markets. Expansion in the demand for meat protein due to real economic growth of the industrialized countries of the world increased commerce in meat products approximately 40 percent in the decade ending in 1972. Total trade volume in the international meat market reached a record in 1972.[3] There was a decided decrease in 1974 and 1975, but a noticeable recovery in 1976.

The major markets for red meats during the last decade have been the Western European countries, Japan, and the United States. However, the nine member countries of the EC, because of natural as well as economic circumstances, drastically reduced imports beginning in 1973. In fact, the EC has been a net meat exporter in all categories except mutton and lamb since 1974.

The meat markets of Western Europe, Japan, and the United States have been a major source of revenue for exporting countries of South America, Oceania, and Africa. The African countries have registered a positive trade balance in slaughter animal sales markets and red meat markets. Trade in meat products was also the primary source of capital for the Oceanian countries.

Massive demand pressures generated in the industrialized nations during the last decade have been responsible for increasing international commerce in red meats and other agricultural products. Yet, even with this strong demand, commerce in meat products still remains hindered by a maze of trade barriers. A spirit of coordination among governments to establish a liberal trade policy is still absent in the GATT.

During the past four decades, the most significant intervention in the international trade of meats and meat animals, as well as other agricultural products, has come primarily from nontariff barriers established by industrialized nations. As outlined in earlier chapters, these barriers are in the form of government intervention in trade, customs and administrative entry procedures, standards and specifications, charges on imports, and numerous specific limitations. Because each has been effectively used to manipulate the flow of trade in agricultural products, it is the principal purpose of this chapter to describe and analyze the selected laws, rules, and regulations, under our definition of nontariff barriers, which have a restrictive effect on international trade in the meat and livestock sector of agriculture.

THE EUROPEAN COMMUNITY

The European Community expanded its membership in the fall of

1973 to include the United Kingdom, Denmark, and Ireland. The merging of the economic operations of these countries into a united economic front, a primary goal of the architects of the European Community concept, was programed over a five-year period, ending in 1978. During this period, each of these countries' tariff and nontariff measures affecting trade in live meat animals and red meats was phased into a common program.

The degree of control on imports of live animals and red meats from non-Community countries is an important issue facing the governments of the expanded Community. Traditional tariff and nontariff systems of the newest members are undergoing revision, while standard systems practiced by the original six-member Community are being reevaluated. The volatile nature of this transition makes it necessary to describe import control systems invoked by each of the three new member states. The past dissatisfaction of the United States with their transition into the EC verifies the need to focus on trade programs of the individual states. Therefore, the nontariff barriers affecting trade in animals and meats are separated here into two major sections. The first section focuses on the nontariff systems invoked by the original six-member Community and the second describes the systems employed by each of the new member states and the transition through 1978.

THE ORIGINAL SIX MEMBER STATES

The establishment of the European Community in the late 1950s has acted to unify and coordinate many traditional restrictive policies of the European countries into a common trade front during the last two decades. The protective policies have been most constraining on world commodity markets, because of the creation of the Common Agricultural Policy, the goals of which are the growth in production security of the food-producing sector, equitable incomes for producers, and the achievement of stability in EC markets. In order to support the CAP and its goals, trade policies are designed to insulate domestic producers from competition of foreign agricultural products.

Much has been written about the effects of the CAP on international trade, so it is not necessary here to analyze its effect on the economic equilibrium of the world's commodity markets. Rather, the objective is to describe and examine the most restrictive of the nontariff measures used by Common Market countries to control the importation of livestock and meats. Table 7.1 illustrates the types of nontariff restrictions which may be used to control trade in livestock and meats by the original six members of the European Community. In the following text, these nontariff barriers will be described and examined in greater detail.

TABLE 7.1 Measures Affecting Imports of Livestock and Meats in Member Countries of the Original European Community, March–April 1972

FRANCE

Barriers	Live Animals	Meat (fresh, chilled, and frozen)
Levies	Variable levies or sluice-gate prices, except for sheep[a]	Variable levies or sluice-gate prices, except for mutton and lamb
Quotas	No, except quantitative restrictions for horses and mules	No, except quantitative restrictions for the meat of horses and mules
Agreements	EEC agreements concerning reduced levy or duty on imports of livestock and meat except sheep from Austria, Denmark, Yugoslavia, Turkey, Morocco, Tunisia, and Spain. Import certificates for sheep	None Import certificates for sheepmeat
Licenses	None	None
Border Charges	None	None
Internal Taxes	None	None

TABLE 7.1 *Continued*

GERMANY (FEDERAL REPUBLIC)

Barriers	Live Animals	Meat (fresh, chilled, and frozen)
Levies	Variable levies or sluice-gate prices except for live sheep. For imports from Austria, Denmark, and Yugoslavia, reduced levies may be applied	Variable levies except for mutton and lamb
Quotas	Global quotas for sheep and lamb imports	Global quotas for mutton and lamb
Agreements	EEC agreements concerning reduced levy or duty on imports of livestock and meat except sheep from Austria, Denmark, Yugoslavia, Turkey, Morocco, Tunisia, and Spain. State trading for sheep and lambs	EEC agreements with Argentina for chilled and frozen beef State trading for mutton and lamb
Licenses	None	
Border Charges	Compensatory payments are fixed for all products following the temporary enlargement of the margin of monetary fluctuation in certain EEC member countries	None
Internal Taxes	None	None

ITALY

| Levies | Variable levies or sluice-gate price, except for sheep.[a] Total exemption from levy for calves of 220–300 kg and 80 kg[b] | Variable levies except for mutton and lamb. |
| Quotas | None | None |

TABLE 7.1 *Continued*

Barriers	Live Animals	Meat (fresh, chilled, and frozen)
Agreements	EEC agreements regarding the reduction of import duties for live animls and meat except sheep from Austria, Denmark, Yugoslavia, Turkey, Morocco, Tunisia, and Spain	EEC agreements with Argentina for chilled frozen beef
Licenses	None	Import license from the Ministry of Finance, in agreement with the Ministry of Foreign Trade, is required for imports of frozen beef from third countries and of fresh and chilled beef and veal from Argentina, for which the importer requests the fixing of a levy in advance
Border Charges	Supplementary tax compensatory payments are fixed for all products following the temporary enlargement of the margin of monetary fluctuation in certain EEC member countries	Supplementary tax 3.30% a.v. CAF[c] 2.40% a.v. CAF[d]
Internal Taxes	Veterinary tax lit. 1,000/head; lit. 500 for calves under 300 kg Lit. 400/head swine Lit. 100/head sheep and goats	Veterinary tax lit. 300–1,000 per 100 kg bovine animals. Lit. 100/100 kg swine, sheep, and goats

BELGIUM and LUXEMBOURG

| Levies | Variable levies or sluice-gate prices,[e] except for live sheep. For imports from Austria, Denmark, and Yugoslavia reduced levies may be applied | Variable levies except for mutton and lamb |

TABLE 7.1 *Continued*

Barriers	Live Animals	Meat (fresh, chilled, and frozen)
Quotas	None	A duty-free EEC import quota for frozen meat of 22,000 tons has been allocated
Agreements	EEC agreements concerning reduced levy on imports for livestock and meat except sheep from Austria, Denmark, Yugoslavia, Turkey, Morocco, Tunisia, and Spain	EEC agreements with Argentina for chilled and frozen beef
Licenses	No license for sheep and goat products except for those from state-trading countries, Hong-Kong, and Japan. A license is required for bovine animals falling under classes 01.02–02 01–02. 06–15.02 and 16.02	An import certificate is required for imports of frozen beef (02.01 AIIa 2). The certificate is granted upon payment of a deposit of Fr. 500 per 100 kg
Border Charges	Compensatory payments are fixed for all products following the temporary enlargement of monetary fluctuation in certain EEC member countries	None
Internal Taxes	None	None

THE NETHERLANDS

Levies	Variable levies or sluice-gate prices,[e] except for live sheep. For imports from Austria, Denmark, and Yugoslavia, reduced levies may be applied	Variable levies except for mutton and lamb
Quotas	None	None

TABLE 7.1 *Continued*

Barriers	Live Animals	Meat (fresh, chilled, and frozen)
Agreements	EEC agreements regarding the reduction of import duties for live animals and meat except sheep from Austria, Denmark, Yugoslavia, Turkey, Morocco, Tunisia, and Spain	EEC agreements with Argentina for chilled and frozen beef
Licenses	None	None
Border Charges	None	None
Internal Taxes	None	None

Source: Adapted from Food and Agriculture Organization of the United Nations, *National Regulations Affecting Imports of Livestock and Meat,* CCP: ME 72-8 (Rome, April 1972), pp. 9, 17, 21, 28, 34.

[a] Levies are reduced for imports from Austria, Denmark, and Yugoslavia.

[b] When prices in the Community are higher than the orientation price, calves below 80 kg have a 50 percent reduction in customs duty.

[c] Increased by border taxes except for frozen forequarters and boneless cuts for manufacturing purposes.

[d] Other than meat in airtight containers.

[e] Calves of 220–300 kg and 80 kg are exempt from levy. When the Community price exceeds the guide price, customs duties are reduced by 50 percent for calves of 80 kg. Under certain conditions the levy may be reduced or suspended for slaughter cows for manufacturing purposes from Austria and Denmark and for certain other types.

Government Intervention in Trade

Governments of the member countries of the European Community have instituted the variable levy, one of the most important nontariff barriers faced by exporters of agricultural products. As pointed out in Chapter 5, variable levies placed on imported goods are basically the difference in value between world market price, c.i.f. the frontier, plus import fees, if any, and the price established under CAP to support local agricultural producers. Support prices are established annually. Increases of 10 and 8 percent, for example, were recommended for beef and pork, respectively, in the 1974–75 period but were reduced to 3 and 4 percent for 1977–78 because of the high cost of the program.[4]

The variable levies calculated for beef and veal products are derived on a weekly basis by conversion coefficients from levies on live cattle and calves. The latter live animal levies in turn are calculated as the difference between an orientation (support) price and the computed price of imports (c.i.f., plus duty). This import price is at present computed as the weighted average of wholesale market prices for certain cattle in specified markets. However, if the actual c.i.f. price is significantly below this computed import price, a special import price may be fixed.[5]

The use of the levy on beef products by the EC is designed to restrict the importation of beef for direct consumption in order to protect the European producers of fresh meat. Under quota restrictions negotiated through the GATT, only a marginal volume of frozen meat is allowed to enter the direct consumption meat market. Generally, the cost for imported meats to penetrate the fresh market is prohibitive.

Special provisions, however, allow the levy to be reduced or waived for calves and frozen beef imported for processing. The quantity of the latter imports is strictly controlled by licensing in relation to a quarterly estimate of the needs of the processing industry.

For pork, a basic variable levy is calculated every three months in proportion to the levies on the quantity of feed grains assumed necessary to the production of the given quantity of pork, plus an additional margin of preference. In addition, however, the EC calculates a minimum import or gate price equal to the estimated fair cost of third country production. A supplementary levy is imposed on imports priced below the gate price. Third countries that commit themselves to respect the gate price may be exempted from supplementary levies.[6]

Unlike the CAP support programs established for the beef and pork sector, there is no common EC policy on sheepmeat imports. Each member of the community abides only by the standard EC duties on the importing of live animals and meat products. Belgium, Luxembourg, Italy, and the Netherlands, for example, do not apply any form of a levy system or formal quantitative restrictions on sheepmeat products. France, however, applies a reversement or border charge on fresh or chilled meat. Yet when the weighted average wholesale price of fresh sheepmeat dips below a set threshold price, the French borders are closed to third country imports. In fact, not until 1972 was frozen sheepmeat, based on a global quota of 2,000 tons, allowed into the French meat market.

The Federal Republic of Germany also applies a quantitative import system on sheepmeats from third countries. The German Agricultural Ministry administers a Global Quota, a Fair Quota, and an Import-Export Quota.

The Global Quota allows German importers who have established a past reference system in the trading of lamb to import from any supplying country. The permissible quantitites of imports allowed by the ministry, however, are generally not published. Imports of sheepmeat are also allowed under the Fair Quota. Countries interested in sheepmeat exports are given quota allotments to import meats so they can publicize their products in some international trade fairs in Germany. The last of the quota allowances is based on an import-export scheme. German exporters of sheepmeat may obtain import licenses in relation to proven exports. As of 1973, German meat traders were allowed to import the equivalent of 25 percent of the live weight of sheep or lamb exported, and 50 percent of the quantity of sheepmeat they have exported.[7]

The effect of this import system has been to restrict the expansion of the sheepmeat market. The reference system has a particularly restrictive effect, as it permits a small number of license holders to control the market. This prevents other traders from entering the business simply because they have no history in lamb trade during the reference period. License holders, therefore, under certain circumstances can indulge in price speculation. Profit margins for imported lamb, for example, over the years have become unnecessarily inflated at the wholesale level, which has not, however, meant higher returns for sheepmeat producers.[8]

Customs and Administrative Entry Procedures: Licensing

The standard entry procedures required of exporters of red meats interested in trading with the European Community are the acquisition of import licenses and certificates from authorities of the EC and member states. These procedures have several functions. First, licensing and certification of imports allows recipient countries to record the volume of goods entering their domestic markets. More important, however, it enables countries to control imports by allotting licenses or certificates to meat exporters, which act effectively as a form of quantitative restriction. The issuance of licenses and certificates is also used to enforce health and sanitary rules established by recipient countries. Refusal to meet these rules results in the barring of meat imports across trade frontiers.

Currently, there is no licensing authority or common program sponsored by the EC. Its Council is involved only in the issuance of certificates to exporters of manufactured beef to coordinate and guarantee supplies of beef for the meat-processing industries of the Community. The licensing of meat importers and meat products is under the jurisdiction of the ministries of agriculture and of foreign trade in each country. The objective of the ministries' licensing policy has been primarily the administration and enforcement of health and hygiene standards for imported meat products.

Licenses are required for all imports of fresh beef, frozen beef, and veal by the member states of the EC. When a shipment of meat reaches frontier inspection points, certificates of public health and animal health must accompany the cargo, verifying its origin, destination, and contents (type of cuts), along with a statement of approval by a recognized veterinarian on the health and hygienic standards of the product. The absence of proper certification generally results in the impoundment of the goods by inspection officials.

Special certification is required of imported beef products which receive special import treatment in the form of total or partial suspension of the levy. The issuance of these special import certificates is subject to the lodging of a deposit guaranteeing the commitment to import within a specified period. Proper documents are required if the cargo is to receive special advantages when entering the recipient country.

Requirements for porcine imports are similar to those for beef products. Imports of pork must be licensed by the proper authorities and accompanied by health certificates.

There is great variability in sheepmeat importer licensing procedures practiced by the EC countries. As with other meat products, licenses and health certification must accompany the cargo entering the Community. These are freely available to importers from Belgian, Luxembourg, Dutch, and Italian authorities, as long as the product is certified to meet proper health and hygienic standards. However, additional restrictions are placed on the importation of sheepmeats in France and Germany. In 1972–73, for example, French authorities placed a quantitative restriction on licenses of 10 tons per applicant, valid for two weeks,[9] but licenses were denied when the weighted average wholesale price exceeded the market price. The issuance of import licenses by German authorities is limited to those firms which have a recorded history in trade of sheepmeats, consequently blocking new trade organizations from obtaining licenses.

Standards and Specifications

Standards and specifications of trading nations usually fulfill a dual role. Most apparent is the function of protecting the domestic economy from inferior products, but equally important, these standards also establish a framework within which trade goods can move with limited interference across international borders. These channels of trade, however, meet with opposition in the area of enforcement. Bureaucratic systems established to enforce standards and specifications are often inefficient or trapped in a maze of checks and balances of authority. Thus, delays and conflicts in interpretation of regulations arise as forms of nontariff barriers.

The standards which most influence the channels of commerce in livestock and meat products throughout the European Community lie in the area of health and hygienic regulations. Each government of the member states requires exporting countries seeking trade rights to submit requests to the appropriate government agencies in charge of health standards. Inspection of the livestock sector and accompanying industries of the exporting nations by the licensing agencies is mandatory before any meat products are allowed across EC member borders.

The areas which government agencies of member states investigate are livestock health and the sanitary and hygienic standards of the meat-processing and transportation sectors of exporting countries. Freedom of the exporter's livestock population from epizootic disease is a minimum health condition required by community members. The country or established disease-free zones must be free of foot-and-mouth diseases for twelve months, and of rinderpest for two years. In addition, the veterinary inspection service of the exporting country is required to notify the International Bureau of Epizootics in Paris on a regular basis of the state of health of its livestock.

The establishment by the exporting country of a veterinary service to protect the health of animals within its territory is a standard requirement. This service must also act as the agent for examining live animals for diseases prior to slaughter and in conducting post-mortem examinations to verify the health and conditions of carcasses. Animals or carcasses diagnosed as having or displaying symptoms of infectious communicable animal diseases or contamination must be barred from commercial trade.

Slaughterhouses in the exporting countries need specific approval from *individual importing EC countries*. Slaughtering, storage, and transportation systems employed in the processing and movement of meat must meet specific health and hygienic standards to ensure the trade of meat products.

A paramount problem in the commerce of meats is the lack of a common minimum standard code for the Community. Attempts have been made to establish a standard health and hygienic code but they were blocked by strong opposition from two fronts. Some EC governments objected to liberalizing their standards on specific health regulations, while others were hesitant to allocate additional resources in capital and manpower to upgrade their regulations and systems of inspection to comply with a uniform health code. Consequently, each country still functions independently to establish and enforce health and hygienic standards. This diversity of regulatory jurisdiction places a serious economic burden on exporting countries which have to comply with all aspects of the maze of sanitary standards.

The divergency of standards and practices of EC members ranges from variation in general inspection procedures at the border to variations in the requirement for shipment of organs for veterinarian inspection. For example, in some countries carcass meat must be delivered with all lymph nodes opened by the veterinarian service of the exporting country as proof that they were inspected. In other countries, however, at least one lymph node must be intact so that the veterinary service of the importing country can use it for bacteriological control. On the other hand, current provisions in the U.S. allow entry of imported meat without lymph glands, as long as an official certificate from the exporting veterinary service verifies the healthiness of the meat.[10]

Another example of the disruption of the smooth flow of trade by variations in health standards is the ban by Italian health authorities on meats sprayed with chlorine, a common practice of U.S. processors of meat for domestic and foreign markets. To date, no other countries have banned chlorine-sprayed meats.

Variations in packaging requirements also exist among EC countries. In France, each unit of frozen beef must have polythene inner wrappings, jute outer wrapping with blue white plastic, and weigh 20 to 30 kg. Belgium and Luxembourg require similar packaging material, but weight classifications for approved shipment are 40 to 50 kg for jute packs and 30 to 35 kg for cartons. The packing and marking practices required by Italian authorities, based on the Italo-Argentine Meat Agreement of September 7, 1970, Annex IX, Sections 42 and 43, are another hindrance to trade. Shipments of boneless beef must have an inner packing made from colorless, transparent, odorless sterile material (polythene, cryovac film, etc.) and an outer pack of cardboard or wood. These requirements have not been very favorably received by the trade, which prefers the cheaper and traditional jute packing.[11]

Attempts to improve transportation and packaging systems to reduce risks of meat spoilage and contamination have been met with varying reactions by importing EC countries. While container shipment has been accepted by the United Kingdom and the Federal Republic of Germany, other EC countries have not accepted it because they lack port facilities for unloading container ships. This doesn't explain, however, their support for additional restrictions on containerized meat shipments.

They require that for inland deliveries, meat in containers must be refrigerated, even though the thermal quality of containers probably maintains proper temperatures up to forty hours. In addition, veterinary procedures in some EC countries require that refrigerated vans must be opened at the frontiers, thereby increasing the risk of meat contamination and spoilage. Equally odd, some countries require that red meat shipped by sea be held at -18° F throughout the voyage, although modern containerized ships maintain a temperature of -10° F.[12]

The general policies behind sanitary and hygienic requirements to protect domestic livestock herds from epizootic contamination and to protect human populations from contaminated meats and products are unquestionably legitimate. However, the barriers and the protectionism lie in the administrative interpretation of health standards and regulations set forth by legislative action of importing countries. The criteria for acceptance may lie, not in the specific wording of the regulations or the specific intent of protecting public health standards, but in their interpretation and enforcement by administrators.

Import Charges

Products entering the EC are subject to various charges levied by member governments of the Community. Red meats are no exception; in the last decade these commodity goods have been subject to an extensive array of import fees and levies, including compensatory taxes, municipal taxes, and value added taxes. These are among the most common fees placed on commodities by the Community states.

Compensatory taxes applied to meat imports are a result of the recent monetary crisis and exchange rate variations. The conditions involved were as follows:

During the monetary crisis, exchange rates of EC countries were allowed to appreciate above the rates in calculating variable levies. The levies alone, therefore, were insufficient to offset the difference between EC common national farm price levels set for beef and pork and world levels in terms of national currencies. Consequently, member states are authorized to collect an additional tax to close this gap. This compensatory tax varies in amount among the member countries, depending on the extent of appreciation of the national exchange rate.[13]

Plans were under consideration for the phasing out of these taxes in 1974 or 1975, but acceptance of this move is now under attack by a number of EC members. Because of falling prices for beef in the spring of 1974, France, Italy, and Ireland supported stricter measures to control beef imports. One of the mechanisms proposed by this group of EC members was the use of compensatory payments to help beef raisers by putting an extra tax on imports.

Municipal taxes are devices which local regions, communities, or municipalities use to earn revenues for their treasuries. Taxes are levied on locally produced slaughter animals and meat products as well as on slaughter animals and meat products produced by members and nonmembers of the EC. Generally, a tax rate is set on a fee per quantity basis. For example, in Rome, during 1972 municipal taxes were established on sheepmeats of 50.6 lire per kg of fresh lamb killed there.[14]

Often, countries, regions or municipalities interchange or substitute value added tax systems for municipal tax systems as a revenue earning mechanism. Value added taxes (VAT), which are simply a percentage of the c.i.f. value, generally range between 2 to 8 percent of red meat products c.i.f. value.

Besides the standard import charges previously described, red meat imports are also subject to statistical, veterinary, consular, health inspection, and other fees. Each of these import charges is levied in some form on imports of fresh beef and veal, frozen beef, manufacturing beef, fresh and frozen sheepmeats, and pork products. Although there is some uniformity in the pattern of import charges placed on beef and pork products, since these goods are regulated under a general EC policy, there is a wide diversity in the taxing practices of EC countries in regard to imports of sheepmeat.

In addition to veterinary fees, health inspection charges, etc., value added taxes are prominent in the trade of sheepmeats. During 1972, Belgium, Luxembourg, and the Netherlands instituted a value added tax of 6 percent, while France levied a 7.5 percent value added tax on sheepmeat imports. France also imposes a border tax, or reversement charge, on sheepmeats. French border taxes are shown in table 7.2.

TABLE 7.2   French Border Tax on Sheepmeats, 1972

Market Price Range (francs per kilo)	Reversement[a] (francs per kilo)
Below 11.50	No third country imports permitted
11.50–11.90	3.30
11.90–12.30	2.70
12.30–12.70	2.10
Over 12.70	1.50

Source: New Zealand Meat Producers Board, "New Zealand Meat Seminar," papers presented in London, October 16–18, 1972, p. 58.

[a] The rate of live animals is half that for carcass meat.

During and prior to 1972, Italy operated a complicated system of supplementary purchase, health inspection, purchase, and municipal taxes. Imported sheepmeat from EC countries and third countries was subject to each of the taxes listed in table 7.3. Domestic meat, however, was exempt from supplementary purchase and health inspection taxes. The complicated nature of this tax system prompted authorities to propose a replacement system based on a single value added tax of 6 percent.

Special Limitations

Because a host of special restraints and limitations are imposed on red meat imports by the member states of the EC, it would be a herculean task to categorize every item which interferes with the commerce across their borders. However, some highly visible special limitations within the EC pose some of the most restrictive constraints of the potpourri of special regulations now enforced. These nontariff barriers function in the areas of health standards, agricultural protectionism, agricultural marketing, and political favoritism.

Regulations established by the EC require that frozen beef imports be packaged in anatomical sections. These regulations place an added economic burden on the Community's meat industry,

TABLE 7.3 Italian Import Tax System on Sheepmeats, 1972

Tax	Mutton		Lamb[a]	
	Fresh	Frozen	Fresh	Frozen
Conguaglio (supplementary purchase tax)	3.3%[b]	3.3%[b]	3.3%[b]	3.3%[b]
Health inspection tax	Lire 33/kg	Lire 33/kg	Lire 33/kg	Lire 33/kg
Imposta generale entrata (Purchase tax)	Lire 21/kg	Lire 21/kg	Lire 33/kg	Lire 33/kg
Municipal tax in Rome[c]				
Killed in Rome	Lire 16/kg	Lire 10.67/kg	Lire 50.6/kg	Lire 33.6/kg
Killed elsewhere	Lire 19.2/kg	Lire 12.8/kg	Lire 60.48/kg	Lire 40.32/kg

Source: New Zealand Meat Producers Board, "New Zealand Meat Seminar," p. 28.

[a] Includes *agnelloni.*

[b] Calculated on c.i.f. price plus import duty.

[c] Municipal tax varies from place to place.

since the processors must thaw and recut the frozen sections in order to process the product for the commercial market.

Although these measures may act in some situations as a safeguard to public health, they are primarily a protective device to protect EC fresh meat producers from Third Country competition by preventing the use of frozen meats for direct consumption.

Similar EC regulations on the admissibility of carcass sections also affect imports of fresh, chilled, and frozen sheepmeats. The original six members prohibit shipment of sheepmeats, other than saddles, shoulders, and legs, in portions smaller than quarters. In 1972, this restriction was relaxed by German authorities to allow certain cuts of sheepmeats produced in New Zealand and processed by certain New Zealand exporters to enter the German meat market. This liberalization in trade was achieved only after an exhaustive inspection by German health authorities of New Zealand sheepmeat slaughter facilities.

Advances in trade liberalization for New Zealand sheepmeats are also underway in Italy. An agreement similar to the German-New Zealand arrangement would allow certain types of cuts to enter the Italian meat market. Yet, exporters of sheepmeat still face a unique barrier there: legislation prohibits the sale of frozen and fresh sheepmeats in the same shop.

Other forms of limitations to trade are the numerous special agreements or arrangements which favor particular exporting nations. More favorable treatment by EC members of some exporters resembles a form of nontariff barrier by placing nonfavored exporters of live slaughter animals and red meat products at an economic disadvantage. The EC, for example, is involved in special agreements with Argentina for chilled and frozen beef. Agreements are also in effect regarding the reduction of EC import duties for live animals and meat products, except for sheep, from Austria, Yugoslavia, Turkey, Morocco, Tunisia, and Spain.

The individual member states also issue favored-nation status to exporting countries of live slaughter animals and red meat products. Under certain conditions, Belgium may reduce variable levies for slaughter cows for manufacturing purposes from Austria and for certain types of animals and meat from Yugoslavia (table 7.1). Similarly, Italy reduces variable levies of sluice-gate prices for imports of live animals, except sheep, from Austria and Yugoslavia (table 7.1). Germany, meanwhile, has had a special agreement with

Denmark on importing slaughter cattle, and has also entered into agreements with New Zealand to allow special cuts of sheepmeat and beef to enter the German retail meat market.

The basis for granting favorable treatment often depends on the public health and hygienic conditions of the exporting nation's livestock and meat industries, but political considerations are also prevalent. Most-favored-nation status offers a form of political suasion which can be used by importing nations on governments of favored, or to-be-favored, exporting countries.

RECENT CHANGES AFFECTING BEEF

In late 1976, EC farm ministers agreed on plans for the resumption of beef imports after April 1, 1977. Despite the obvious conflict between the beef-exporting and the beef-importing countries of the Community, concessions on processing beef imports ensured that the British, West Germans, and Italians agreed to a higher level of import levies than has ever operated before.

The Council agreed that when the beef import ban was lifted, beef should be allowed to be imported under a scale of levies ranging from nil to 114 percent of the basic levy. However, the system for calculating the basic levy has not been substantially altered.

Basic levies—equal to the difference between the world prices and the EC guide price—will still be set monthly. Despite earlier French and Irish demands, there will be no special levy for frozen beef. Indeed, it is possible that the new system may be more liberal as far as frozen beef imports are concerned, because frozen beef will now be subject to the same scale of import levies as fresh and chilled beef, whereas under the old system levies on frozen beef could never be less than 100 percent of the basic levy.

The new levy system, which lifted the safeguard clause and ended jumelage, operates at up to 106 percent of the guide price, above which there is no levy. The basic levy will still be calculated monthly in the manner shown in table 7.4.

TRADE PROGRAMS OF THE NEW MEMBER STATES

The United Kingdom through the years has been a lucrative market for exporters of meat products, which have represented

TABLE 7.4   European Beef Imports Levy Scale

Reference Price as Percentage of Guide Price	Percentage of Basic Levy Applied[a]
Less than 90	114
90–96	110
96–98	105
98–100	100
100–102	75
102–104	50
104–106	25
Over 106	nil

Source: USDA, Foreign Agricultural Service.

[a] Basic levy = difference between lowest world market offer price and EC guide price.

approximately 20 percent of total British payments for commodity goods during the past decade.

During the nineteenth century, the United Kingdom followed a national cheap food policy. In order to maintain minimum price levels, the British government opened domestic markets to foreign competition and embarked on liberal trade programs with Commonwealth and other agricultural exporting nations. These liberal trade practices, however, have been tarnished in the last few years as protective agricultural programs have been increasingly applied. Balance-of-payments difficulties, among other economic problems, have pressured the United Kingdom into a more autarchic attitude toward agriculture. Price support programs were established to improve incomes of British farmers and to stimulate production, while various protective devices were instituted against foreign competition. Imports of livestock and meat products, for example, were subject to duties, variable levies, licensing, and health and hygiene certification, among other hindrances to commerce (table 7.5). Membership in the EC, therefore, was the final scenario of the movement to insulate and protect agriculture in the United Kingdom.

Ireland, on the other hand, has traditionally followed an extremely protective agricultural import policy. Restriction of imports has been a primary goal of its trading policy, because agriculture is an important sector of the total economy, and a high proportion of domestically produced agricultural goods is exported. Approximately 26.5 percent of the population is engaged in agriculture and total agricultural exports account for 40 percent of gross national output,[15] with cattle and beef constituting the primary export of Ireland. Exports of Irish beef were restricted primarily to the United Kingdom and the United States, since as a third country, Irish exports to the EC were severely regulated.

The similarity of agricultural goals in Ireland and the EC is easing the way for Irish adoption of the CAP because protection of agriculture, particularly the livestock sector, is essential for the Irish economy. An added benefit to EC membership is the opening of the channels of commerce for Irish livestock and meat exports to the Continent.

The opening of the EC to exports of meat and dairy products was a major factor in the decision of Danish authorities to apply for and accept membership in the Community. The value of Danish exports of these products is approximately 40 percent of the country's total export earnings. Markets for these products include the Americas as well as nations bordering the EC states. However, to maintain an active trade program, Denmark established agricultural subsidy programs in which treasury payments were made into an Agricultural Disposal Fund and a Grain Equalization Fund. These were used for market promotion, quality production schemes, subsidies to stabilize the grain market, freezing and storage of beef, stabilization of the pork market, and quantitative rebates on canned meats and milk.[16]

Consequently, government protection and intervention in the livestock industry became a common practice. Membership in the EC offers Danish producers a comparable degree of support and insulation, while opening the lucrative meat markets of Germany, Belgium, Luxembourg, Italy, France, and the Netherlands.

TRANSITION TO THE EEC SYSTEM OF NONTARIFF BARRIERS

The United Kingdom. Prior to British admission into the EC,

TABLE 7.5 Measures Affecting Imports of Livestock and Meat into the United Kingdom, January 1972

Items	Levies[a]	Quotas	Licenses[b]	Agreements and Arrangements
Live animals	Chargeable on all fat cattle imports except from Irish Republic. Charged on all poultry imports except from Denmark and Irish Republic		Individual licenses required for imports from Eastern Area (including Republic of China)	Anglo-Irish Trade Agreement
Meat (fresh, chilled, or frozen)	Chargeable on all imports except from Irish Republic. Charged on all poultry imports except from Denmark and Irish Republic	On pigmeat from Eastern Area countries[c]	Individual licenses required for imports from Eastern Area. Import restriction on poultry meat	
Meat (bacon, etc.)[d]		On pigmeat products from Eastern Area. Imports of bacon regulated by Bacon Market Sharing Understanding.	Imports of uncanned whole hams from outside sterling area prohibited. Individual licenses required from Eastern European countries	Bacon Market Sharing Understanding
Meat (canned)[e]	On pigmeat products from Eastern Area countries		Individual licenses required for imports from Eastern Area countries	

Source: Adapted from Food and Agriculture Organization of the United Nations, *National Regulations Affecting Imports of Livestock and Meat*, CCP: ME 72–8 (Rome, April 1972), pp. 9, 17, 21, 28, 34.

[a] Including other regulating duties not under customs duties or border charges in table 7.1.

[b] Quota import deposits, etc.

[c] Fresh, chilled, and frozen poultry imports were liberalized on January 1, 1972.

[d] Meat dried, salted, or smoked, whether or not in airtight container, and bacon, ham, and other dried, salted, or smoked pigmeat.

[e] Meat in airtight containers, n.e.s., and meat preparations whether or not in airtight containers.

commerce in livestock and red meat products within the United Kingdom operated under a system of duties and nontariff restrictions composed of variable levies, licensing practices, health and hygienic certification, import charges, special limitations, and special agreements (table 7.5). These trade mechanisms were the foundations of government policy to control foreign meat imports. However, since Britain's entrance into the EC, major transitions have been taking place in the U.K. system of trade control. Paramount among the formulas of change are transitions in variable import levies, special agreements with Commonwealth and third country nations, and special specifications on health and hygienic conditions.

The United Kingdom on July 3, 1971, placed in effect a system to stabilize the beef market by means of minimum import prices enforced by variable levies on such imports as fresh, chilled, and frozen beef and veal and of fat cattle. These import prices were related to the annual target indicator price for fat cattle in the U.K. market. Levies were chargeable if in any week the average market price fell below the target indicator price for the week. Levies were payable at the time of importation or upon withdrawal from bonded warehouses.[17]

Although Community trade regulations now supersede British ones, the transition of jurisdiction in trade is taking place over the period 1973–78. British commodity trade systems have been phased out in favor of the common import duty, variable levy, special meat import certification, and quantitative constraints on meat imports instituted by the European Economic Council. The transition is based on a four-step formula which stipulates that the United Kingdom will initiate the common tariff in steps of 8, 12, 16, and 20 percent and will institute levy, certification, and quota regulations of the EC Council while its own levy is reduced in a similar four-step process.

Another of the many critical areas is the negotiated disposition of favorable trade agreements with Commonwealth nations, members of the European Free Trade Association (EFTA) and other nations. These countries have enjoyed preferential treatment through the decades and have become dependent on the British market, as table 7.6 shows.

Various assurances of continuing adequate and remunerative access to the United Kingdom have been given by British authorities

TABLE 7.6   U.K. Customs Duties, January 1972

Item	Most Favored Nations and European Free Trade Association	Commonwealth
Meat (fresh, chilled, or frozen)		
bovine animals	£.311–.350/cwt	free
sheep and goats	£.9335/cwt	
swine	10% ad valorem	free
Meat (dried, salted, or smoked)	0–20% ad valorem	free

Source: Adapted from Food and Agriculture Organization of the United Nations, *National Regulations Affecting Imports of Livestock and Meat,* CCP: ME 72-8 (Rome, April 1972), pp. 9, 17, 21, 28, 34.

to traditional sources of supply. However, the volatile nature of negotiations in the arena of international trade creates complications which can negate such assurances. The entry of Britain into the Common Market has not been smooth for the livestock industry with respect to its traditional trade channels with Commonwealth, EFTA, and South American nations. After July 1974, the only beef EC traders were allowed to import was under special arrangements—the nil levy GATT quota, the reduced levy arrangements for beef from African, Carribean, and Pacific (ACP) countries, and the jumelage arrangements. It is an understatement to suggest that such major meat exporters as Argentina, New Zealand, Australia, and Brazil are continually concerned about the outcome of negotiations on trade policies regarding red meats. Within the British meat trade as well as among its traditional meat suppliers, it is increasingly recognized that the 1977 commodity changes affecting beef and other meats will not mean more free trade. Imports of beef from third countries are likely to continue to be extremely restricted. This will be the case despite the fact that as of April 1, 1977, import levies for the import of third country meat were available for the first time since July 1974.

The British government has followed a policy of strict control of epizootic disease, and outbreaks of such diseases over the last eighty years have been combatted by slaughter programs. As a result, the livestock population of Great Britain has had little chance to build up needed immunities.

Because of the lack of immunity to epizootic contamination, sporadic outbreaks of foot-and-mouth disease have had disastrous economic effects on the livestock sector. In 1968, the animal population of the British Isles was subject to a severe series—2,364 recorded outbreaks. This again focused the attention of British health authorities on the necessity for adequate and progressive control policies.

A recent economic assessment by Power and Harris of alternative methods of controlling foot-and-mouth disease in Great Britain used cost/benefit analysis to measure the economic aspects of the slaughter control method practiced in Great Britain and the vaccination method used extensively on the European continent.[18] The results of the study revealed that on purely quantifiable factors the traditional slaughter policy would be less costly, but adding in the true costs to society (measures of nonquantifiable effects included), would probably make vaccination cost-effective.

It is apparent that for the last seven years there has been a growing concern in Britain over the threat of epizootics and the methods of controlling them. This concern also manifests itself in currently strict policies on shipment of red meats from exporting areas in which many epizootic diseases are endemic.

Only a few countries under the 1954 Importation of Carcasses and Animal Products Order as amended—those free from foot-and-mouth disease—receive unconditional admittance to the meat and livestock markets of Great Britain. Other countries with a history of foot-and-mouth disease must apply for special licenses to gain access to the British market. During the early 1970s licenses were available for imports of beef, mutton, and lamb (but not pork) from Belgium and France but were denied to Luxembourg, Germany, and Italy.[19]

One of the basic principles of the concept of the European Economic Community is free trade among member states. This principle implies a program of unconditional admission, subject, of course, to public health standards for red meat and meat product exports for the British market. Demand not filled by Irish fresh meat exports, for example, could be open to European producers. Since the European continent is an endemic area where epizootics are controlled by vaccination programs, the liberalization of health standards appears to be inevitable. The extent or degree of liberalization, of course, is subject to further negotiations among British and EC representatives.

An additional requirement of British health authorities stipulates that frozen meat products originating from foot-and-mouth disease areas be deboned, minus lymph glands, and shipped in anatomical sections. This regulation was a result of the 1968 foot-and-mouth disease epidemic. Since then, major exporters of beef have modernized their plants for deboning (although it is not required by other EC countries) and much red meat is shipped in deboned form. However, difficulties arising from admission policies concerning the importation of bone or deboned meats do not appear to be a barrier in the formulation of a common meat import system between the EC and the United Kingdom.

Similarly, other health and hygienic standards regulating trade in red meats do not appear to be a barrier in the transition of the United Kingdom into the EC. Since the EC does not function under a common health and hygiene code, British health and hygienic standards, like those of other member states, will remain intact and under the scrutiny of state officials.

All red-meat-exporting nations, for example, must continue to make a formal approach at the governmental level for a trade license from the British Ministry of Agriculture, Fisheries and Food. The ministry must be satisfied with regard to the disease situation in the exporting country; the control measures and organization for dealing with diseases; public health measures relating to slaughter, transportation, and storage facilities; and meat inspection arrangements (ante- and post-mortem checks). Additionally, the 1968 Imported Food Regulation prohibits importing into the United Kingdom for sale for human consumption any meat or meat product without an official certificate recognized by the Ministry of Agriculture, Fisheries and Food. The certificate must verify (1) that the meat was derived from an animal inspected before and after death in the country of origin and passed in accordance with criteria satisfactory to the minister; (2) that dressing and other meat preparation was carried out with all necessary precautions to prevent danger to public health.

Ireland. Ireland's restriction of agricultural imports, prior to its admission into the EC, relied primarily on discretionary licensing as the principal nontariff barrier. It was administered by the Department of Agriculture and Fisheries, supplementing a host of health and sanitary regulations combined with import calendars and fiscal charges applying to red meat imports. But its entrance into the EC is being accompanied by the abolition of such licensing controls.

Under the EC, CAP support prices for Irish agricultural products will be insulated from foreign competition by the introduction of the variable import levy. Prices for feeder cattle and sheep, for example, which have been supported under the British guaranteed price plan, are being administered by the EC Council under the transition plan. Upon complete transition into the CAP framework, import levies will act as the major mechanism controlling competition from live meat animal and red meat imports.

Health and sanitary regulations, to remain under the jurisdiction of Ireland's Ministry of Agriculture and Fisheries, are similar in purpose and administration to those of British authorities in the hygienic and health areas of the slaughter, transportation, and storage of imported meats. Standards are also enforced regarding the health of slaughter animals and admission of meats from areas with a history of epizootic disease contamination.

Denmark. Before Denmark's entrance in the EC, its agricultural trade policy operated under a restrictive import system composed of discretionary licensing, global quotas, import surcharges, value added taxes, and health and sanitary regulations. Because of the importance of the dairy and beef industries to Denmark's economy, livestock and meat products were among the agricultural commodities most restricted. During 1972, global quotas and discretionary licensing were strictly administered on meat products; in addition, there was a value added tax of 15 percent and a temporary import surcharge of 10 percent on prepared meats.[20]

The future course of Denmark's trade policy regarding livestock and meat products is now also dominated by its participation in the European Community. All quantitative import restrictions on red meat products, whether on other EC members or on Third Countries, are being abolished. Intervention purchases of beef and pork products currently come under the current EC regulations, and exports to Third Countries are eligible for EC export subsidies.

Adjustments to the EC level of beef and livestock prices for new member countries, which are protected by variable import levies toward third countries, are taking place in a six-step program during the five-year transition period which has been underway for the Danish beef and dairy industry since April 1, 1973. Tariffs protecting cattle, beef, and veal against imports from EC members are being discontinued in five equal steps. However, fixed levies or restrictions corresponding to the difference between intervention prices in the individual importing and exporting countries allow fluctuations of 10 percent in price adjustments at the individual steps of transition.[21]

THE UNITED STATES

The United States ranks first among major industrialized countries in the consumption of red meats and red meat products, with annual consumption averaging 36 billion pounds during the last five years. This demand by Americans is placing a growing burden on domestic producers to supply the market adequately with red meats, although to date, producers have met this challenge. Domestic production in the last five years has met approximately 95 percent of national demand, leaving a 5 percent deficit to be filled by imports. When transformed into physical measurements, however, this seemingly low figure constitutes a substantial volume of imports, placing the United States just behind the first-place United Kingdom as an importer of red meats.

Imports of red meats and red meat products into the United States increased steadily during the late 1960s and early 1970s. Major supply sources of beef were Australia, New Zealand, Argentina, and Mexico. The Oceanic countries of Australia and New Zealand were also the major suppliers of lamb and mutton, imports of which reached 92.9 million pounds in 1972. Pork imports in the last few years have come largely from Denmark, Canada, Poland, and the Netherlands.

Even though imports of red meats have increased in volume during the last decade, commerce in meat products is still subject to numerous constraints and restrictions erected by the United States government. One cause of this restrictive position is the underlying policy of the federal government to insulate domestic agriculture from excessive foreign competition. Consequently, imports of red meats and meat products, like those of other agricultural commodities, are subject to the quota, along with administrative customs procedures and health and hygienic regulations. The latter are among the most restrictive of all agricultural nontariff barriers.

Government Intervention in Trade

Import controls on agricultural commodities during the last four decades have been invoked by the United States under the authority invested in the president by Section 22 as amended of the Agricultural Adjustment Act, enacted on August 4, 1935 (Chapter 5). This stipulated that the president is authorized to impose fees or quotas in addition to the basic duty on any article or articles which in the judgment of the secretary of agriculture and/or the president: (a) render or tend to render ineffective or materially interfere with any price support or other program, relating to agricultural commodities, undertaken by the Department of Agriculture, or (b) reduce substantially the amount of any product processed in the United States from any agricultural commodity or product thereof with respect to which any program or operation is being undertaken. Since the enactment of Section 22, import controls have been placed on eleven commodities or groups of commodities. These commodities include cotton products, cereal grain products, dairy products, almonds, peanuts, and vegetable oil products, all of which are subject to various government support programs.

Unlike the commodities subject to import control, because imports of red meats could not be controlled under the specifications of Section 22 the meat-producing industries of the United States were not tied to governmental assistance programs. They therefore faced minor restrictions and impediments. Not until 1963–64, when red meat imports reached record highs while U.S. farm prices for meat products declined, was Congress spurred to enact legislation to control these imports.

The 88th Congress passed special legislation in 1964 which established a quota on imports of red meats (fresh, chilled, and frozen cattle meats and fresh, chilled, and frozen goat and sheepmeats) while entrusting to the president additional executive powers regarding the control of the importation of such meats into the United States. The initial quota set by this bill (PL 88-482) was based on the average volume of imports during the period 1959–63. This figure was 725,400,000 pounds, or approximately 4.6 percent of domestic production during the base period. Quotas for the years following 1964 were thereby set at levels also representing 4.6 percent of the commercial domestic production of the same year, and imposition of these quotas was triggered when imports exceeded 110 percent of the base quota.

But imposition was unnecessary during the 1965–67 period, since actual imports did not reach base quota levels. During 1968 and 1969, persuasion by the U.S. government encouraged exporting nations to use voluntary restraints on exports to make quotas again unnecessary. However, they were invoked in 1971 and then suspended upon the setting of a new voluntary restraint level of 1,160 million pounds.

The manipulation of restraint levels of quota systems is empowered to the president under the proclamation clause of PL 88-482:

The President may suspend any proclamation under subsection (c), or increase the total quantity proclaimed under each subsection, if he determines and proclaims that—

(1) Such action is required by overriding economic or national security interests of the United States, giving special weight to the importance to the nation of the economic well-being of the domestic livestock industry;

(2) The supply of articles of the kind described in subsection (a) will be inadequate to meet domestic demand at reasonable prices; or

(3) Trade agreements entered into after the date of the enactment of this act ensure the policy set forth in subsection (a) will be carried out.

Any such suspension shall be for such period, and any such increase shall be in such amount, as the President determines and proclaims to be necessary to carry out the purposes of this subsection.[22]

The most sweeping action taken under the executive powers of PL 88-482 with regard to imports of red meats and red meat products was the complete relaxing of quotas in June 1972, when inflationary pressures on red meat prices during late 1971 and early 1972 moved the president to this *nonrestrictive* trade position. The duration of this nonquota trade posture on red meat imports is a variable factor, since such presidential actions maintain a high degree of flexibility. For example, because of the depressed conditions in the U.S. livestock feeding industry, political pressures in 1974 demanded a change in the country's meat import policy. Discontent among the producers of livestock again resulted in a coordinated effort to restrict imports of red meats. As we have seen earlier in this chapter, voluntary agreements were worked out with Australia and New Zealand, but in October 1976 the president imposed import quotas.

In addition to meat import quotas, the United States operates a quota system for the importation of animals crossing Mexican and Canadian borders. The use of this quota has been unnecessary, however, since both Canada and Mexico enforce export quotas on live animal movement which are more restrictive than those of the United States. Suffice it to say, in addition to beef and substantial imports of hams and variety meats, the United States historically has imported large numbers of stocker cattle, largely from Mexico. Such a situation with respect to the marketing of livestock and livestock products makes this industry very susceptible to trade impediments in the United States, as is the case in all developed market economies.

Customs and Administrative Entry Procedures

Licensing and Health and Hygienic Standards. Every nation which desires to obtain the right to export red meats, red meat products, or slaughter animals to the United States must first make a formal approach to the Department of State. Once an application for a license to trade is registered there, officials from the Department of Agriculture are sent to the applying country to investigate the health and hygienic conditions of its meat-processing industry and its livestock population. USDA health authorities focus attention on the procedures and techniques used for animal slaughter. Also examined are facilities for the processing, packaging, storage, and transportation of red meats. The exotic disease situation in the prospective exporting country is studied carefully. Compliance with the U.S. Code of Federal Regulations on Health and Hygienic Standards by the exporting country, as measured by the investigating officials, determines the country's eligibility for a license to export to the United States.

The health and hygienic standards required of export meat-processing industries under the U.S. Code of Federal Regulations and those health standards required of the livestock population of the meat-exporting countries are among the most restrictive of the industrialized trading countries. For example, under Section 306 of the Tariff Act of 1930, as amended, the importation of cattle, sheep, swine, and forms of meats of these animals is prohibited from all countries where rinderpest or foot-and-mouth disease exists. Currently, U.S. imports of these animals and/or meat products in a fresh, chilled, or frozen state are limited to North and Central America, Australia, New Zealand, the Fiji Islands, Japan, the Republic of Ireland, Norway, Iceland, the Channel Islands, and Northern Ireland. As a consequence of Section 306, U.S. imports from the important meat-producing countries of South America in recent years have been virtually all in the form of cooked, canned, or cured meats.[23]

In addition to the strict posture of the U.S. government on the exotic disease situation in exporting countries, every country exporting meats in fresh, chilled, frozen, cooked, canned, or cured state must have an adequate local veterinary and health inspection service. This service must have an adequate staff and facilities to perform ante- and post-mortem checks of meat animals slaughtered for export, to maintain health and hygienic standards of processing plants, and to report accurately to U.S. authorities on the contagious and exotic disease status of its livestock population. To guarantee proper supervision of the meat-exporting industry by the local veterinary and health inspection services, each country is also subject to periodic checks by the United States. In some countries, U.S. inspection officials are on assignment in the country to oversee the supervision of these health standards by local agencies. However, as long as Federal Code of Health and Hygienic Regulations are being met, exporting nations will continue to be licensed to ship red meats, red meat products, or slaughter animals into the United States.

The primary intent of the licensing procedures practiced by the United States is clearly to protect its consuming public and domestic livestock sector from diseased or contaminated meat imports, and licenses have not been overtly used as a form of a quota. This is because quotas have been a common mechanism used by the United States to control meat imports during the last decade, so license manipulations have been unnecessary. Yet the avoidance of using licenses as an overt control doesn't preclude its potential as an effective nontariff barrier. This has been most apparent with respect to imports of meat products from South America after the relaxation of the quota system in June 1972. Although the United States became a ready market for South American red meats, the licensing mechanism, guided by the strict health and hygienic standards (regarding exotic diseases), banned South American exports of fresh, chilled, or frozen meats and meat products.

Entry Procedures. The customs and entry procedures administered by the U.S. port and customs authorities on imports of red meat and slaughter animals represent another form of nontariff barrier. These imports must be accompanied by numerous documents to verify health and hygienic conditions, including certification by the official health inspector of the exporting nation regarding ante- and post-mortem checks on slaughtered animals, verification of proper processing of meat under the United States Federal Code, information on the origin of slaughter animals, identification of the slaughter plant, and papers relating to proper labeling of the cargo according to cuts, type of meat, and weight. All this information is completed and checked by an official application examiner to ascertain whether all the proper documentation has been completed by the exporters before the shipment is allowed entry into a U.S. port.

Once the documentation is completed and checked, random samples are taken from the cargo, to be examined for wholesomeness and bacteria levels. Frozen (boned or unboned) meats are checked by cutting a piece away from the carcass, defrosting it, and inspecting it at a proper facility. Canned meats are also randomly checked. Cans are opened, the product examined for wholesomeness, and the weight checked. Contamination of samples or labeling or weight irregularities result in the confiscation of the cargo at the port of entry by U.S. customs officials.

The extent of hindrance these procedures cause in the movement of imports depends, of course, on the intensity of interpretation with which the custom and entry procedures are administered. Excessively strict interpretation can be an effective nontariff device, especially when there are undue delays in meat distribution; minor errors or documentation problems with respect to perishable imports such as fresh, chilled, or frozen meats can cause problems which may be economically disastrous for the exporter.

JAPAN

Densely populated Japan is a major importer of agricultural goods and products. Since World War II, it has relied heavily on commodity imports to support its domestic demand for food products. Imports of food and animal products have increased steadily since the early 1960s.

The expansion of imports of red meats and meat preparations resulted in part from a liberalization of agricultural trade policy by the Japanese government. Advances achieved in quota regulations resulted in the elimination of some quotas on commodities, although others were enlarged. In addition, numerous other nontariff impediments were removed or relaxed in trade negotiations. Despite this progress in the last few years, the Japanese government still maintains an active role in the regulation of trade. This intervention emanates from a long-standing policy of government support of and protection for its domestic agricultural sector, along with a general concern about its international balance-of-payments position. Thus, many restrictive and highly constraining tariff and nontariff barriers still greatly affect the free movement of agricultural goods into Japan.

Government Intervention in Trade

The primary nontariff barriers used by the Japanese government to control imports of red meat animals, red meats, and red meat products are quotas. In 1971, they were placed on imports of beef, veal, and horse meat as well as on pork. However, constant economic and political pressures exerted by numerous major trading nations moved Japan in late 1971 and early 1972 to a more conciliatory position regarding quotas on these products, and they were removed on pork, ham, and bacon products and were expanded for general-quality and high-quality beef until the international buildup of red meat surpluses moved the Japanese government again to establish controls on red meat imports. In June 1974, the Japanese government invoked a complete ban on red meat imports, which has since been relaxed.

These moves toward trade liberalization prior to the June 1974 ban on red meat imports were misleading, since in numerous cases the Japanese government instituted variable levy systems on the import items which were granted immunity from quotas. For example, a new variable levy system on pork assured that imports would enter free of the levy only when domestic pork prices were high.

The movement to variable levy systems assured the Japanese of having one of the most diversified groups of nontariff regulations with respect to meat imports, proving that regulation and intervention remained the underlying factors influencing Japanese foreign trade policy.

Customs and Administrative Entry Procedures

Licensing. All red meat animal and meat imports are subject to licensing under a three-code system before being allowed into Japan. The three codes are designated: Automatic Approval (AA), Automatic Import Quota (AIQ), and Import Quota (IQ). Of these three types, the AA and AIQ systems are the most liberal, since licenses are issued freely by certain banks authorized by the government and the Ministry of International Trade and Industry. Meat products eligible for the AIQ and AA license are ham, bacon, pork, and live swine, which are regulated by the variable levy system.[24]

Meat and offals of bovine animals, fresh, chilled, or frozen, are subject to the IQ system, the most restrictive of Japan's licensing procedures. Applications for licenses must be made directly to the Ministry of International Trade and Industry. The issuance of licenses is conducted on a limited basis, thereby regulating the quantities of beef imports. The amount of the quota usually is not officially announced, although generally it is obtainable on an unofficial basis.[25]

Health and Hygienic Standards. The establishment by the Japanese government of health and hygienic regulations to regulate slaughter animal and red meat imports focuses on the traditional principles of consumer protection and insulation of domestic agricultural industries from health hazards. The list of procedures followed by Japanese authorities to maintain these health standards is similar to that of many importing nations. Common to the health procedures of other countries are wholesomeness inspections at ports of entry by Japanese officials, investigation of the storage and slaughter facilities of exporting nations to verify that proper health precautions are in operation, examination of the livestock populations for exotic diseases, and periodic checks of licensed exporting facilities to ascertain whether health standards are being maintained according to Japanese health requirements. Even though these are common international procedures, variations which create formidable nontariff barrier possibilities still exist in the interpretation and enforcement of these health regulations by Japanese authorities.

Japan, in some cases, cites health standards and regulations as justification for general restrictive action on meat imports. A case in point was the Japanese position on imports of poultry meat. In June 1971, officials began to analyze meat for salmonella virus, even though the same tests were not applied to domestic poultry.[26] This action resulted in a decrease in the volume of imports allowed to enter.

There currently appears to be no overt action based on vague health and hygienic grounds to control imports of red meats into Japan. However, it must be stressed that criteria for acceptance by Japanese authorities of such imports do not necessarily depend on the specific wording and specific intent of health regulations, but frequently depend on domestic issues.

OTHER DEVELOPED NATIONS

The description of the impediments to commerce characterizing the trade programs of the major meat-importing regions of Japan, the United States, and the European Economic Community serves to identify many nontariff barriers used to regulate red meat and slaughter animal imports. Variable levys, quotas, licensing, border charges, and enforcement of health and sanitary regulations are found to be the most common devices regulating trade. These nontariff barriers, however, are not unique to the trade programs of these three major meat-importing regions because they also characterize the trade of numerous other industrialized nations.

Austria, Switzerland, and the Scandinavian countries have established a system to control imports of red meats and red meat products similar to that operated by the European Community. The variable levy system is an important mechanism in the regulation of meat imports. (Norway calls its levy mechanisms a

minimum price system.) In addition to levy systems, these northern European countries also invoke quotas on imports of specific
red meat items, issue licenses, practice discretionary licensing, levy
border charges, and enforce strict health and sanitary regulations.
Clearly, these nontariff mechanisms at times unduly restrict competition in domestic markets from foreign-produced meat goods.

Eastern European governments' strict control on imports of
red meats and slaughter animals is manifested by the authority of
state trade monopolies or state trade committees whose officials
enforce the parameters of trade which their government will allow
under bilateral agreements with exporting nations. The degree of
regulation is, therefore, absolute and clearly defined in the agreements.

Barriers affecting trade in red meats and slaughter animals are
not as severe in a number of the Mediterranean countries. Spain
and Yugoslavia, however, do impose excessively rigid restrictions
on red meat imports. Spain operates under a system of variable
levys, quotas, licenses, and enforcement of strict health and sanitary regulations, combined with numerous special bilateral agreements. With the exception of the variable levy system, Yugoslavia follows a program comparable to the Spanish system of
regulations. Greece and Portugal, meanwhile, control red meat
import levels by licensing or state trading. Greece maintains
regulatory powers on the import of pork and bovine meats, while
Portugal maintains import restrictions on beef, pork, mutton,
and lamb. Turkey operates its red meat import program under a
system of excessively high tariff and customs duties rates, plus
nontariff regulations that focus on health and sanitary factors
designed to protect Turkish consumers from contagious and exotic
diseases.

Health and sanitary regulations pose the principal nontariff
barrier affecting imports of red meats into Canada. Its import
regulations operate on a veterinary import permit system based on
rigid and strictly enforced health and hygienic standards. Only
seven countries currently meet Canadian health requirements for
the production, slaughter, processing, and exportation of fresh,
chilled, and frozen red meat products. The issuance of import
permits for cooked and canned meats is equally dependent on the
acceptability of the health and sanitary conditions of the exporting meat industries.

Similar restrictions on imports of red meats result from the barriers created by the enforcement of strict health and sanitary regulations established by Australian health and trade authorities. Under the provisions of quarantine legislation, uncanned meats or uncanned products containing edible parts of animals may be imported only from New Zealand. A complete ban, however, is placed on imports of uncanned meat or pigs. The effect is to insulate clearly Australian red meat markets from foreign-produced and -processed fresh, chilled, and frozen products.

More liberal trade conditions exist in the commerce of canned products. Canned meat, with the exception of pigmeat, may be imported from any country, subject to the provisions on health conditions listed in the quarantine and commerce regulations. South American, European, and Asian meat exporters are, therefore, given an opportunity to penetrate the canned meat markets of Australia. Only a few countries qualify to export canned pigmeat under the current provisions: New Zealand, Canada, the United States, Ireland, and Northern Ireland.

New Zealand imposes a more diverse array of regulations than Australia on red meat imports. Although variable levies are not used, quotas, restrictive licensing, and preferential trade agreements with Australia and other Commonwealth nations dominate the commercial policy employed. Quotas and restrictive licensing are applied to poultry, sausages, and meat preparations. Special trade agreements range from movements of live slaughter animals and red meats between New Zealand and Australia, to trade in fresh, chilled, frozen, and canned bovine and sheep meats with the United Kingdom.

DEVELOPING NATIONS

Information compiled by the Committee on Commodity Problems, Food and Agriculture Organization of the United Nations,[27] on tariff systems employed by developing nations showed less extensive nontariff barrier systems in them. Quotas, variable levys, restrictive licensing, and restrictive special trade agreements were used much less frequently than in developed countries. Only occasionally were direct nontariff regulations on animal and meat imports enforced, with the import license most common, particularly in cases where local governments wished to protect domestic livestock industries during their infant states of development from bordering nations. Kenya, for example, employs restrictions on pigmeat and poultry primarily against imports from Uganda, Ethiopia, Somaliland, and Tanganyika. The only nontariff regulations common to all developing nations are health and sanitary requirements to control diseases. The maintenance of health standards is of greatest importance, of course, to those developing countries which are also major exporters of red meat products. In order to secure trading rights with major meat-importing nations, proper health precautions and disease protection rules must be observed by meat exporters. Argentina, Brazil, and Chile, for example, employ strict and comprehensively enforced health regulations to assure licenses to trade in red meat with Europe (frozen, chilled, canned, and processed) and the United States (processed). Protection is sought by these South American countries from contamination of processed products and from epidemics of exotic diseases crossing their borders which might infect local livestock. Contamination of this nature would immediately result in the revocation of licenses to trade with Western industrialized countries.

For example, when Uruguay in 1969 fell victim to foot-and-mouth disease contamination, the disease was transported in the bone of red meat products imported by the United Kingdom. Upon verification of the disease, U.K. officials, in June 1969, stripped Uruguay of the right to export beef products to the United Kingdom. The loss of trade in Uruguay was almost 33,500 tons in 1970.

Actually, the primary means of regulating imports of red meat and slaughter animals for most developing countries is excessively high customs rates combined with various systems of internal or border taxation. General customs duties range from 10 to 100 percent ad valorem, with various border, global, turnover, and internal taxes levied at 5 to 15 percent ad valorem. A simple system to administer, this avoids the administrative complications associated with sophisticated nontariff systems of regulation.

Chapter 8.

NEGOTIATIONS ON NONTARIFF AGRICULTURAL BARRIERS

The thesis of this study has been that agricultural trade barrier problems residual to the Kennedy Round negotiations, buttressed by the nature of their uniqueness, are likely to become more complicated and important in the next few years. This position is taken despite the respite in traditional trade restriction activity which occurred in the years 1972–75. The likelihood of international trade breakdown will increase proportionately to the unwillingness of the major agricultural producing and trading nations to reduce the adverse impact of their domestic farm policies upon international trade. This is particularly true of developed industrial countries such as the United States, the Western European countries, and Japan. But it is also true of Australia, Canada, and New Zealand, and holds for developing countries and wherever state trading predominates. Succinctly put, domestic farm policies are the root cause of the major restrictions in international commerce of farm products. Our treatment of Japanese quotas, and Section 22, and the Common Agricultural Policy variable levy demonstrate this.

Though it appears unlikely that positive major steps to eliminate agricultural trade restrictions will be taken except as part of a general international agreement, it is hypothesized that in the case of many nontariff barriers alluded to in this study, particularly administrative types of harrassments and related measures, protection could be eased by bilateral agreement and mutual consent. In short, there would be little need to enter the "big arena" of negotiations on major trade strategies in order for some countries to make progress on selected nontariff barriers.

As a brief digression, one must take issue with Gale Johnson and his "there's nothing-new-in-the-world" implication about agricultural protection, i.e., that since the fifteenth century, protection has been the rule, and that today's instruments to carry out protectionist policies are about the same as they have been throughout history.[1] To be sure, as Solomon told us in Ecclesiastes, there is nothing new under the sun, and in principle that is true. Instruments of protection have varied over time, however, and so has the volume of trade during the last five centuries. The point should not be pressed either in principle or philosophically; but, technically, there is a major point which this study has been trying to make: technology and administrative bureaucracy have made some commercial problems of the twentieth century unique.

For example, market-differentiating factors such as grades, standards, and labeling; health and sanitary laws and regulations supported by rigorous border inspections; rapid mass transport; and instantaneous communication—these and many other factors, buttressed by the powers of administrative bureaucracies described in Chapter 2, clearly make for *methods* of trade restriction which necessitate different techniques and modalities for negotiating. Furthermore, the large public payrolls in this sense are essentially a twentieth-century phenomenon because, perhaps for the first time since the fifteenth century, many trade barriers are used in part to justify the existence of the bureaucracies raising them. Johnson is correct in that there has never been much difference in terms of results between various historical methods of agricultural protection. It is also true that one of the main consequences of such protection throughout history has been to increase agricultural rents.

NEEDS AND REQUIREMENTS FOR NEGOTIATIONS

The need for negotiations to avoid or to mitigate major conflicts in agricultural trade policies becomes pressing when taking into account world food needs, the tendency toward internationalization of world production, the changing world trade structure, the evolution of the CAP and the Western European trading bloc, the rapid rise of Japan as an economic superpower, and the emergence of the Soviet Union and Eastern Europe on the international trading scene. In all these developments, the politics and the economics of liberal trade policies go hand in hand. For example, farm groups in the United States, heavily dependent on exports, are strong supporters of trade expansion policies and are generally opposed to protectionism. Solving their fundamental problems in a world of economic disorder would have a desirable political as well as a desirable economic outcome. The same could be said, but with a different slant, about Western European farm interests. Agricultural adjustment there is basic not only to harmony in Europe but to international political stability.

Currently, while the world as a whole has a great capacity to produce food and fiber—perhaps enough for all its inhabitants—the present trading system does not distribute products equitably. Furthermore, efficiency (not just the distribution of assets, but their earning power) is also obstructed by many of the trade barriers referred to and described in this study. Despite temporary appearances to the contrary, many trade and development problems are getting worse, not better. There is a real danger of another trade breakdown such as the world endured during the 1930s. Current monetary instability, exacerbated by market uncertainty and low productivity, is a danger signal. At such times, govermnents often feel obliged to intervene directly in their domestic agricultural production and marketing sectors with the alleged objectives of improving farm incomes, increasing self-sufficiency ratios in food production, improving balance-of-payments positions, fighting inflation, and for other attendant reasons such as improving diets, etc. Unilateral intervention in an economic world which is increasingly technological, commercial, and administratively interdependent means that governments will assume the nationalistic posture of garnering and preserving sales by imposing rigid control of imports and exports.

This is not to imply that negotiators should throw up their hands in despair when the going gets rough—when, for example, Japan closes its borders to beef imports from the West, as it did in the summer of 1974; or when the European Economic Community threatens a tax on American soybeans, and member countries subsidize shipments of a beef surplus to the Soviet Union; or if the United States were to drastically revise its beef quota. Indeed not. The negotiations must go on. But it must be recognized that the post-World War II bargaining mechanisms do not suffice to solve many problems of a nontariff nature, whether in agriculture or in other sectors of the world economy.

As many experienced officials have pointed out, it takes time to negotiate.[2] But in the area of nontariff barriers and agricultural trade policies, the process inevitably will be slow. As shown in Chapter 3, agricultural protection has its roots planted in several centuries of agrarian fundamentalism. Moreover, the administrative bureaucracies which have been built around domestic farm programs and related matters in all countries of the world are tenacious. Hence, progress through liberalizing actions in future rounds of GATT negotiations will depend on the degree to which the bargaining governments can move away from the air of unreality which sometimes accompanies discussions of nontariff barriers and the extent to which they can move beyond the deliberations on "policy" to the harsher world of political action.[3]

The need for hardheadedness in approaching the problem of negotiating, the need for non-self-deluding tactics on the part of negotiators, and the need for openness in the discussion has been well put by Brian Hindley:

What goes wrong (in academic discussion of nontariff barriers and of commercial policy in general) is that the logic of self-interest which suggests that such-and-such would be a good thing from a world point of view, or even from that of the nation, also suggests that such things will be largely irrelevant to political units. Optimal allocation of world resources must seem a pale creature to non-economists at the very best of times; and when it appears to be in competition with the evident and politically charged manifestations of unemployment, balance-of-payments problems, depressed regions and industries and lagging growth, it is surely not the horse that policy-makers should be expected to back.

Beyond the exigencies of policy are the harsher ones of politics. An arrangement which effects a gift in such a way that the ultimate donor does not notice his loss means, in political terms, a friend gained or maintained and none lost. A tariff here, a health regulation there, and anti-dumping investigation: each provides a gift without any need for those who foot the bill to be aware of their munificence. And, indeed, should they know it, they may be prepared to give, either because the fresh application of the principle makes more secure their own protection, or because they may themselves want to call for protection in the future.

. . . .
. . . Statements of principle have been easier to obtain than commitments to action. It is hard to find an adequate "quid," in political terms, for the "quo" given up by renunciation of protective devices.

. . . .
. . . there is a strong case for bringing . . . disagreements into the light of day for criticism and analysis; and for initially creating a framework of

international discussion and negotiation which does not commit the participating governments to action. Trade is restricted because governments believe it is their interest to restrict it. That belief, if it can be dislodged at all, will not disappear overnight. But the process of discussion of what is harmful, and the policies available to deal with ostensible harm, may lead to an atmosphere in which the worst interferences could be eliminated and the application of the rest improved.[4]

In brief, negotiations will not move without the political will of governments, and without the constant prodding of negotiators by officials with the power to effectuate breakthroughs and solutions. Exploratory processes could well evolve into a part of the negotiated settlements. In fact, one of the critical ingredients to problem solving could be the emergence of on-going consultative machinery.[5] To be sure, such machinery may be necessary because of the complex nature of agricultural protection and the innumerable and seemingly endless nontariff techniques which nations use to implement that protection. It is not likely, therefore, that the next round of negotiations will end in the dramatic way as did the Kennedy Round.

APPROACHES TO NEGOTIATION

It should be reemphasized that one of the difficulties in negotiating agricultural protection lies in the nature of agrarian fundamentalism. Added to this, nontariff instruments of protection will be hard to negotiate because most of these trade-distorting practices are deeply rooted in the political and social policies and in the laws, rules, and regulations of each nation. The fact that agricultural and nontariff trade impediments remain after so many years of negotiations is evidence of the hard-core problems of these areas.

Negotiators, therefore, must remember that nontariff barriers are directly associated with domestic and social objectives. One of these has been mentioned already—the employment factor in national administrative bureaucracies. Others are promotion of employment in low-wage unemployment areas, protection of key political constituencies, protection of priority sectors in national growth plans, preservation of government control of production and distribution of certain types of products, protection of a minimum production capability for national security reasons, import substitution for balance-of-payments reasons, protection of consumers, and similar objectives. Sometimes these barriers are intended by governments to discriminate against international competitors, but at other times they have been inadvertent, often an outgrowth of some decision on domestic policy which never took its trade effects into account.

The GATT

The principal negotiations on all trade barriers since World War II have come through the GATT. Its Agricultural Committee during its intermittent deliberations since the end of the Kennedy Round has produced a series of reports relating to trade negotiations. Specifically, for example, a Working Group has met on various occasions since 1970 "to examine various techniques and modalities for future negotiations as they relate to agriculture." This group focuses its general search for solutions on problems which have been defined in four particular sectors: (1) measures which affect exports; (2) measures which affect imports; (3) measures which affect production; and (4) other relevant measures, health and sanitary regulations in particular. Working sessions preparatory to new negotiations like those held on many occasions in 1972 produced documents which thoroughly examined the principal measures of concern, including export assistance; tariffs, variable levies, and other special charges; quantitative restrictions; health and sanitary regulations, marketing standards, and licensing; specific production measures; international stabilization arrangements; codes of good conduct; self-sufficiency ratios; and margin of support *(montant de soutien)*.

Much of the work of this GATT Working Group has been done on a theoretical plane in the sense that no reference was made to the position of a particular product or country. This, plus the fact that the group didn't discuss objectives of future trade negotiations, placed definite limitations on the pragmatic value of its work.

The decision made to open new trade negotiations in the GATT, which led off with the Tokyo Declaration of September 1973, was in part a response to obvious needs developed in such working groups and in response to the strains resulting from rapid changes in the world economic environment. To solve specific problems of international trade posed by such needs and changes, the GATT has continued to search for solutions to the many questions brought before it. In a first agreement concerning the technical work to be carried out in the early months of the negotiations and the procedural arrangements to be made, a detailed program of analytical work to be undertaken in six specialized subgroups has been established.

Still many doubt the relevance of negotiations in the GATT, arguing that the tradition of negotiations within the GATT framework reflects world conditions that no longer prevail. Barriers are irrelevant, they say, in a world in which the rate of annual inflation exceeds the existing general rate of protection—about 8 percent. Fluctuating exchange rates, supply shortages, and the determination of governments to negotiate when their balance-of-payments positions are so insecure are other reasons for doubting the relevance of the forthcoming negotiations.

GATT Director-General Oliver Long has countered these doubts with some positive arguments for moving ahead on the negotiations.[6] First he poses the traditional argument for lower import duties, adding that the reduction of import duties offers a direct means of countering inflation. A second argument is of great current importance: secure markets are a key to secure supplies. Many shortages of agricultural commodities have their origin in previous underinvestment in the agricultural sector. Investment, particularly the long-term kind required for agricultural and other primary commodities, will not be undertaken without assurances that the product can find a market. Seen in this light, the removal of obstacles to imports is an excellent way of improving the security of essential trade flows and of ensuring greater stability in prices.

Long goes on to say, correctly, that the third argument applies to nontariff obstacles in the same way as to import duties, probably with even more force. Nontariff measures are by their nature a greater source of uncertainty in trade than tariffs, which are at least quantifiable and published. Moreover, comparatively little has been done about such measures in the past.

The GATT preparatory work on nontariff measures has shown that most statutory and regulatory activities are legitimate and essential. Governments must, for example, protect their citizens against imports that are infected or unsafe, or that are subsidized to such an extent that they drive otherwise competitive domestic producers out of business. What is required is to ensure that such measures do not unduly restrict trade. The general GATT point of view is that the practical solution will in many cases be to agree on codes of conduct, as was done during the Kennedy Round negotiations, so that the trade-restricting effects of anti-dumping action might be reduced.

Excellent references to the work of the GATT are available, along with some excellent analyses of issues to be raised in forth-coming negotiations.[7] One recurrent theme appears in these and other analyses: little will be gained in future GATT negotiations if the participants concentrate on tallying each others' violations of some theoretical norm or idealized view of world trade and make these violations the main topic of conversation in trade negotiations. More preparation and more documentation, as well as more patience and good-will, are necessary. Perhaps an entirely new set of guidelines will be required as a fundamental beginning.

In answer to other criticisms of the GATT and its negotiating procedures, it should be pointed out that this organization and its operating procedure are but reflections of interests of participants. The most likely result of any new negotiating forum would be a confrontation of the same protagonists on the same issues that have evolved within the GATT. Reformation of the GATT and its procedures holds out about as much hope for reducing nontariff trade barriers and for trade liberalization as does the creation of new international forums and negotiating procedures.

Harmonization and Collective Responsibility

Various proposals for the liberalization of trade would result in the extension of existing international rules and the elimination of certain protection policies. These are but variants of the proposal for treaty-bound codes of good conduct, because negotiations aimed at the formulation of such codes would likely result in elaborating existing rules, while eliminating policies would require some form of multilateral treaty.

Another related proposal has attracted attention—*harmoniza-tion* of national policies, a term with different meanings, depend-ing on who proposes it. Malmgren, perhaps more than others, has probed the possibilities of this approach.[8]

The key principle implied by these and related approaches is that governments must cease trying to pass on to other countries the costs of domestic farm policies. At the same time, it is argued that agricultural protection and problems related thereto are not so very different from those arising because of industrial nontariff barriers. That is, harmonization or regularization of economic policies in some orderly framework lies at the heart of any sensible new departures in trade liberalization.

Central to most statements on harmonization is the idea of negotiating with a greater respect for intergovernmental cooperation than has existed in the past. Proponents of collective responsibility[9] and harmonization imply, as do so many other writers, that a conceptual debate couched in terms of free-trade-versus-protection is irrelevant to current trade negotiations. They say bluntly that it is no longer sufficient to assume that the international agricultural market will somehow take care of itself, and that the best trade policy is one of minimum intervention. Governments, instead, should be guided by general economic concepts for facilitating a high level of production, trade, and prosperity in a dynamic world economy, a procedure involving elements of deliberation, decision making, and coordination. Governments would agree to continual multilateral public hearings. There would be no façade of multilateral decision to be struggled for and then ignored. All governments would be committed to cooperation to accomplish the public purpose of their actions after having considered them through their own constitutional processes.

The hard question for those who argue for harmonization and coordination is, How do nations get beyond the rhetoric—beyond even a transitional period when, no doubt, some type of access commitments, price arrangements, subsidy limits, etc., will be necessary—and beyond the seemingly interminable sessions of administrative bureaucrats, to the harder ground of actual trade liberalization? One writer says that "given [the present trade situation] there is urgent need for governments to intervene to restrain themselves, and to restrain each other."[10] How do nations go about "intervening to restrain themselves?" What does this and other such language mean in the hard world of trade negotiation?

It appears, therefore, that harmonization and related approaches to trade liberalization might have to proceed, like many other proposals, on the basis of treaty-bound agreements—unless there is created for such purposes an international agency with supranational powers. Prospects for the latter seem highly unlikely, especially in light of the experiences of GATT and UNCTAD.

There is also a variant of the harmonization-cooperation theme. Since some form of treaty-bound rules of competition appears to be the only feasible course for dealing with nontariff trade barrier

problems, Hindley suggests that a particular format for negotiation
is in order.[11] The first stage would aim at obtaining international
accord on a set of general rules of competition based on Part II of
the General Agreement covering nontariff barriers. In that case,
it would be necessary to dispense with the Protocol of Provisional
Application (the so-called grandfather clause).

Hindley's second stage of negotiation would consist of listing
in order (outside the country applying them) those forms of
intervention in trade flows most damaging to the rest of the world.
This process would lead to one of four outcomes with respect to
the instrument:

1. Its outright elimination.
2. Its elimination by the substitution for it of instruments farther down the list—for example, substitution of subsidies to
   import-competing production for import quotas or tariffs.
3. Its conversion to a form which would allow it to be shifted to
   a lower level on the list—for example, the conversion of
   simple restrictive quotas to quotas with rights allocated to
   foreign governments.
4. Control of its application.

As soon as one of these outcomes was achieved, Hindley points
out, negotiations could focus on the second instrument on the list
and so on to the third, fourth, and so on. Before the process could
start, it would be necessary to construct the list of instruments to
be negotiated. And the first thing to remember in constructing the
list is that not everything designated as a nontariff barrier should
be on the same negotiating list. For example, health and sanitary
regulations are not instruments of policy with the same power and
flexibility as quotas. A second thing to be remembered is that such
a list must be ordered, which might be a topic in itself for negotiating.

The Atlantic Council Approach

A number of national and international organizations have taken
positions on, or made proposals with reference to, trade negotiations. One such organization is the Atlantic Council of the United
States. A Special Advisory Panel to the Trade Committee of the
council on "Reform of the International Trade System" outlines a

code of trade liberalization in an interim report.[12] The proposed code would supplement the GATT and would at the outset apply to the United States, the European Community, Japan, and perhaps the more developed EFTA members, Canada and Australia. It would provide for a common pattern and time schedule for tariff reduction, with exceptions referred to vaguely in an annex, and with variable levies not mentioned at all. "Major agricultural products," not further defined, would be given special treatment, which could include limitations on the total amount of protection in any form. These arrangements could also include stockpile goals, perhaps jointly financed, and food aid levels. An agriculture committee would administer commitments.

The imposition of quota restrictions, surcharges, or similar measures for balance-of-payments reasons would be subject to prior International Monetary Fund approval, and future customs unions or free-trade areas would be subject to prior code-member approval. Export restrictions for short supply reasons would require prior consultation and nondiscriminatory application. Export subsidies are not mentioned, and nontariff agreements would be worked into the code later. The GATT escape clause provisions would continue to apply, but the report is uncertain whether or how they might be changed. Reverse preferences from the less developed countries would disappear; special preferences would not, "in general," discriminate among less developed countries.

The proposed code supposedly would supplement the GATT, but might in practice devalue and supplant it. Tariff-reduction/commodity-arrangement negotiations among an industrial elite might replace the customary GATT round. To an extent, this would be merely a recognition of present reality, but the general idea that GATT obligations represent at least a goal would appear to be abandoned. Principle apart, the question of which countries would be expected to adhere to the code raises practical difficulties. Reductions negotiated under the code would extend to all GATT members, but they could be suspended for products supplied principally by "an industrialized country which, although able to do so, refused to accept the obligations of the code."

A separate treatment by the Council regarding the agricultural trade question addresses principally the special situation of the United States.[13] Chapter 4, "Agriculture in General Trade Negotiations," of that study offers an excellent discussion of the basic problem of agricultural trade negotiations, and its most specific contribution, after reviewing codes of conduct, is to distinguish two alternative methods of approaching trade negotiations. The main difference between the two alternatives is that one gives major emphasis to the negotiation of international arrangements as a means of stabilizing and expanding trade in farm products; the other emphasizes trade liberalization and the elimination of restraints on consumption and government-financed incentives to production as the guiding principles for organizing trade in farm products.

There is a related difference between the two methods in the way they deal with tactics of negotiations. These tactics are detailed in the study, and the positions of the United States and Western Europe are obvious, both as to the alternative methods as well as the tactics of negotiation. Though the agricultural study presents a more sophisticated treatment of the international trade problem of agriculture than the "Reform" study, neither gives a very obvious or heavy role to the GATT. It will be interesting to observe how the suggestions and recommendations which derive from such studies will be utilized in the forthcoming GATT negotiations.

An Integrated Eco-Political Approach

It is essential to any GATT negotiations that all participants recognize the nature of the disease they are trying to cure, so that too much time and energy won't be spent in dealing with symptoms. National domestic policies are the root cause of agricultural protection and for the interference in the free flow of international trade. Instruments described in this study—quantitative restrictions, variable levies, licensing requirements, mixing regulations, health and sanitary standards, and others—are but manifestations and an outgrowth of basic protective elements in national policies. Various price and income objectives, particularly on the part of nations in the industrialized world, have necessitated trade-interfering measures to assure their attainment. To doctor the disease, therefore, treatment must be applied to the basic problem, not to its symptoms. It is quite evident that the participants in the negotiations recognize this. It is even more evident to the international organizations such as FAO, the International Monetary Fund (IMF), OECD, and others. Hence, there appears to be little patience for another round of bargaining in which trade barriers alone are the main subject of discussion. This is said even though one of the main theses of this study has been that certain nontariff barriers need special attention in the next round, and that particular trade impediments such as administrative rules and interpretations might be dealt with even on a bilateral basis.

World, regional, and national agricultural adjustment, effective protection, new guidelines, and basic research which reveals the economic truth about a nation's agricultural policy objectives— these must be the fundamental topics of the discussions and negotiations. Gale Johnson, who has elaborated the effective protection idea, predicates his entire framework for negotiations on defining effective protection so as to give defensible answers to fundamental questions about national agricultural policies.[14]

The role of effective protection for agriculture would be the first criterion for meaningful negotiation, to be followed by a criterion as to the effects of particular price and income supports for agriculture upon output and consumption. A considerable amount of research preparation is suggested for negotiating on the basis of these criteria, because answers are not known to some of the important questions regarding the effects of farm policies on production, prices, incomes, and consumption. However, it is doubted whether governments want an objective and competent evaluation of their agricultural policies.

After a proper study of effective protection composed essentially of economic analyses, there must follow the development of a code of conduct or a set of rules for domestic agricultural policies and trade barriers. This would be essentially a political question. Major attention would be given to devising a code to cover *acceptable* trade barriers. For example, one rule that might be considered is that import quotas must be increased whenever the effective degree of protection goes above an agreed-upon level for three months.

One drawback to negotiating proposals such as those made by Johnson is the time and expense involved. Not only would it take several years for economic studies, but perhaps an equally long period would be needed to effectuate the codes of conduct and policies that the research suggests. This time horizon, however, does not differ materially from that involved in other proposed approaches to negotiations, especially those of the harmonization proponents, who suggest perpetual negotiations on agricultural policies and nontariff barriers.

CRITICAL ISSUES

It is appropriate to conclude this study by outlining and briefly commenting on some of the crucial options and courses to be considered when dealing with nontariff and agricultural restrictions in the context of international trade negotiations. These options and courses of actions are available to negotiators in the Tokyo Round and beyond:

1. Foremost to be decided is whether agricultural trade negotiations will be carried on primarily under the GATT or whether there will be supplemental institutions or arrangements for bargaining. Though there has been criticism of GATT's accomplishments on nontariff and agricultural barriers during the Dillon and Kennedy Rounds, demands for abandoning the GATT have not yet been taken seriously.

2. Assuming that all negotiations will take place predominantly under the GATT auspices, will it be feasible to conduct those of the agricultural and industrial sectors jointly? There is considerable disagreement on this point. Many interest groups and experts feel that the concept of joint negotiations is a fundamental element of the international trade negotiation process, and believe that the failure to adhere to it during the Kennedy Round led to many problems. In other words, they feel agriculture must be treated in the same manner as the other sectors. Others feel strongly that separate negotiations on agricultural trade issues are necessary, and say that the existing rules of the GATT as they apply to agriculture must be modified so as to get at the principal obstacle to international trade liberalization—namely, domestic farm policies. In this view, agriculture is different and must be treated differently.

3. A third major issue is the basis for negotiation. There seems to be general agreement among the experts that *some* method must be devised to measure the degree of protection—to quantify it in monetary terms—that nations give to their agricultural sector through domestic policies. Also, this economic calculation, though expensive and time-consuming,

must precede any realistic, politically determined codes of conduct which might cover restrictive trade devices.

4. A very critical issue is codes of conduct, including rules of competition. Governments must be convinced that many of their present nontariff barriers and farm policies are of little value, although enormously costly, if there is to be a basis for successful negotiations on agricultural restrictions. In this regard, little can be gained by having trade barriers themselves the main topic of discussion during the negotiations. In such an atmosphere—as witnessed in the GATT and before that in the Reciprocal Trade Agreement Acts of the United States—it has been difficult for a country to find an adequate quid, in political terms, for the quo given up when it renounces its protective devices. Prospective poor results in the swapping of trade concessions, therefore, may be an argument against holding agricultural and nontariff negotiations separately.

5. The concept of harmonization of policies is likely to be more successful when countries and industries can agree on issues which can be supported by treaty-bound agreements. This might be possible in the broad areas of health and sanitary regulations, grades, standards, food codes, etc., and even in the administrative interpretation of legislative intent.

6. Ultimately, the fundamental issue is, How do governments obtain the necessary authority to negotiate meaningfully on such questions as nontariff agricultural trade barriers and related matters? As has been strongly noted in this study, agricultural protection has been associated for at least two centuries with social and philosophical issues related to agrarian life and its values. In addition to this, nontariff barriers not only touch on economic policies but in many cases relate to vast administrative bureaucracies in which public employment is an issue. Here the outcome of trade negotiation could, ex ante, be affected by some perceived effect it might have on the authoritarian mechanism.

In sum, both nontariff and agricultural trade barriers are tied up in all kinds of domestic laws, rules, and regulations managed by many different parts of each government. In the United States, for example, there is much congressional resistance to giving the executive branch a blank check; yet, the executive cannot effectively negotiate without some kind of mandate. Because within the executive branch there is competition among the departments as to who will wield the power, here is where the administrative bureaucracies come into play.

7. Finally, there is the necessity of patience. Because of the complexity of the issues in the nontariff and agricultural fields, it is likely to take several years of work to get very far. Perhaps during this time it will be possible to conduct the necessary studies on levels and degrees of protection which almost everyone deems essential for a positive outcome. The length and complexity of the negotiations must be recognized, and time must be allowed for interaction between governments and their parliaments, as well as among governments themselves.

NOTES

CHAPTER 1

1. See GATT, *International Trade, 1975-76* (Geneva: GATT, 1976), pp. 9-19. For more basic observations, see Commission on International Trade and Investment Policy, *United States International Economic Policy in an Interdependent World* (Washington, D.C.: U.S. Government Printing Office, 1971), 1:631 ff.; H. B. Malmgren and D. L. Schlecty, "Rationalizing World Agricultural Trade," *Journal of World Trade Law* 4 (July-August 1970):515-47; and D. Gale Johnson, *World Agriculture in Disarray* (London: Fontana-Collins, 1973), chap. 3, pp. 44-64.

2. Unless otherwise noted, data are from the United Nations *Monthly Bulletin of Statistics* and related United Nations sources. Data include intra-European trade.

3. This position is taken despite the events of the 1973-76 period in countries such as the United States where "free trade" pushed agricultural exports to higher and higher levels—to $21.5 billion in fiscal 1975 and to a record $23 billion in fiscal 1976.

4. To be sure, the long-run effects of support measures on overall levels of economic activity are rather difficult to discuss without evidence. Analysis and discussion might be tied to the extent to which the effective support tends to be associated with flexible or inflexible production factors and whether these are just as flexible or inflexible everywhere else. In the short run, a distinction might be made between those that automatically tend to pump money into the economy as soon as they are taken out—ceteris paribus; e.g., if the external price of beef falls, a variable levy tends to rise and the money raised may not be spent immediately but is lost to traders; a variable deficiency payment will put extra money into the system as well as allowing more goods to come in. Presumably, the role of export promotion and conversion of produce to inferior uses is less negative. This may promote certain kinds of economic activity which may be wasteful but at least qualify as activity.

5. Johnson, *World Agriculture*, pp. 24-27 (my emphasis).

6. See references in Chapter 2.

CHAPTER 2

1. Besides the many hundreds of shorter articles and references, a few of the major studies which grapple with the subject are: Robert D. Baldwin,

Nontariff Distortions of International Trade (Washington, D.C.: Brookings Institution, 1970); H. B. Malmgren, *Trade Wars or Trade Negotiations: Nontariff Barriers and Economic Peacekeeping* (Washington, D.C.: Atlantic Council of the United States, 1970); Gerard and Victoria Curzon, *Hidden Barriers to International Trade* and *Global Assault on Nontariff Trade Barriers,* and Geoffrey Denton and Seamus O'Cleiracain, *Subsidy Issues in International Commerce,* Thames Essays nos. 1, 3, and 5, Trade Policy Research Center (London: Ditchling Press, 1970-72); Commission on International Trade and Investment Policy, *United States International Economic Policy in an Interdependent World,* vol. 1, sec. 5, pt. 2, pp. 617-90; and U.S. Tariff Commission, *Nontariff Trade Barriers,* T. C. publication no. 665 (April 1974).

2. Denton and O'Cleiracain, *Subsidy Issues,* p. 1.

3. Though this is a large number of items, it is, as Gardiner Patterson points out, an arbitrary one to which no special significance should be attached. "In the numbering, the quantitative restrictions of most countries, which may run to fifty or a hundred individual four-digit tariff items, count as one or perhaps two items, and similarly a country's government procurement policy, though it affects many different products, counts as one barrier. At the other extreme, some notifications counted as 'an item' affect only a few products, or even one product when imported from one country" (see Commission on International Trade and Investment Policy, *United States International Economic Policy in an Interdependent World,* 1:621n).

4. Denton and O'Cleiracain, *Subsidy Issues,* pp. 2-4.

5. H. B. Malmgren, *Trade Wars or Trade Negotiations,* p. 13.

6. *Trade* is placed in quotes here because a situation is being described in which the physical process of exchange is negligible or nonexistent.

7. J. S. Hillman, "Economic Aspects of Interstate Agricultural Trade Barriers in the Western Region" (Ph.D. dissertation, University of California, Berkeley, 1954); J. S. Hillman and J. D. Rowell, *A Summary of Laws Relating to the Interstate Movement of Agricultural Products in the Eleven Western States,* report no. 109 (Tucson: University of Arizona Agricultural Experiment Station, 1952).

8. For a more complete discussion of this problem, see John B. Condliffe, *The Reconstruction of World Trade* (New York: Norton, 1940), pp. 31 ff.

9. For some comments on particular regulations and the implications of their administration, see Gerard and Victoria Curzon, *Hidden Barriers,* pp. 26-33.

10. F. Bane, "Administrative Marketing Barriers," *Law and Contemporary Problems* 8, no. 2 (Spring 1941): 376-90.

11. Available transport facilities presumably depend in the main on the historic flow of goods. One may agree that national frontiers are moderately permanent and may have limited the present network of crossings of frontiers. There are, however, offsetting situations which may make trading out of

the country relatively profitable: (a) Production of internal companies engaged in carrying trade within the country. External navigation acts are no longer tolerated except on aid shipments. (b) Colonial-type structures with heavy past investment in ports, etc. (These—combined with considerations about market splitting by big firms—*may* lead to choice of trading site with more external activity than is justified in an ideal world after a long adjustment period.) For instance, suppose that only a minor part of the expansion of grain farming in the United Kingdom since 1938 were due to support measures; there still might be a residual handicap arising from a concentration of marketing facilities at port. The principal point is that domestic sales as well as trade expansion can meet what appear as unnatural obstacles.

12. A most useful treatment is found in W. M. Corden, *The Theory of Protection* (Oxford: Clarendon Press, 1971). Theoretical treatments of special cases of less than completely free trade based on the assumed existence of market or infant industry distortions or on cases which assume different economic objectives have been developed in recent literature. Two examples are: J. Bhagwati, "The Generalized Theory of Distortions and Welfare," in *Trade Balance of Payments and Growth,* ed. Bhagwati et al. (Amsterdam: North Holland, 1971), pp. 69-90; and H. G. Johnson, "An Economic Theory of Protectionism, Tariff Bargaining and the Formulation of Customs Unions," *Journal of Political Economy* 73 (June 1965): 254-83.

13. For a more complete elaboration of certain difficulties, see: Denton and O'Cleiracain, *Subsidy Issues,* chap. 2, "Theory of Distortions and Interventions"; Brian Hindley, "Negotiations on Nontariff Barriers," chap. 6 in *Towards an Open World Economy* (London: Macmillan, 1977), pp. 127-32; and Baldwin, *Nontariff Distortions,* as well as references cited in those publications.

14. It is difficult to form a sound judgment concerning the degree to which a country makes unfair use of biological precautions and marketing standards which are legitimate in certain circumstances. For example, as originally provided in the U.S. Tariff Act of 1930, the legislation enacted to check the spread of rinderpest (foot-and-mouth disease) was, no doubt, largely protective in intent (see Percy Bidwell, *The Invisible Tariff* [New York: Council on Foreign Relations, 1939], pp. 211-12). Over the years, the precaution and legitimate exercise of government intervention in this matter have appeared to be more economically rational and acceptable.

15. See FAO, *Processed Agricultural Products and Agricultural Adjustment,* C73/LIM/11 (Rome, November 1973).

16. I am indebted to Brian Hindley's treatment in "Negotiations on Nontariff Barriers" in formulating this point.

17. J. Tobin, "Economic Growth as an Objective of Government Policy," *American Economic Review* 54 (1964): 11.

18. G. Ohlin, "Trade in a Non-Laissez Faire World," in *International*

Economic Relations, ed. Paul Samuelson (London: Macmillan, 1969), p. 174.

19. Ibid.

20. Hindley, "Negotiations on Nontariff Barriers," p. 129.

CHAPTER 3

1. For more definitive studies and detailed treatments of agricultural protection and adjustment problems in Western Europe and the United States, see the following: M. R. Benedict, *Farm Policies of the United States, 1790-1950* (New York: Twentieth Century Fund, 1953); J. B. Condliffe, *The Commerce of Nations* (London: George Allen and Unwin, 1951); E. M. Ojala, *Agricultural and Economic Progress* (London: Oxford University Press, 1952); W. Röpke, *German Commercial Policy* (London: Longmans, 1934); M. Tracy, *Agriculture in Western Europe* (London: Jonathan Cape, 1964); P. L. Yates, *Food, Land and Manpower in Western Europe* (London: Macmillan, 1960).

2. This point was made in private conversation with the author.

3. Benedict, *Farm Policies,* pp. 58-60.

4. H. Leipmann, *Tariff Levels and the Economic Unity of Europe* (London: George Allen and Unwin, 1938).

5. Tracy, *Agriculture in Western Europe,* pp. 27-32, 120-22.

6. P. L. Yates, *Forty Years of Foreign Trade* (London: George Allen and Unwin, 1959).

7. T. Mun, *England's Treasure by Forraign Trade* (London and Oxford, published for the Economic History Society by B. Blackwell, 1949).

8. W. M. Corden, "Tariffs and Protectionism," in *The International Encyclopedia of Social Sciences,* vol. 8 (New York: Macmillan Co. and Free Press, 1968), pp. 113-21.

9. Illustrative of the measures and of the involvement of various administrative and regulatory agencies is the title page of the report by a Study Group of the British Coordinating Committee for International Studies, "Memorandum on British External Economic Policy in Recent Years, Part II" (1939), which contains the following outline:

A. Financial Policy
B. Commercial Policy
   (i)   General Tariff Administration
        a) Protective Duties and the Import Duties Advisory Committee
        b) Retaliatory Duties
        c) Revenue Duties
        d) Merchandise Marks Acts
   (ii)   Statutory Quotas
        a) In connection with Marketing Schemes
        b) Under Ottawa Agreements Act

c) Under Sea Fishing Industry Act
d) Dyestuffs
e) Importation of Cinematograph Films
f) Admission of Aliens
(iii) Processing Duties
a) Wheat Act
b) Empire Cotton Growing Corporation
(iv) "Voluntary" Administrative Machinery
a) "Voluntary" Quantitative Restrictions of Imports
b) "Voluntary" action by Cartels
c) "Voluntary" cooperation in Statutory Import Quotas
(v) Administration of Government Subsidies
a) North Atlantic Shipping
b) British Shipping (Assistance) Act, 1935
(vi) Developing Trade Relations
a) Credits for Export
b) Department of Overseas Trade
c) Marketing Schemes
(vii) Administrative Protection

10. E. M. Ojala, "Europe and the World Agricultural Economy," conference paper no. 1., Agricultural Adjustment Conference, University of Newcastle-upon-Tyne, July 1972, p. 17.

11. Ibid., p. 20.

12. G. Haberler, et al., *Trends in International Trade* (Geneva: GATT, 1958), pp. 81-84.

CHAPTER 4

1. Commission on International Trade and Investment Policy, *United States International Economic Policy in an Interdependent World*, 1:621.

2. Ibid.

3. Working groups representing major trading countries were set up in GATT, not only on import restriction but also in other sectors such as measures affecting (1) exports, (2) production, (3) other relevant areas, in particular, health and sanitary regulations.

4. B. Balassa, *The Structure of Protection in Developing Countries* (Baltimore: Johns Hopkins University Press, 1971).

5. Ibid.

6. U.S. Department of Agriculture, Economic Research Service, *Prospects for Agricultural Trade with the USSR*, Foreign Series report no. 356 (Washington, D.C., 1973), especially the article by D. Gale Johnson, pp. 43-50.

CHAPTER 5

1. For example, W. M. Corden, *Trade Policy and Economic Welfare* (London: Oxford University Press, 1974).

2. For an up-to-date statutory statement of Section 22, see Appendix A.

3. President Nixon asked for a temporary suspension of the quota on wheat in early 1974. He also increased the import quota on cheeses by 100 million pounds for the three-month period January 3–March 31, 1974.

4. Johnson, *World Agriculture*, p. 25.

5. Quotas through Section 22 have been imposed on eleven different commodities or groups of commodities since its enactment. Only four of these remained as of 1973.

6. For good treatments of tariff and quota theory, see Corden, *Theory of Protection*, chap. 9; and C. P. Kindleberger, *International Economics*, 3d ed. (Homewood, Ill.: Irwin, 1963), chap. 13.

7. "Special Report on Examination of Divided Authority over Agricultural Import Quotas under Section 22 of the Agricultural Adjustment Act, as Amended," by the Comptroller General of the United States, 1961; "Study Group Review of the Special Report on Examination of Authority over Agricultural Import Quotas under Section 22 of the Agricultural Adjustment Act, as Amended," USDA, October 1962 (prepared in response to the foregoing report).

8. See UNCTAD, TD/B/C, 2/83, November 13, 1969, p. 6.

9. The following objectives of the Common Agricultural Policy correspond closely to national policies of member countries and to the underlying reasons given for government intervention in agriculture and trade elsewhere in the world, namely: (a) to increase agricultural productivity by developing technical progress and by ensuring the rational development of agricultural production and the optimum utilization of the factors of production, particularly labor; (b) to ensure thereby a fair standard of living for the agricultural population, particularly by the increasing of the individual earnings of persons engaged in agriculture; (c) to stabilize markets; (d) to guarantee regular supplies; and (e) to ensure reasonable prices in supplies to consumers. Other parts of Article 39 of the Treaty of Rome state that account should be taken of the social structure of agriculture, the structural and natural disparities between various agricultural regions, the need to make appropriate adjustments gradually, and that agriculture in each of the member countries is an important sector within the economy as a whole.

10. T. Josling, "The EEC and the World Market for Temperate Zone Agricultural Products," paper presented at the Royal Economic Conference, York, England, September 25-28, 1972.

11. The EEC concepts are based on T. Josling, "More Problems and Less Prospects in the EEC," in *Agriculture and Britain's Trade Policy Dilemma,*

Thames Essay no. 2, Trade Policy Research Center (London, Ditchling Press, 1970).

12. There is another opinion as to the operative classifications of the variable levy. The difference with the authors' interpretation may be more apparent—or semantic—than real. Ernest Koenig, U.S. agricultural attaché in Geneva, says, "I do not believe that the variable levy acts like a quota. It does not limit imports quantitatively but only indirectly via its price effects. If demand is inelastic, the variable levy does not limit imports. It must not be forgotten that the variable levy raises the world price to, or somewhat above, the internal EC price. Hence, the incidence of the levy is high as a percentage of the world market price but generally not too high as a percentage of the domestic price. I believe the variable levy can be considered to be a *variable specific duty*" (private correspondence with the author, 1977).

13. Malmgren and Schlechty, "Rationalizing World Agricultural Trade," p. 517.

14. Malmgren, *Trade Wars or Trade Negotiations*, p. 40.

15. Newsletter on the Common Agricultural Policy, no. 11, November 1968.

16. I am indebted to Dr. D. Gale Johnson for this and other general observations on government export intervention. See "Are High Farm Prices Here to Stay?," *The Morgan Guaranty Survey* (New York: Morgan Guaranty Trust Co., August 1974), pp. 9-14.

17. The Cocoa Agreement, which became effective June 30, 1973, has had little influence over the cocoa market. The purpose of the agreement was to stabilize cocoa bean prices within a given range by using, in the six major producing countries, export quotas which are reduced as prices fall, and a buffer stock from which sales are to be made when prices approach the upper end of the range. Quotas have never been implemented, as cocoa prices have remained well above the price range, and the buffer stock has not accumulated because of tight supplies.

18. The *Wall Street Journal* of October 9, 1974, in an editorial, "The Risks of Export Controls," put it this way: "The danger lies principally in the beguiling political appeal of seemingly simple solutions to economic problems. If you want to bring down the price of doughnuts what could be more simple than cutting off exports of wheat? And since that is such a good idea why not shut off exports of lots of other things, too, so we can have more of everything at home and prices will come down? Indeed, prices might come down and so would jobs, profits, stock prices and all that other economic structure that rapidly expanding world trade has built in the postwar era. No one would find it to their liking."

19. Heavy reliance is placed on published materials for these cases. Specifically, very helpful were U.S. Department of Agriculture Foreign Agricultural Service circulars ATP-1-72 to ATP-10-72, GATT documents of the

Agricultural Committee, and FAO Committee on Commodity Problems (CCP) reports on particular commodities.

20. Commission on International Trade and Investment Policy, *United States International Economic Policy in an Interdependent World*, 2:186.

21. This is on the basis of four-digit Brussels Tariff Nomenclature (BTN). A warning should be given, however, with respect to the relevance of the numbers of different headings as a measure of the degree of total protection by quantitative barriers for a country's agriculture. Other factors must be weighed. For example, while the United States has quantitative restrictions falling within only nine different headings (meats and dairy products [4], wheat [1], peanuts [1], sugar [2]) of the 177 in the agricultural part of the BTN (compared to 34 for Japan), these products accounted for almost half of its total agricultural output.

22. The United States, which had been demanding further liberalization in the Japanese market, had a special interest in the following products which were liberalized: fresh grapefruit, apples, grapes, lemon juice, soybean meal, vegetable oils, margarine and shortening, live cattle and swine, pork and sausages, canned corn, and instant potatoes.

23. Commission in International Trade and Investment Policy, *United States International Economic Policy in an Interdependent World*, 2:186.

24. Specifically, under Sections XII and XVIII of the GATT regulations.

25. Since the citrus quotas are limited principally to the third quarter, this rules out European countries as major beneficiaries. It might be argued that the position of the Caribbean is being protected in that a bargaining counter is being retained which might be used to promote its interest in United States trade. It seems more likely that the United Kingdom is protecting its capital abroad. One may note that both the citrus and banana markets in the United Kingdom have been less buoyant than might have been expected, looking ahead from 1955. One of the reasons may be an adverse dynamic trend associated with population structure (a kind of vintage model of housewives) whose effect may be as high as -.6 percent per annum for oranges, -2.0 percent for other citrus, and -.7 percent for bananas. Clearly, over periods of ten years this can cut into presumed expansion from income growth and from the cheaper supplies available and tend to strengthen the hand of those (in the Caribbean, etc.) who want to protect what market they have.

26. All data are from the Foreign Agricultural Service, USDA.

CHAPTER 6

1. United States Tariff Commission, *Nontariff Trade Barriers*.

2. Selected from *Nontariff Trade Barriers,* part 2 of a Report to the Committee on Finance, U.S. Senate, and Its Subcommittee on International Trade; also from United States Department of Commerce, *International*

Commerce (Washington, D.C.: U.S. Government Printing Office, 1971), p. 10, which contains an inventory of all the impediments mentioned for all commodities and import practices; this, and inventories for sixty-nine other countries, are contained therein; it was based on a detailed list of trade practices contained in a study by the United States House Ways and Means Committee.

3. Frank G. McKnight, *Foreign Agriculture* (Washington, D.C.: USDA, FAS), March 13, 1972, p. 12.

4. The anomalous agricultural trade situation which began in 1972 has resulted in many accommodations—and even reversals—in trade programs. As noted elsewhere, in early 1974 the United States temporarily suspended its import quota on wheat and expanded the import quota on cheese.

5. Josling, *Agriculture and Britain's Trade Policy Dilemma*, pp. 18–34.

6. Great Britain Ministry of Agriculture, Fisheries and Food, *Annual Review and Determination of Guarantees, 1969* (London: HM Stationery Office, 1969), p. 5.

7. For more information on the general subject of the United Kingdom and the EEC, see D. K. Britton "Problems of Adapting U.K. Institutions in the EEC," Conference Paper no. 9, Agricultural Adjustment Conference, University of Newcastle-upon-Tyne, 1972.

8. U.S. Department of Agriculture, Foreign Agricultural Service, "Nontariff Barriers Affecting Trade in Agricultural Products—United Kingdom," *Agricultural Trade Policy*, FAS circular ATP-8-72, 1972, p. 3.

9. M. Auge-Laribe, Conseil National Economique, *La Politique agricole de la France de 1880 à 1940* (Paris: Presses Universitaires de France, 1950).

10. A detailed classification of European Community nontariff agricultural barriers may be found in "Nontariff Barriers Affecting Trade in Agricultural Products—EEC," *Agricultural Trade Policy*, USDA, FAS circular ATP-10-72, December 1972. Much of the following commentary comes from that circular.

11. Probably the most significant analytical treatment of EECV agricultural protection—and that of selected other countries—can be found in T. Josling and J. S. Hillman, *Agricultural Protection and Stabilization Policies: A Framework of Measurement in the Context of Agricultural Adjustment*, FAO C75/LIM/2 (Rome, FAO: 1975).

12. For a recent summary of Japan's trade policy and protection, see FAO, *International Agricultural Adjustment: A Case Study of Japan*, C73/LIM/3, November 1973, pp. 24–28.

13. Ibid., p. 26.

14. U.S. Department of Agriculture, Foreign Agricultural Service, "Japan Institutes New Trade Measures, Cuts Tariffs on Some Agricultural Products," *Agricultural Trade Policy*, FAS circular ATP-7-72, December 1972.

15. U.S. Department of Agriculture, "Nontariff Trade Barriers Affecting

Trade in Agricultural Products—Japan," *Agricultural Trade Policy*, FAS circular ATP-2-72, June 1972, pp. 2-4.

CHAPTER 7

1. I am grateful for the assistance of William J. Hanekamp, former research associate, Department of Agricultural Economics, University of Arizona, in preparing this chapter.

2. U.S. Department of Agriculture, FAS, *Foreign Agriculture*, Vol. XII, No. 29 (Washington, D.C., July 15, 1974), p. 3.

3. U.S. Department of Agriculture, Foreign Agricultural Service, *World Agricultural Production and Trade* (Washington, D.C.: USDA, December 1973), p. 15.

4. Information obtained from Foreign Agricultural Service, USDA.

5. U.S. Department of Agriculture, Foreign Agricultural Service, "Nontariff Barriers Affecting Trade in Agricultural Products—EEC," *Agricultural Trade Policy*, FAS circular ATP-10-72, October 1972, p. 2.

6. Ibid.

7. New Zealand Meat Producers Board, "New Zealand Meat Seminar," papers presented at seminar held in London, October 16-18, 1972, p. 64.

8. Ibid., p. 65.

9. Ibid., p. 57.

10. International Trade Centre, *The Market for Manufacturing Grade Beef in the United Kingdom and the European Economic Community* (Geneva: UNCTAD, GATT, 1971), p. 53.

11. Ibid., pp. 76, 85, 99, 127.

12. New Zealand Meat Producers Board, "New Zealand Meat Seminar," p. 133.

13. U.S. Department of Agriculture, Foreign Agricultural Service, "Nontariff Barriers Affecting Trade in Agricultural Products—EEC," *Agricultural Trade Policy*, FAS circular ATP-10-72, October, 1972, p. 3.

14. New Zealand Meat Producers Board, "New Zealand Meat Seminar," p. 28.

15. Peter J. Needham, "How Ireland Conquered the British Beef Market," *CALF News* 12, no. 3 (March 1974): 54, 55, 82.

16. U.S. Department of Agriculture, Foreign Agricultural Service, "Nontariff Barriers Affecting Trade in Agricultural Products—Denmark," *Agricultural Trade Policy*, FAS circular, ATP-5-72, September 1972, p. 1.

17. International Trade Centre, *Market for Manufacturing Grade Beef*, p. 65.

18. A. P. Power and S. A. Harris, "A Cost/Benefit Evaluation of Alternative Policies for Foot-and-Mouth Disease in Great Britain," *Journal of Agricultural Economics* 24, no. 3 (1973): 573-98.

19. As of 1971, licenses were available for imports from the following countries other than South America:

Beef only	Beef, mutton, lamb	Beef, mutton, lamb, pork	Miscellaneous
Austria	Bulgaria	Denmark	Cuba
Botswana	France		Rumania
Holland	Poland		Republic of South Africa
Hungary	Yugoslavia		Sweden
South West Africa			
Switzerland			
United States			

20. FAO, *National Regulations Affecting Imports of Livestock and Meat*, CCP: ME 72-8, April 1972, p. 11.

21. U.S. Department of Agriculture, Foreign Agricultural Service, "Nontariff Barriers Affecting Trade in Agricultural Products—Denmark."

22. *United States Statutes at Large*, 88th Cong. 2d sess. (1964), vol. 78 (Washington, D.C.: U.S. Government Printing Office, 1965), pp. 594–95.

23. U.S. Tariff Commission, *Summaries of Trade and Tariff Information*, vol. 1, *Animals and Meat*, T.C. publication No. 250 (Washington, D.C.: U.S. Government Printing Office, 1968).

24. U.S. Department of Agriculture, Foreign Agricultural Service, "Nontariff Barriers Affecting Trade in Agricultural Products—Japan," *Agricultural Trade Policy*, FAS circular ATP-2-72, June 1972, p. 3.

25. Ibid.

26. Ibid.

27. FAO, *National Regulations*, pp. 14, 22, 31, 37, 38, 42, 47, 52.

CHAPTER 8

1. Johnson, *World Agriculture*, pp. 250 ff.

2. For example see Malmgren, *Trade Wars or Trade Negotiations*, pp. 74 ff. Malmgren spent two years immediately after the Kennedy Round leading U.S. delegations to the GATT work on nontariff barriers, agricultural trade problems, and border taxes.

3. All five rounds of negotiations which took place between 1947 and 1952 were concerned almost entirely with tariffs. Methods of negotiating weren't very different from prewar bilateral bargaining, even though they took place in a multilateral framework. The Kennedy Round of negotiations which began in 1962 exposed the degree to which governments were involved in a whole range of policies of intervention that, either by design or by practical effect, distorted the market processes of international trade. The Smithsonian Agreement of 1971 broke an international monetary logjam, and

following intensive bilateral negotiations, there emerged an increasing commitment from the United States, the European Community, and Japan to another full-scale trade negotiation, under GATT auspices.

4. Brian Hindley, *Britain's Position on Non-Tariff Protection* (London: Trade Policy Research Center, 1972), pp. 45, 49.

5. A specific suggestion is the establishment of machinery to review price developments in various countries (1) with respect to their influence on trade and the level of self-sufficiency and (2) with a view to coordinating the transfer of resources to products for which there was demand. Machinery of this kind would be an important addition to the GATT function of arbitrating trade disputes in that it would include a significant measure of mutual discussion of domestic farm-support policies. This might prove an effective forum for discussion of the European grain price level or the quantitative restrictions on American dairy imports. (Trade Policy Research Center, "British, European and American Interests in International Negotiations on Agricultural Trade," Staff Paper no. 3 [London, 1973], p. 11.)

6. Oliver Long, "The Multilateral Trade Negotiations in a Changing World Economy," address to the Swedish National Committee of the International Chambers of Commerce, Stockholm, March 19, 1974.

7. For references, see Trade Policy Research Center, "British, European and American Interests," pp. 12-13. One of the best of the analyses is Sidney Golt, *The GATT Negotiations, 1973-75: A Guide to the Issues* (London, British-North American Committee, April 1974), p. 88.

8. H. B. Malmgren, "Negotiating Nontariff Barriers: The Harmonization of National Economic Policies," in *U.S. Foreign Economic Policy for the 1970s: A New Approach to New Realities* (Washington, D.C.: National Planning Association, 1971), pp. 79-109. See also H. B. Malmgren, *Trade Policy and Negotiations in the 1970's*, a statement prepared for hearings before the Subcommittee on Foreign Economic Policy of the Joint Economic Committee, U.S. Congress, March 17, 1970, pp. 38-42.

9. This term is used by Robert B. Schwinger. See his "New Concepts and Methods in Foreign Trade Negotiations," *American Journal of Agricultural Economics* 51, no. 5 (December 1969): 1338-49.

10. Malmgren, *Trade Policy and Negotiations in the 1970's*, pp. 40.

11. Hindley, *Britain's Position on Non-Tariff Protection*, pp. 46-47.

12. The final report of this panel was not available to me when this manuscript was drafted. I am grateful to Barbara Sharkey, Foreign Agricultural Service, USDA, Washington, D.C., for comments on the code.

13. Atlantic Council, *U.S. Agriculture in a World Context: Policies and Approaches for the Next Decade* (Washington, D.C.: Praeger, 1973), p. 117.

14. Johnson, *World Agriculture*, pp. 257 ff.

APPENDIX A

Section 22 of the Agricultural Adjustment Act
of 1933 as Reenacted and Amended[1]

(a) Whenever the Secretary of Agriculture has reason to believe that any article or articles are being or are practically certain to be imported into the United States under such conditions and in such quantities as to render or tend to render ineffective, or materially interfere with, any program or operation undertaken under this title or the Soil Conservation and Domestic Allotment Act, as amended, or section 32, Public Law Numbered 320, Seventy-fourth Congress, approved August 24, 1935, as amended, or any loan, purchase, or other program or operation undertaken by the Department of Agriculture, or any agency operating under its direction, with respect to any agricultural commodity or product thereof, or to reduce substantially the amount of any product processed in the United States from any agricultural commodity or product thereof with respect to which any such program or operation is being undertaken, he shall so advise the President, and, if the President agrees that there is reason for such belief, the President shall cause an immediate investigation to be made by the United States Tariff Commission, which shall give precedence to investigations under this section to determine such facts. Such investigation shall be made after due notice and opportunity for hearing to interested parties, and shall be conducted subject to such regulations as the President shall specify.

(b) If, on the basis of such investigation and report to him of findings and recommendations made in connection therewith, the President finds the existence of such facts, he shall by proclamation impose such fees not in excess of 50 per centum ad valorem or such quantitative limitations on any article or articles

which may be entered, or withdrawn from warehouse, for consumption as he finds and declares shown by such investigation to
be necessary in order that the entry of such article or articles will
not render or tend to render ineffective, or materially interfere
with, any program or operation referred to in subsection (a) of
this section, or reduce substantially the amount of any product
processed in the United States from any such agricultural commodity or product thereof with respect to which any such program or operation is being undertaken: *Provided,* that no proclamation under this section shall impose any limitation on the total
quantity of any article or articles which may be entered, or withdrawn from warehouse, for consumption which reduces such permissible total quantity to proportionately less than 50 per centum
of the total quantity of such article or articles which was entered,
or withdrawn from warehouse, for consumption during a representative period as determined by the President; *And provided further,*
That in designating any article or articles, the President may describe them by physical qualities, value, use, or upon such other
bases as he shall determine.

In any case where the Secretary of Agriculture determines and
reports to the President with regard to any article or articles that a
condition exists requiring emergency treatment, the President may
take immediate action under this section, without awaiting the
recommendations of the Tariff Commission, such action to continue in effect pending the report and recommendations of the
Tariff Commission and action thereon by the President.[2]

(c) The fees and limitations imposed by the President by proclamation under this section and any revocation, suspension, or
modification thereof, shall become effective on such date as shall
be therein specified, and such fees shall be treated for administrative purposes and for the purposes of section 32 of Public Law
Numbered 320, Seventy-fourth Congress, approved August 24,
1935, as amended, as duties imposed by the Tariff Act of 1930,
but such fees shall not be considered as duties for the purpose of
granting any preferential concession under any international
obligation of the United States.

(d) After investigation, report, finding, and declaration in the
manner provided in the case of a proclamation issued pursuant to
subsection (b) of this section, any proclamation or provision of

such proclamation may be suspended or terminated by the President whenever he finds and proclaims that the circumstances requiring the proclamation or provision thereof no longer exist or may be modified by the President whenever he finds and proclaims that changed circumstances require such modification to carry out the purposes of this section.

(e) Any decision of the President as to facts under this section shall be final.

(f) No trade agreement or other international agreement heretofore or hereafter entered into by the United States shall be applied in a manner inconsistent with the requirements of this section.[3]

NOTES

1. See also section 202(a) of the Agricultural Act of 1956. Section 22 was added by the act of August 24, 1935 (49 Stat. 773). Action under this section, as originally enacted, could be taken only with respect to articles the importation of which was found to be adversely affecting programs or operations under the Agricultural Adjustment Act of 1933. Section 22 has been amended several times and was revised in its entirety by section 3 of the Agricultural Act of 1948 (62 Stat. 1247) and again by section 3 of the act of June 28, 1950 (64 Stat. 261). Regulations governing investigations under this section are set forth in Executive Order 7233, dated November 23, 1935, and in 19 CFR 201, 204.

2. Paragraph added by section 104 of the Trade Agreements Extension Act of 1953 (67 Stat. 472).

3. The provisions of this subsection (f) were substituted for earlier provisions by section 8(b) of the Trade Agreements Extension Act of 1951, approved June 16, 1951 (65 Stat. 72, 75).

APPENDIX B
THE TOKYO DECLARATION
OF GATT MINISTERS[1]

1. The ministers, having considered the report of the Preparatory Committee for the Trade Negotiations and having noted that a number of governments have decided to enter into comprehensive multilateral trade negotiations in the framework of GATT and that other governments have indicated their intention to make a decision as soon as possible, declare the negotiations officially open. Those governments which have decided to negotiate have notified the Director-General of GATT to this effect, and the Ministers agree that it will be open to any other government, through a notification to the Director-General, to participate in the negotiations. The Ministers hope that the negotiations will involve the active participation of as many countries as possible. They expect the negotiations to be engaged effectively as rapidly as possible, and that, to that end, the governments concerned will have such authority as may be required.

2. The negotiations shall aim to:

— achieve the expansion and ever-greater liberalization of world trade and improvement in the standard of living and welfare of the people of the world, objectives which can be achieved, *inter alia,* through the progressive dismantling of obstacles to trade and the improvement of the international framework for the conduct of world trade.

— secure additional benefits for the international trade of developing countries so as to achieve a substantial increase in their foreign exchange earnings, the diversification of their exports, the acceleration of the rate of growth of their trade, taking into account their development needs, an improvement in the possibilities for these countries to participate in the expansion of world trade and a better balance as between developed and developing countries in the sharing of the advantages resulting from this expansion, through, in the largest possible measure, a substantial improvement in the conditions of access for the products of interest to the developing countries and, wherever appropriate, measures designed to attain stable, equitable and remunerative prices for primary products.

To this end, co-ordinated efforts shall be made to solve, in an equitable way the trade problems of all participating countries, taking into account the specific trade problems of the developing countries.

3. To this end, the negotiations should aim, *inter alia,* to:

(a) conduct negotiations on tariffs by employment of appropriate formulae of as general application as possible;

(b) reduce or eliminate nontariff measures or, where this is not appropriate, to reduce or eliminate their trade restricting or distorting effects, and to bring such measures under more effective international discipline;

(c) include an examination of the possibilities for the co-ordinated reduction or elimination of all barriers to trade in selected sectors as a complementary technique;

(d) include an examination of the adequacy of the multilateral safeguard system, considering particularly the modalities of application of Article XIX, with a view to furthering trade liberalization and preserving its results;

(e) include, as regards agriculture, an approach to negotiations which, while in line with the general objectives of the negotiations, should take account of the special characteristics and problems in this sector;

(f) treat tropical products as a special and priority sector.

4. The negotiations shall cover tariffs, nontariff barriers and other measures which impede or distort international trade in both industrial and agricultural products, including tropical products and raw materials, whether in primary form or at any stage of processing including in particular products of export interest to developing countries and measures affecting their exports.

5. The negotiations shall be conducted on the basis of the principles of mutual advantage, mutual commitment and overall reciprocity, while observing the most-favoured-nation clause, and

consistently with the provisions of the General Agreement relating to such negotiations. Participants shall jointly endeavour in the negotiations to achieve, by appropriate methods, an overall balance of advantage at the highest possible level. The developed countries do not expect reciprocity for commitments made by them in the negotiations to reduce or remove tariff and other barriers to the trade of developing countries, i.e., the developed countries do not expect the developing countries, in the course of the trade negotiations, to make contributions which are inconsistent with their individual development, financial and trade needs. The Ministers recognize the need for special measures to be taken in the negotiations to assist the developing countries in their efforts to increase their export earnings and promote their economic development and, where appropriate for priority attention to be given to products or areas of interest to developing countries. They also recognize the importance of maintaining and improving the Generalized System of Preferences. They further recognize the importance of the application of differential measures to developing countries in ways which will provide special and more favourable treatment for them in areas of the negotiation where this is feasible and appropriate.

6. The Ministers recognize that the particular situation and problems of the least developed among the developing countries shall be given special attention, and stress the need to ensure that these countries receive special treatment in the context of any general or specific measures taken in favour of the developing countries during the negotiations.

7. The policy of liberalizing world trade cannot be carried out successfully in the absence of parallel efforts to set up a monetary system which shields the world economy from the shocks and imbalances which have previously occurred. The Ministers will not lose sight of the fact that the efforts which are to be made in the trade field imply continuing efforts to maintain orderly conditions and to establish a durable and equitable monetary system.

The Ministers recognize equally that the new phase in the liberalization of trade which it is their intention to undertake should facilitate the orderly functioning of the monetary system.

The Ministers recognize that they should bear these considerations in mind both at the opening of and throughout the negotiations. Efforts in these two fields will thus be able to contribute effectively to an improvement of international economic relations, taking into account the special characteristics of the economies of the developing countries and their problems.

8. The negotiations shall be considered as one undertaking, the various elements of which shall move forward together.

9. Support is reaffirmed for the principles, rules and disciplines provided for under the General Agreement.[2] Consideration shall be given to improvements in the international framework for the conduct of world trade which might be desirable in the light of progress in the negotiations and, in this endeavour, care shall be taken to ensure that any measures introduced as a result are consistent with the overall objectives and principles of the trade negotiations and particularly of trade liberalization.

10. A Trade Negotiations Committee is established, with authority, taking into account the present Declaration, *inter alia:*

(a) to elaborate and put into effect detailed trade negotiating plans and to establish appropriate negotiating procedures, including special procedures for the negotiations between developed and developing countries;

(b) to supervise the progress of the negotiations.

The Trade Negotiations Committee shall be open to participating governments.[3] The Trade Negotiations Committee shall hold its opening meeting not later than 1 November 1973.

11. The Ministers intend that the trade negotiations be concluded in 1975.

NOTES

1. Adopted on September 14, 1973, by the ministers of about one hundred countries represented at a GATT ministerial conference in Tokyo. The text is reproduced from the *International Economic Report of the President,* together with the *Annual Report of the Council on International Economic Policy* (Washington, D.C.: U.S. Government Printing Office, February 1974), pp. 112-13.

2. This does not necessarily represent the views of representatives of countries not now parties to the General Agreement. (Footnote in original.)

3. Including the European Communities. (Footnote in original.)

APPENDIX C
PUBLIC LAW 88–482,
AUGUST 22, 1964

AN ACT

To provide for the free importation of certain wild animals, and to provide for the imposition of quotas on certain meat and meat products.

Be it enacted by the Senate and House of Representatives of the United States of America in Congress assembled, That (a) item 852.20 of title I of the Tariff Act of 1930 (Tariff Schedules of the United States; 28 F.R., part II, August 17, 1963) is amended to read as follows:

"852.20 Wild animals (including birds and fish) imported for use, or for sale for use, in any scientific public collection for exhibition for scientific or educational purposes.........Free Free"

(b) Headnote 1 of part 4 of schedule 8 of such title I is amended by striking out "item 850.50," and inserting in lieu thereof "items 850.50 and 852.20,".

(c) The amendments made by this section shall take effect on the tenth day after the date of the enactment of this Act.

Sec. 2. (a) It is the policy of the Congress that the aggregate quantity of the articles specified in items 106.10 (relating to fresh, chilled, or frozen cattle meat) and 106.20 (relating to fresh, chilled, or frozen meat of goats and sheep, except lambs) of the Tariff Schedules of the United States which may be imported into the United States in any calendar year beginning after December 31, 1964, should not exceed 725,400,000 pounds; except that this quantity shall be increased or decreased for any calendar year by the same percentage that estimated average annual domestic commercial production of these articles in that calendar year and the two preceding calendar years increases or decreases in comparison with the average annual domestic commercial production of these articles during the years 1959 through 1963, inclusive.

217

(b) The Secretary of Agriculture, for each calendar year after 1964, shall estimate and publish—

(1) before the beginning of such calendar year, the aggregate quantity prescribed for such calendar year by subsection (a), and

(2) before the first day of each calendar quarter in such calendar year, the aggregate quantity of the articles described in subsection (a) which (but for this section) would be imported in such calendar year. In applying paragraph (2) for the second or any succeeding calendar quarter in any calendar year, actual imports for the preceding calendar quarter or quarters in such calendar year shall be taken into account to the extent data is available.

(c) (1) If the aggregate quantity estimated before any calendar quarter by the Secretary of Agriculture pursuant to subsection (b) (2) equals or exceeds 110 percent of the aggregate quantity estimated by him pursuant to subsection (b) (1), and if there is no limitation in effect under this section with respect to such calendar year, the President shall by proclamation limit the total quantity of the articles described in subsection (a) which may be entered, or withdrawn from warehouse, for consumption, during such calendar year, to the aggregate quantity estimated for such calendar year by the Secretary of Agriculture pursuant to subsection (b) (1).

(2) If the aggregate quantity estimated before any calendar quarter by the Secretary of Agriculture pursuant to subsection (b) (2) does not equal or exceed 110 percent of the aggregate quantity estimated by him pursuant to subsection (b) (1), and if a limitation is in effect under this section with respect to such calendar year, such limitation shall cease to apply as of the first day of such calendar quarter; except that any limitation which has been in effect for the third calendar quarter of any calendar year shall continue in effect for the fourth calendar quarter of such year unless the proclamation is suspended or the total quantity is increased pursuant to subsection (d).

(3) The Secretary of Agriculture shall allocate the total quantity proclaimed under paragraph (1), and any increase in such quantity pursuant to subsection (d), among supplying countries on the basis of the shares such countries supplied to the United States market during a representative period of the articles described in subsection (a), except that due account may be given to

special factors which have affected or may affect the trade in such articles. The Secretary of Agriculture shall certify such allocations to the Secretary of the Treasury.

(d) The President may suspend any proclamation made under subsection (c), or increase the total quantity proclaimed under such subsection, if he determines and proclaims that—

(1) such action is required by overriding economic or national security interests of the United States, giving special weight to the importance to the nation of the economic well-being of the domestic livestock industry;

(2) the supply of articles of the kind described in subsection (a) will be inadequate to meet domestic demand at reasonable prices; or

(3) trade agreements entered into after the date of the enactment of this Act ensure that the policy set forth in subsection (a) will be carried out. Any such suspension shall be for such period, and any such increase shall be in such amount, as the President determines and proclaims to be necessary to carry out the purposes of this subsection.

(e) The Secretary of Agriculture shall issue such regulations as he determines to be necessary to prevent circumvention of the purposes of this section.

(f) All determinations by the President and the Secretary of Agriculture under this section shall be final.

Approved August 22, 1964.

BIBLIOGRAPHY

Annual Report of the Council on International Economic Policy. Washington, D.C.: U.S. Government Printing Office, February 1974.

Atlantic Council. *U.S. Agriculture in a World Context: Policies and Approaches for the Next Decade.* Washington, D.C.: Praeger, 1973.

Auge-Laribe, M. *La Politique agricole de la France de 1880 à 1940.* Paris: Presses Universitaires de France, 1950.

Balassa, B. *The Structure of Protection in Developing Countries.* Baltimore: Johns Hopkins University Press, 1971.

Baldwin, Robert D. *Nontariff Distortions of International Trade.* Washington, D.C.: Brookings Institution, 1970.

Bane, F. "Administrative Marketing Barriers." *Law and Contemporary Problems* 8, no. 2 (Spring 1941): 376-90.

Benedict, M. R. *Farm Policies of the United States, 1790-1950.* New York: Twentieth Century Fund, 1953.

Bhagwati, J., et al. *Trade Balance of Payments and Growth.* Amsterdam: North Holland, 1971.

Bidwell, Percy. *The Invisible Tariff.* New York: Council on Foreign Relations, 1939.

Britton, D. K. "Problems of Adapting U.K. Institutions in the EEC." Conference Paper no. 9, Agricultural Adjustment Conference, University of Newcastle-upon-Tyne, 1972.

Commission on International Trade and Investment Policy. *United States International Economic Policy in an Interdependent World.* Vols. 1 and 2. Washington, D.C.: U.S. Government Printing Office, July 1971.

Condliffe, J. B. *The Commerce of Nations.* London: George Allen and Unwin, 1951.

_____. *The Reconstruction of World Trade.* New York: Norton, 1940.

Congressional Record. Washington, D.C.: U.S. Government Printing Office, June 1968.

Corden, W. M. "Tariffs and Protectionism." In *The International Encyclopedia of Social Sciences,* vol. 8. New York: Macmillan Co. and Free Press, 1968. Pp. 113-21.

____. *The Theory of Protection.* Oxford: Clarendon Press, 1971.

____. *Trade Policy and Economic Welfare.* London: Oxford University Press, 1974.

Curzon, Gerard and Victoria. *Global Assault on Nontariff Trade Barriers.* Thames Essay no. 3, Trade Policy Research Center. London: Ditchling Press, 1970.

____. *Hidden Barriers to International Trade.* Thames Essay no. 1, Trade Policy Research Center. London: Ditchling Press, 1970.

Denton, Geoffrey, and O'Cleiracain, Seamus. *Subsidy Issues in International Commerce.* Thames Essay no. 5, Trade Policy Research Center. London: Ditchling Press, 1972.

EEC Commission. *Fourth General Report on the Activities of the Communities, 1970.* Brussels: EEC, February 1971.

Ehrich, Rollo L. and Usman, Mohammad. *Demand and Supply Functions for Beef Imports.* Bul. 604. Laramie: Agricultural Experiment Station, University of Wyoming, January 1974.

FAO. *Developments in Agricultural Price Stabilization and Support Policies, 1965-1970.* Committee on Commodity Problems, CCP 71/15. Rome, August 1971.

____. *International Agricultural Adjustment: A Case Study of Japan.* C/73/LIM/3. Rome, 1973.

____. *National Regulations Affecting Imports of Livestock and Meat.* CCP: ME 72-8. Rome, April 1972.

____. *Note on Tariff and Nontariff Measures Affecting International Trade in Meat and Poultry.* Committee on Commodity Problems, CCP: Mah 70/b. Rome, May 1970.

____. *Processed Agricultural Products and Agricultural Adjustment.* C73/LIM/11. Rome, November 1973.

GATT. *International Trade, 1975-76.* Geneva: GATT, 1976.

Golt, Sidney. *The GATT Negotiations, 1973-75: A Guide to the Issues.* London: British-North American Committee, April 1974.

Great Britain Ministry of Agriculture, Fisheries and Food. *Annual Review and Determination of Guarantees.* London: HM Stationery Office, 1969, 1971.

Haberler, G., et al. *Trends in International Trade.* Geneva: GATT, 1958.

Hill, B. E. "The World Market for Beef and Other Meat." In *World Animal Review,* no. 4-1972. Rome, 1972.

Hillman, J. S. "Economic Aspects of Interstate Agricultural Trade Barriers in the Western Region." Ph.D. dissertation, University of California, Berkeley, 1954.

Hillman, J. S., and Rowell, J. D. *A Summary of Laws Relating to the Interstate Movement of Agricultural Products in the Eleven Western States.* Tucson: University of Arizona Agricultural Experiment Station, 1952.

Hindley, Brian. *Britain's Position on Non-tariff Protection.* London: Trade Policy Research Center, 1972.

____. "Negotiations on Nontariff Barriers." Chapter 6 in *Towards an Open World Economy*. London: Macmillan, 1972.

Hoover, Edgar M. *The Location of Economic Activity*. 1st ed. New York: McGraw-Hill Book Co., 1948.

International Trade Center. *The Market for Manufacturing Grade Beef in the United Kingdom and the European Economic Community*. Geneva: UNCTAD, GATT, 1971.

Jasiorowsky, H. A. "Twenty Years with No Progress?" In *World Animal Review*, no. 4-1972. Rome, 1972.

Johnson, D. Gale. "Are High Farm Prices Here to Stay?" *The Morgan Guaranty Survey*. New York: Morgan Guaranty Trust Co., August 1974.

____. *World Agriculture in Disarray*. London: Fontana-Collins, 1973.

Johnson, H. G. "An Economic Theory of Protectionism, Tariff Bargaining and the Formation of Customs Unions." *Journal of Political Economy* 73 (June 1965): 254-83.

Josling, T. *Agriculture and Britain's Trade Policy Dilemma*. Thames Essay no. 2, Trade Policy Research Center. London: Ditchling Press, 1970.

____. "The EEC and the World Market for Temperate Zone Agricultural Products." Paper presented at the Royal Economic Conference, York, England, September 25-28, 1972.

Josling, T., and Hillman, J. S. *Agricultural Protection and Stabilization Policies: A Framework of Measurement in the Context of Agricultural Adjustment*. FAO C75/LIM/2. Rome: FAO, 1975.

Kindleberger, C. P. *International Economics*. 3rd ed. Homewood, Ill.: Irwin, 1963.

Leipmann, H. *Tariff Levels and the Economic Unity of Europe*. London: George Allen and Unwin, 1938.

Long, Oliver. "The Multilateral Trade Negotiations in a Changing World Economic." Address to the Swedish National Committee of International Chambers of Commerce, Stockholm, March 19, 1974.

McArthur, M. H. "Australia's Role in the World's Beef Future." San Antonio: Paper presented at meeting of the American National Cattlemen's Association, January 1973.

McKnight, Frank G. *Foreign Agriculture*. Washington, D.C.: USDA, FAS, 1972.

Malmgren, H. B. "Negotiating Nontariff Barriers: The Harmonization of National Economic Policies." In *U.S. Foreign Economic Policy for the 1970s: A New Approach to New Realities*. Washington, D.C.: National Planning Association, 1971. Pp. 79-109.

____. *Trade Wars or Trade Negotiations: Nontariff Barriers and Economic Peacemaking*. Washington, D.C.: Atlantic Council of the United States, 1970.

Malmgren, H. B., and Schlecty, D. L. "Rationalizing World Agricultural Trade." *Journal of World Trade Law* 4 (July-August, 1970): 515-47.

Mun, T. *England's Treasure by Forraign Trade*. London and Oxford, published for the Economic History Society by B. Blackwell, 1949.

Needham, Peter J. "How Ireland Conquered the British Beef Market." *CALF News* 12, no. 3 (March, 1974): 54, 55, 82.

New Zealand Meat Producers Board. "Annual Report and Statement of Account for Year Ended September 30, 1971." Wellington, 1972.

_____. *New Zealand Meat Markets, 1970*. Wellington, March 19, 1971.

_____. "New Zealand Meat Seminar." Papers presented in London, October 16-18, 1972.

OECD. *Policy Perspectives for International Trade and Economic Relations*. Paris: OECD, 1970.

Ohlin, G. "Trade in a Non-Laissez Faire World." In *International Economic Relations*. Edited by Paul Samuelson. London: Macmillan, 1969. Pp. 157-75.

Ojala, E. M. *Agricultural and Economic Progress*. London: Oxford University Press, 1952.

_____. "Europe and the World Agricultural Economy." Conference paper no. 1. Agricultural Adjustment Conference, University of Newcastle-upon-Tyne, July 1972.

Patterson, Gardiner. *Commission on International Trade and Investment Policy*. Vol. 1. Washington, D.C.: U.S. Government Printing Office, 1971.

Power, A. P., and Harris, S. A. "A Cost/Benefit Evaluation of Alternative Policies for Foot-and-Mouth Disease in Great Britain." *Journal of Agricultural Economics* 24, no. 3 (1973): 573-98.

Röpke, W. *German Commercial Policy*. London: Longmans, 1934.

Schwinger, Robert B. "New Concepts and Methods in Foreign Trade Negotiations." *American Journal of Agricultural Economics* 51, no. 5 (December 1969): 1338-49.

Study Group of the British Coordinating Committee for International Studies. "Memorandum on British External Economic Policy in Recent Years, Part II." 1939.

Tobin, J. "Economic Growth as an Objective of Government Policy." *American Economic Review* 54 (1964): 1-200.

Tracy, M. *Agriculture in Western Europe: Crises and Adaptation since 1880*. London: Jonathan Cape, 1964.

Trade Policy Research Center. "British, European and American Interests in International Negotiations on Agricultural Trade." Staff Paper no. 3. London, 1973.

United Nations. Conference on Trade and Development. *Commodity Problems and Policies: Access to Markets. A Report by the UNCTAD Secretariat*. Santiago, Chile: UNCTAD, 1972.

_____. TD/120/Supp. 1. January 31, 1972.

United States. Department of Agriculture. *Code of Agriculture. Section 22 of the Agricultural Adjustment Act of 1933 as Reenacted and Amended.* Washington, D.C., January 1972.

____. *Measures of the Degree and Cost of Economic Protection of Agriculture in Selected Countries.* Washington, D.C., 1967.

United States. Department of Agriculture. Economic Research Service. *Prospects for Agricultural Trade with the USSR.* Foreign Series report no. 356. Washington, D.C., 1973.

United States. Department of Agriculture. Foreign Agricultural Service. *Foreign Agriculture* 12, no. 29 (July 15, 1974).

____. "Japan Institutes New Trade Measures, Cuts Tariffs on Some Agricultural Products." *Agricultural Trade Policy,* FAS circular ATP-7-72, December 1972.

____. "Nontariff Barriers Affecting Trade in Agricultural Products—Canada." *Agricultural Trade Policy,* FAS circular ATP-3-72, July 1972.

____."Nontariff Barriers Affecting Trade in Agricultural Products—Denmark." *Agricultural Trade Policy,* FAS circular ATP-5-72, September 1972.

____. "Nontariff Barriers Affecting Trade in Agricultural Products—EEC." *Agricultural Trade Policy,* FAS circular ATP-10-72, June 1972.

____. "Nontariff Barriers Affecting Trade in Agricultural Products—Ireland." *Agricultural Trade Policy,* FAS circular ATP-9-72, December 1972.

____. "Nontariff Barriers Affecting Trade in Agricultural Products—Japan." *Agricultural Trade Policy,* FAS circular ATP-2-72, June 1972.

____. "Nontariff Barriers Affecting Trade in Agricultural Products—Norway." *Agricultural Trade Policy,* FAS circular ATP-4-72, September 1972.

____. "Nontariff Barriers Affecting Trade in Agricultural Products—Spain." *Agricultural Trade Policy,* FAS circular ATP-6-72, September 1972.

____. "Nontariff Barriers Affecting Trade in Agricultural Products—Sweden." *Agricultural Trade Policy,* FAS circular ATP-1-72, March 1972.

____. "Nontariff Barriers Affecting Trade in Agricultural Products—United Kingdom." *Agricultural Trade Policy,* FAS circular ATP-8-72, December 1972.

____. *World Agricultural Production and Trade.* Washington, D.C., December 1973.

United States. Department of Commerce. *International Commerce.* Washington, D.C.: U.S. Government Printing Office, 1971.

United States. Senate. *Nontariff Trade Barriers.* Report to the Committee on Finance. T.C. publication no. 665. Washington, D.C., 1974.

United States Statutes at Large. 88th Cong., 2d sess., 1964. Vol. 78. Washington, D.C.: U.S. Government Printing Office, 1965.

United States. Tariff Commission. *Nontariff Trade Barriers.* T.C. publication no. 665, April 1974.

____. *Summaries of Trade and Tariff Information.* Vol. 1, *Animals and Meat.* T.C. publication no. 250. Washington, D.C.: U.S. Government Printing Office, 1968.

Yates, P. L. *Food, Land and Manpower in Western Europe.* London: Macmillan, 1960.

____. *Forty Years of Foreign Trade.* London: George Allen and Unwin, 1959.